D0874130

ALL THE SWEETS OF BEING

All the Sweets of Being

— A LIFE OF —

JAMES BOSWELL

ROGER
HUTCHINSON

MAINSTREAM PUBLISHING

EDINBURGH AND LONDON

First published in Great Britain in 1995 by
MAINSTREAM PUBLISHING COMPANY (EDINBURGH) LTD
7 Albany Street
Edinburgh EH1 3UG

ISBN 1 85158 702 0

A catalogue record for this book is available from the British Library

Subsidised by THE SCOTTISH ARTS COUNCIL

Typeset in Palatino by Servis Filmsetting Ltd
Printed and bound in Great Britain by Butler & Tanner Ltd, Frome,
Somerset

TO BRIAN MONTAGUE

Here Boswell lies! drop o'er his tomb a tear,
Let no malignant tongue pursue him here;
Bury his failings in the silent grave,
And from unfriendly hands his memory save.

Robert Boswell (cousin),
unused verse from a proposed memorial tablet

CONTENTS

PREFACE

The village of Sollacaro stands at 1,600 feet above sea-level, at the head of a valley so broad and flat and fertile that it is best described as the flood-plain of the River Tavaro, which flows down from wooded sub-Alpine mountain ranges to the Gulf of Valinco on the south-western coast of the island of Corsica.

Sollacaro is a stern, shuttered and cobbled Corsican hill-town, with thickly pointed granite fronts and an apparent indifference to the outside world. Like many of its type, it appears hardly to have changed in two or three centuries. What developments have occurred since the advent of electricity and the internal combustion engine are muted there, stilled beneath limitless skies. There is a post-office, though, and across the road from the post-office a bronze plaque has been set at head height into a stone wall. The words on the plaque read:

JAMES BOSWELL

ECRIVAIN BRITANNIQUE

ET AMI DE LA CORSE

RENCONTRA DANS CE VILLAGE

DU 22 AU 29 OCTOBRE 1765

PASQUALE PAOLI

'BABBU DI A PATRI'

'British writer and friend of Corsica'. There are many ways of seeing a man. Those modern Corsicans – and there are a few – who recognise the name of James Boswell are likely to know nothing whatsoever of an eighteenth-century lexicographer and essayist named Samuel Johnson. If they were asked to offer word-associations with the noun 'Boswell', the results would be entirely uncluttered by terms such as 'drunkenness', 'lechery' and 'sycophancy'. Other qualities would certainly come to their minds – half-remembered virtues, such as loyalty, honour, courage and idealism. Neither his Corsican admirers nor his British detractors can properly claim the perfect portrait of James Boswell, of course. Both are guilty of a similar failing: they invest in him all of the qualities of his age. In Corsica it was an heroic age, a time of noble struggle and self-sacrifice, and Boswell, more than any other Briton, reflected that. In Britain it was a time of free-flowing claret and sexual anarchy, of strange rituals at secret clubs, of garish bucks, of duels, riots, and the ever-present ignobility of an urban death. James Boswell, more than any other Briton, wrote also of that. He was not an uncritical friend of his period – towards the end of his life he considered 'the world a fool' – but he was its uncensorious, unremitting biographer, and for his pains too many of the inhabitants of posterity have chosen to see in Boswell the most unpleasant embodiment of a reprehensible epoch. Largely lacking his intelligence and tolerant good humour, they have failed to appreciate that the past is truly another country, and to damn uncomprehendingly the customs of its natives is to be guilty of a kind of historical missionary colonialism.

The result has been, in Britain if not in Corsica, a popular distortion of the busy life of an accomplished citizen. 'How can you not dislike,' it was said to me, 'a man who spends all his time crawling around after another?' A distinguished introduction to a modern edition of his most famous work ends with the words: 'It is the story of a great life, told by one whose own life was otherwise shabby and disconsolate.' There is, according to another scholar of the time, such a thing as 'the Boswellian disease' of living one's own life through the achievements of acquaintances.

Such nonsense was started in the malicious streets which were ruled over by George III. Every notable figure of the time was subject to caricature and slander and worse – it was one of the charms of the eighteenth century – and those notables of the age, including James Boswell, knew how to look after themselves when the barbs began to fly. They did so, largely, by firing other barbs back. It made for a lively social scene, but it should never have been used as the basis for dispassionate historical account one and two centuries afterwards.

But perhaps we should forget about dispassionate history. I first approached the life of James Boswell by travelling from a house a hundred yards from the churchyard in which he stood and contemplated Scottish Highland life in the late summer of 1773 to that village in the deep south of Corsica where he first discovered that the sweets of life were all around him, hanging like the chestnuts to be plucked and enjoyed. He was at his passionate best during each of those adventures. They were the times of which, during a mainly cheerful later life, he liked best to be reminded. They repaid rediscovery.

It would be, if not easy, an easier task than that accomplished by James Boswell to reconstruct his life in the immense detail that he applied to Samuel Johnson: thanks to the work of Yale University, and especially of the redoubtable Professor Frederick A. Pottle, an overflowing cornucopia of material is available to the researcher. I have not tried to outdo the great biographer. What follows is an extended essay on his character and his times. Those who wish to spend a rewarding six months (and several hundred pounds) on acquainting themselves with a day-by-day account of Boswell's life should buy the academic editions of Yale's comprehensively researched and compiled anthologies. This is a simple story, which began – fortunately, I think – on a summer's day in Sollacaro.

It would probably never have been written if David Robinson of the *Scotsman* Weekend magazine had not commissioned a couple of articles on the subject. I owe him many thanks. Peter Stockham of the Staffs Bookshop in Lichfield was immensely helpful, to my profit and, I like to think, to his. I am fortunate to live within easy distance of the excellent libraries at the Clan Donald Centre in Armadale, Skye, which has been built by the descendants of those who were fleeing from Sir Alexander Macdonald to Upper America in 1773, and the Sabhal Mor Ostaig, the Gaelic college which has grown up just a few hundred yards from the heap of old stones which is all that remains of one of Johnson and Boswell's lodging places in the Highlands. Neither man would have believed that these places could, within a mere 200 years of their depressing visit to Sleat, be built in this area; both of them – in particular Samuel Johnson – would be delighted beyond measure by such cultural progress. Inverness Library, Glasgow University Library and, of course, the wonderful National Library of Scotland in Edinburgh helped me to complete my researches.

My father, William Hutchinson, first showed me, 30 years ago, the volume of Boswell's work which he, like so many others, had bought as a student 30 years before that. Has the man ever, I wondered then, been out of print? My family, Caroline MacKechnie, and my friends were all typically interested and encouraging – Richard Adams in particular took his usual pains to point me towards the light. I love the publishers, Bill Campbell and Peter MacKenzie, better than life itself, and Peter Frances's editing has been, once again, exemplary. Finally, I would like to thank the Scottish Arts Council and the Society of Authors for their generous help with travel and research grant aid.

Roger Hutchinson, Skye, 1995

Chapter One

THE DANCER'S BELLS

*The Baron was one of the most powerful lords in Westphalia; his castle
had both a gate and windows; and his great hall was even adorned with
tapestry. The dogs of his outer yard composed his hunting pack upon
occasion, his grooms were his huntsmen, and the vicar of the parish
was his chief almoner. He was called My Lord by everybody, and
everyone laughed when he told his stories.*

VOLTAIRE, *CANDIDE*

If, as he would later claim, omens of his future greatness lit up
the northern skies on the occasion of his birth, they were noted
by none of his fellow citizens. He spilled on to his mother's bed on
29 October 1740, in the heart of a tall town house at the boisterous centre of an Edinburgh with other things on its mind. The
merchants of the town, his father's friends, were deeply fearful for
the safety of their investments in the Silesian coal-mines following
the death of the German Emperor of a flux and vomiting caused
by eating mushrooms stewed in oil. Their anxieties would shortly
be justified when Silesia was seized by the ambitious new tyrant
of Prussia, Frederick II – the same great Frederick whose patron-
ising words in later years helped send the young man groping for
inspiration among the peerless, shimmering crags of an alien
southern land. If there were omens, they cast eccentric shadows.

The babble on the streets in the hours after his nativity was not of northern lights, but of civic unrest in the distant Highland market town of Dingwall, of urban grain seizures following the crop failure on such as his grandfather's Ayrshire estate in 1739, of the war with Spain. It was the hectic, raucous clamour of the second city in Britain; a truculent city no longer certain of its role but always shrill, if not entirely confident, in protest, haggle, and debate; a high-rise city of combustible 14-storey tenements and dark wynds littered with human dung; a city wherein eight serious riots occurred between the year of his birth and the year of his death – Protestants rioted against papists, footmen rioted against a play which was insulting to footmen, and almost everybody rioted against body-snatchers. He came from a rich family of the landed establishment, which had been blessed for 230 years with ownership of one of the most placid agricultural vales in Great Britain; but he was born and brought up in the compressed energy of the most densely populated hillside in the western world. The whoop and hum of the city streets were his cradle-songs; the electricity of Edinburgh was his inheritance. The city formed James Boswell, the city thrilled him, and the city left him – a reluctant, guilty ingrate – always seeking more.

There probably were no Boswells in Britain until Sieur de Bosville – 'our ancestor who came over with William the Conqueror,' the young man would casually note – arrived from Beuzeville in Normandy and assumed his lieutenancy at the foot of Senlac Hill, five miles inland from Hastings, in the early winter of 1066. He was rewarded, like so many others after William's shotgun coronation, with an English estate.

During the Anglophile reign of David I of Scotland, Sieur de Bosville's great-grandchildren moved north to Berwickshire, and in the late twelfth century Robert Bosville acquired land at Oxmuir. A tradition of squirarchy, thus established, rolled smoothly through the ages. Adam de Bosville de Oxmuir inherited from Robert, and he bequeathed to Roger, who handed over to William de Bosville (who we find, in 1296, swearing allegiance to Edward I after the English king's bloody rout of Berwick – a slaughter which only ended, William might have noted with some conflict of sympathy, when the Francophone monarch called out, 'Laissez! Laissez!' from the castle ramparts).

Following the revenge of Bannockburn, however, William's son, Richard, gained the favour of Robert the Bruce, and as a consequence obtained additional lands near Ardrossan in Ayrshire. Richard's second son had become, by 1320, Roger de Boswell, and he carried this newly corrupted surname into a profitable marriage with the heiress of the barony of Auchterderran in Fife in south-eastern Scotland. The Fifeshire Boswells were a clever, quietly successful clan. Their younger males became respectable magistrates and ministers, while the first-born nursed the titles. They kept the favour of the Court, they accumulated land, and they continued to marry well – none of those three things being, of course, unconnected. By the beginning of the fifteenth century they had achieved the substantial Fifeshire barony of Balmuto, and in 1458 David Boswell of Balmuto was granted by charter from James II the great estate of Glasmont.

David Boswell married twice. His second bride, Lady Margaret Sinclair, daughter of the Earl of Orkney and Caithness, first bore him a son. Thomas Boswell became a particular favourite of King James IV. His role at the Scottish Court is uncertain now, and it may have been uncertain 500 years ago. James IV gifted a series of unusual objects to Thomas Boswell. A loan of 18 shillings was repaid to him on 15 May 1504. On 2 August he was given 56 shillings for his part in a raid against Eskdale reivers. Most impenetrably, on the first day of 1505, Thomas Boswell and Pate Sinclair were given 28 shillings from the Treasury 'to buy them dancing gear', and on the last day of that year the crown settled a bill for '30 dozen of bells for dancers, delivered to Thomas Boswell, £4 10s'.

Was he the minstrel, this significant ancestor? Was he the Court jester? Did he clown, did he prance, did he make the monarch smile? His post, if it was master of the king's recreations, was not uncommonly given to men of high family. He need not have played the fool, merely have been robust good company. He must have been amiable and ready to entertain, easy to laugh and quick in conversation; comfortable with all men but happiest, perhaps, at the table of the great and the good. As well as bells and dancing gear, Court minstrels were traditionally given land for their favours. On 20 November 1504, a royal charter was issued from Edinburgh. It granted to Thomas Boswell and his family the 'terras et baroniam de Auchinlek'. Seven months later, in June 1505, James IV visited Ayr, and from that seat he issued a second charter which further extended Boswell's land and barony of Auchinleck in the western Lowlands; and in 1507 his holding was elevated to a free burgh and barony.

The name of Boswell would be attached to some part of Auchinleck for the next five centuries, but Thomas Boswell and his wife, Annabella, the daughter of Sir Hugh Campbell of Loudoun, enjoyed their Ayrshire pastures together for just nine years. Royal favours had their price, and in August 1513, following an appeal from the auld ally, Louis XII of France, an appeal which was seductively enhanced by gifts and flattery from his queen, James IV of Scotland called up the largest army his country had ever raised to march south against the forces of Henry VIII.

For the second time, and for the last time bearing arms, a Boswell invaded England. Thomas rode with his liege into Northumberland. On 9 September their army of 20,000 men engaged with the coequal army of the Earl of Surrey on the flanks of Branxton Hill near the village of Flodden. English bowmen and English billmen took a vicious toll of Highland foot and Lowland horse, and in a foolhardy attempt to rescue the day James rode headlong towards the Earl of Surrey. When they inspected his body they found it to be stuck with a dozen arrows, one hand was connected to the wrist by an inch of flesh, and his head had been half-severed from its shoulders by the clean scything stroke of a bill. More than 10,000 Scottish dead lay about him. They included Thomas Boswell of Auchinleck and his half-brother Sir Alexander Boswell of Balmuto.

But family lines did not end as easily as a couple of human lives in the sixteenth century. At Balmuto and at Auchinleck, new heirs arose to claim and continue the inheritance. Thomas's young son David received in 1514 confirmation of his own right to his dead father's barony at Auchinleck, confirmation which came by charter from the two-year-old scion of the fallen king, James V.

Auchinleck, which was – despite its guttural Gaelic origin of 'Achadh na leac', or field of flagstones – softly abbreviated to 'Affleck' in the sixteenth century, is a broad and fertile strath, which is cupped at its eastern head between upland marshes and high scrub and sweeps from there across rolling, generous arable land westward towards the Firth of Clyde and the distant, gun-metal-grey southerly outposts of the Scottish Gaidhealtachd: the Mull of Kintyre and the Isle of Arran. From that island, the first link in the Hebridean chain, the Christian name James entered the Boswell family. On 13 February 1531, David Boswell of Auchinleck married Lady Janet Hamilton, the daughter of James, the first Earl of Arran. David and Janet had two sons, and they called the younger after her father.

But it was the older son who succeeded in the early 1560s, and a weird laird of Affleck was John Boswell. He sued his stepfather (for Janet remarried) in the criminal court for allegedly torching a byre. And in 1591 John was himself arraigned by the Privy Council, who determined that he 'not only has often and divers times consulted with witches, but also he himself practised witchcraft, sorcery, enchantment and other devilish practises, to the dishonour of God, sender of his word, and great contempt of his Highness, his authority and laws'. Ten months later an alleged diabolist named Richard Grahame confessed, shortly before being burned alive in Edinburgh, to having raised the devil 'in the Laird of Auchinleck's dwelling-place'.

Few men or women survived such accusations in the late six-teenth century. By the 1590s the fever of Reformation had touched even Auchinleck, which had had a Protestant minister since 1574. Elsewhere in Scotland, people were being pilloried, imprisoned, tortured and killed for the merest hint of idolatry. The Privy Council insisted upon an audience with John Boswell, an audience which would probably have proved fatal for the

Laird of Auchinleck, so he simply failed to show up and was denounced as a rebel.

But nothing more occurred. He kept his land, his title and his life. His family's breeding doubtless helped to save him: all those good marriages had accrued a valuable dividend, and perhaps the latest of the Stuart line, James VI, was not entirely unaware of his great-grandfather's attachment to the amusing, brave and loyal Boswell of a hundred years before, the man he paid in bells and dancing gear, who died beside him on an autumnal English weald.

So John Boswell was left to perish from natural causes in 1609, and his first son, James, succeeded to the estate. James Boswell, the fourth Baron Auchinleck, was in late middle-age when his reprobate old father died. He had dabbled in the law, acting as counsel for at least one murder suspect. He would have a short administration, the historical highlight of which came in 1615 when James VI sent him to the southern Hebrides as a battalion commander on a punitive raid against the insurrectionist remnants of the old Lordship of the Isles. James Boswell returned from that eventful mission in one piece, to the comfort of the modest new fortified towerhouse which he had raised three years earlier on a knoll of meadowland two miles west of the village of Auchinleck, overlooking the home farm, the peaceful scattered hamlets of the rolling champaign, and the distant sea. After a century in Ayrshire, the Boswells considered themselves there to stay.

James died in his towerhouse in 1618, leaving his eldest son 'and apparent heir', David, to pick up the reins in the orderly routine of things, leaving his 'son natural', Matthew, three of the best cows in the byre, and leaving instructions to the other four sons 'to quit claim and discharge other portions and parts of the guides'.

David Boswell would be – aside from the brief, scandalous flirtation with Rome of his most famous successor a hundred years later – the last Catholic, ardently Jacobite Boswell of Auchinleck. The religious and political life of Scotland took a sea-change during his lifetime, and this fervent supporter of

Charles I found himself living in the heart of covenanting Scotland, surrounded by ten thousand fiery devotees of a single Presbyterian Kirk. It cost him little more than a 10,000-mark fine for refusing to sign the National Covenant of 1638, that epochal document which challenged in Scotland the divine right of kings and the power of an undemocratic Church, but when David died in 1661 he left four daughters and no sons, and the estate consequently passed over to his nephew, another David Boswell, but one who was at least sympathetic to the Presbyterian claim, and one who certainly recognised that the long Stuart day was fast approaching night, and that with it must fade the 400-year-old regal patronage of the Boswell family. By the time of this David Boswell's death, and the inheritance of his son, the second James, the Boswells had effectively spurned Rome and the high, cavalier politics of Jacobite Toryism. The minstrel's descendants had become Orange, Whig, and Presbyterian. And they were still one of the richest and best-connected families in Scotland. The long brawl of Scottish history had left them comparatively unbloodied, entirely unbowed, and owners of virtually all that they surveyed.

James Boswell, grandfather of the most famous member of his line, was at the same time the most successful lawyer the family had yet produced and possibly the most diligent laird. 'My grandfather,' the ninth chief of Auchinleck would say, 'thought it heroism to restore his family.' What small parcels of the Kyles of Carrick had been sold or willed away by his predecessors were bought back into his seisin, until the laird of Auchinleck could once more boast of being able to ride for ten uninterrupted miles on his own land. After studying law at Leyden in Holland, he returned to become an eminent member of the Scottish Faculty of Advocates, and in 1704 he married the daughter of the Earl of Kincardine. Elizabeth and James had two sons, Alexander and John, and a daughter, Veronica, who would marry one David Montgomerie and give birth to a girl christened Margaret; a dark, bold, witty girl whose surname would, in the fullness of time and the warp and weft of human affections, revert from Montgomerie to Boswell.

He worked hard, this astute and rigorous man, so hard that after his death his son told his grandson that, 'My worthy father, whom you justly notice had a melancholic turn, was never troubled with it in Session time. Business drove it away. In the vacation, indeed, as he had not acquired tastes for amusing himself to fill up the vacancies in his mind, melancholy frequently got hold of him.' James Boswell gave to his grandson his name, his estate, an open door into the profitable Edinburgh legal profession, and – in a roundabout manner – his wife; but his grandson would credit him most frequently for handing down, over the head of a single generation, the least welcome legacy of them all: the 'black foe' of depression, the numbing melancholia which crept up on them both like summer thunder and haunted their lives from cradle to terrifying grave.

But to his eldest son, Alexander – an altogether more stable legatee – James Boswell gave merely the land, the law, education at Leyden, and a set of increasingly Presbyterian convictions. The homely sermons of Bishop Latimer were their Sabbath text, the brave and simple works of the Protestant martyr who, when about to be burned by a Catholic queen in 1555, turned to his quailing comrade at the stake and said, 'Be of good comfort, Master Ridley, and play the man; we shall this day light such a candle by God's grace in England as I trust shall never be put out.' Hugh Latimer was the reading in the towerhouse on those stern eighteenth-century Scottish Sunday afternoons, leavened perhaps by an essay or two from 'good old Erasmus', as Alexander Boswell would refer to the Dutch philosopher Erasmus Desiderius, who 'laid the egg which Luther hatched'. The Boswells of Auchinleck had travelled a long way in a short time, from bells and dancing gear at the Court of James IV and witchcraft and sorcery in the reign of James VI, to respectful study of the principled revisionism of 'Moriae encomium', while a staid and sentimental Hanoverian filled the Protestant throne of the United Kingdom of Great Britain.

Alexander Boswell was born on All Fool's Day 1706, and never was a birthday more impertinent. By the age of 21 he had graduated from the university of Leyden, and at the age of 23 he was welcomed into the Faculty of Advocates in Edinburgh. He was an accomplished classicist, fluent in Greek and Latin, who read the odes of Horace and Anacreon for fun. He wrote English with clarity and style, and for one of his social position he spoke in a Scots dialect so unusually broad and unashamed that it was the subject of amused – and, in those schizophrenic Scottish Lowlands after the Union, not entirely unadmiring – anecdote, even in his own time. 'Can we not go a little faster?' his eldest son asked him impatiently as they rode one time together. 'Just a little faster: it's not the exercise that fatigues, but the hanging upon a beast.' 'What's the matter, man,' the storytellers reported Alexander Boswell to have replied, 'what's the matter how a chield hings, if he dinna hing upon a gallows?'

That sharp mind and dour brogue made him a formidable opponent in debate. When the Whiggish Presbyterian finally met the High Tory and Jacobite sympathiser Samuel Johnson – whom he instantly, wonderfully, dubbed 'Ursa Major' – the two men relaxed their guards briefly and the predictable argument flared from the unlikely source of Alexander Boswell's coin collection. It featured one from the Commonwealth, bearing the head of Oliver Cromwell. Cromwell had not been such a bad fellow, remarked Auchinleck. No? said Johnson. And what did Cromwell ever do for his country? 'God, Doctor,' spat Alexander Boswell, 'he gart kings ken that they had a lith in their neck.' He let kings know that they had a joint in their necks. Who was then the master of riposte, who was the lord of the last word? Which one most influenced the young James Boswell?

Alexander Boswell's legal and administrative career surpassed even that of his own father. By the age of 26 the nearby coastal town of Prestwick had made him a burgess, or borough magistrate, 'for good services done and to be done'. He became the sheriff-depute of Wigtownshire, and in 1750 he represented the Burgh of Ayr at the General Assembly in Edinburgh. He was raised to the Scottish bench as a Lord of Session on 15 February 1754, assuming the professional title of Lord Auchinleck, and in the following year he was appointed to the Court of Justiciary as one of only five judges at the supreme criminal court in Scotland.

The great thing for a judge, he said, was to steer a case like a ship's pilot: 'The agents always endeavour to keep a cause afloat. But I keep my eye upon the haven, and the moment I have got him fairly in order I give one hard push, and there he's landed.'

He was a handsome man. He had a full, square, open face which never, even in late middle-age, ran overly to fat. His lips were sensual and laughter-lines creased the edges of his mouth. Beneath a high and balding brow, large black eyes looked calmly out upon an interesting world. His religion, that too-often mocked and misrepresented Scottish Presbyterianism, was as much a secular as a spiritual compass. He did believe that 'a poor Church is a pure Church', but so did Saint Francis of Assisi and posterity has not derided him as a miserly curmudgeon. Alexander Boswell was neither mean nor narrow minded. He was an honest man with a deeply felt dislike of the divine pretensions of popes and kings. There was an Englishman in Edinburgh, he told friends, called Jack Bowes – mad, actually, really mad, but humorous. This Jack Bowes got up one day on the lady's steps below the New Kirk and began to preach. 'You will find my text,' he told the gathering crowd, 'in the 2nd Epistle of Saint Paul to Timothy, 4th chapter, 13th verse: "The cloak that I left at Troas with Carpus, when thou comest, bring with thee, and the books, but especially the parchments."

'We insist upon the first clause,' Jack Bowes told his wayside congregation. 'We see, gentlemen, from these words that Paul was a presbyter, for he wore a cloak. He does not say "the gown which I left at Troas", but "the cloak that I left at Troas with Carpus, when thou comest, bring with thee". Timothy, we all know, was a bishop. Now, my friends, the doctrine I would inculcate from this is that a presbyter had a bishop for a baggageman.'

Alexander Boswell loved a drink and a story and a joke. They could be told against his Church, his father, or the English; or occasionally all together, as with the tale about John McLaren, the old minister at Edinburgh's Tolbooth Church, whose opening sermon lines in his later, failing years were prepared for him by Alexander's father, James. McLaren would read them out and pursue the plot extempore: 'Lord, bless thy churches abroad – in

Hungary, Bohemia, Lithuania, Poland. Lord, pity thy poor servants in France. Thou had once glorious churches there; but now they are like dead men out o' mind. And as for the restoring of the Jews, Lord, shovel awa' time. Pity poor Scotland.' Here Alexander Boswell would explain, laughing, that old John McLaren hated the Union. 'Our rowers have brought us into deep waters. May we have a pure ministry and pure ordinances – and let the bane o' Scotland never be a little-worth, lax, frothy ministry, that ken little o' God, less o' Christ, and are full of themselves.'

He would not succeed to the estate at Auchinleck until his father's death in 1749, and so Alexander Boswell established himself early in a town house in Parliament Close at the very nucleus of Edinburgh. From there he pursued his legal career in Courts of Session, where leading judges got the gownkeepers drunk and laid wagers on them subsequently walking a straight line on the floor of the parliament house, where the last wish of leading advocates was that their friends and colleagues should be 'filled a' fou' with wine until 'there wasna ane o' us able to bite his ain thumb', and where as clear, democratic and dispassionate a justice was dispensed as could be found in Europe.

And in 1739 he married Euphemia Erskine of the famous House of Mar, a direct descendant of the first queen of Robert the Bruce, and took her back to Parliament Close. Euphemia became pregnant almost immediately. At the end of October 1740, she gave Alexander Boswell a male heir to the seat of Auchinleck. They named him after Alexander's father and great-grandfather, and perhaps half-consciously for those rash and rakish kings whose sponsorship had helped the family Boswell to sustain and improve upon their conquerors' claim; they christened him James.

Chapter Two

VRAYE FOY

It is indeed wonderful how very strong the desire of continuing ourselves, as we fancy, by a series of offspring, is in all the human race, when we consider that a child begins to exist and comes into the world, we know not how, and most certainly without our being conscious of any ingenuity or art. There is a good story of a simple gentleman who, on being asked how he had contrived to have so many pretty daughters, declared, 'upon his honour, it was all by chance'. I am afraid that in general parents may make a more extensive declaration; and allow that the formation of their children has been all by chance.

JAMES BOSWELL, 'ON PARENTS AND CHILDREN'

Euphemia Boswell was as nervous and devout as the city outside her drawing-room window was brash and blasphemous. She adored her little son and endeavoured from the moment of his birth to shield him from the physical and moral corruptions which advertised themselves by day and gaudy night in the steep stinking gullies of the usurped capital of Scotland. It was a losing cause.

Jamie Boswell would have heard the city first. The susurrus of pigeons kept for meat in the cotes of neighbouring houses. The shrill cries of 'gardy loo!' – *gardez l'eau* – as maids poured refuse from the windows into the close below; the urgent, anxious, hopeful delaying reply of 'hud yer haund' as pedestrians scampered for shelter in the wynds. The grating of the craw in the porch when visitors announced themselves by rasping the metal ring up and down its notched or twisted rod of iron. The lilt and fall of the chorus of Highland sedan-carriers plying for trade or pleading for space. The calls of hawkers carrying goods from door to door: fish from Musselburgh, fruit and vegetables from the hinterland, roasting-jacks, toasting-forks, heather brushes, doormats, crockery, fourpence-ha'penny blacking, peat and coal; all bringing with them their individual yawp and yell – 'yeee-saaaa, yeeee-saaaaa!', yellow sand, yellow sand from the eastern shore to pour on the stairs and the kitchen floor, and occasionally on the spit-and-worse-sodden flags of the taverns. The infrequent rumble of riots, in which hardly any of the town mob died, the city guards dispensing futile Gaelic oaths at the urchins who mocked their age and their antique Lochaber axes. The gill-bells of St Giles' at 11.30 a.m., tolling the citizens into hostels for a meridian of brandy or ale. The strange, soft cosmopolitan carillons playing the tunes of Ireland, Italy and France at upper-storey windows around the morning town; the tin drums and trumpets of small spoilt boys. The song of a drunk picking his way home in the earlies. 'Oh, Canongate, poor elritch hole! What loss, what crosses dost thou thole . . .' And a cat; and the howl of a dog that had escaped the post-rabies canine genocide.

And on the Sabbath-day the relentless bells chiming not for liquor but to come to Christ; the subdued mutterings on the streets outside of genteel persons clumping in groups to church. The scatter of running feet as a patrol of the Kirk of Session's seizers give chase to a 'vaguer' publicly loitering without intent to worship on the Lord's Day. And then silence.

When the windows were thrown up on summer afternoons he will have smelled the caked ordure wafted on southerly zephyrs through the tall parades. 'How long can it be suffered,' asked John Wesley in 1762, 'that all manner of filth should be flung into the streets? How long shall the capital city of Scotland

and the chief street of it stink worse than a common sewer?' In the evenings of six days of the week both Jamie Boswell and the visiting Wesley would have coughed on the acrid stench of brown paper burned in the hearth to purge the air of those low-ceilinged rooms, 'these chambers ever dull and dark', as one of his poetical sons would write of the tenement blocks of old Edinburgh half a century on, their stuccoed ceilings stained with smoke and hardly visible in the daytime gloom.

The infant who first tottered in his laundered galligaskins to an open window facing Parliament Close looked out through black and starting eyes upon a cramped inner-city of 36,000 apartment-dwellers. They were a tiny proportion of the one-and-a-quarter million people who lived in rural Scotland, but they were concentrated in two square miles of quick-burning dystopia. The High Street tenements which overlooked the Luckenbooths at the mouth of Parliament Close rose to eight and nine storeys, enclosing sunless cobbled canyons, and they were by no means the tallest of Edinburgh's monoliths. Thirty yards from the Boswells' living-rooms, mountainous blocks of masonry towered like a cliff-face over Fishmarket Close, their small windows like gulls' nests or the hides of eastern troglodytes, their reeking smoke-stacks hidden in low cloud. Rare was the man who had more than two rooms of such an edifice; rarer and richer was he who owned a building from basement to chimney-top.

Wretches lay in rags upon the streets and in the night-time stairwells. Disease was commonplace and usually fatal: the mortality rate in Edinburgh in the 1740s was 34 in every thousand. Of the 1,123 souls who died there in 1760, old age accounted for just 274. The remainder were carried off by consumption, fever, measles, smallpox, and the score of strange, uncertainly christened maladies that fell from nowhere onto eighteenth-century men and women and swept them with blank, bewildered countenance under a mortcloth and down St Mary's Wynd to the Calton Burying Place.

There was much for a high-born, fragile and doting mother to keep from her elder son. James Boswell was brought up tenderly. As the result, he later surmised, 'I began at an early age to be indisposed, and people pitied me as a very delicate child. My mother was extremely kind, but she was too anxious when I had some small ailment. If I did not feel well, I was treated with excessive attention. I was not made to go to school, which I detested. She gave me sweetmeats and all sorts of pretty things to amuse me. When my health was restored, my slavery would begin again. I knew it, and I preferred being weak and ill to strong and healthy.'

It does not make a pretty picture. While the mother palely lies in labour with a second boy, or nurses the new child through his dangerous early weeks of life, the three-year-old brother lolls in armchairs and mopes in pretty linen shirts around the stuffy, gilded chambers with his face hung towards the floor in order to induce a headache.

But he never lied, about sickness or – he would claim – anything else. 'My worthy father had impressed upon me a respect for the truth which has always remained firm in my mind.' His worthy father; and the fervid Calvinist instruction of Euphemia Boswell, for Jamie's mother was even more deeply concerned with the destination of her family's souls than was the secular, worldly Alexander.

The eternity of punishment in hell was, consequently, 'the first great idea that I ever formed', and the thought of it made the child actually shudder in his steps. It seemed the only end to life. He knew what fire was – it burned in the grates of his home – but heaven? What unattainable fantasy was heaven? 'I had heard that one passed one's time there in endless praise of God, and I imagined that that meant singing psalms in church; and singing psalms did not appeal to me. I should not have wished to go to heaven if there had been any other way of not going to hell. I imagined that the saints passed the whole of eternity in the state of mind of people recently saved from a conflagration, who congratulate themselves on being in safety while they listen to the mournful shrieks of the damned.' Presbyterian worship, he would later say, made him from childhood onwards think of hell.

For the first eight years of his life Jamie was in limbo: between illness real and imagined; between a detested elementary school and a claustrophobic home; between the prospect of an infinite afterlife spent sizzling on sea-coals or alternatively sending up interminable psalms to the sky; between his mother's Calvinist catechisms and the stories told by servants of robbery, murder, witchcraft and the spirit world. 'My imagination,' he would reflect, 'was continually in a state of terror. I became the most timid and contemptible of beings.'

When James Boswell was four years old, his home town of Edinburgh was subjected to a sensational event. This Whiggish, faux-bourgeois, Protestant (less than one per cent of its population was reckoned to be papist), unheroic, elderly merchant city was invaded and occupied by the Jacobite army of Prince Charles Edward Stuart. Jamie was a month short of his fifth birthday when the ragged, romantic Highland hordes moved through the Netherbow gate on 16 September 1745 on their mission to send the Georgians back from London to Hanover and lifted Edinburgh from its doddering city guard without inflicting a single injury. Although the Boswells were certainly in Edinburgh in the autumn of 1745, Euphemia and her two young sons would equally certainly have spent the period of occupation securely within doors at Parliament Close – Mrs Boswell is unlikely to have been counted among the two-thirds of Edinburgh women who were afterwards claimed to have converted overnight to Jacobism. The four-year-old did not, nonetheless, fail to notice this immense disturbance in the routine of daily life. Ten thousand troops occupied the city streets for two days, and the surrounding countryside for a further five weeks. They were not easily forgettable, those unkempt, weatherworn men in plaids, carrying scythes, dirks and cudgels, who kept themselves in such polite good order that the citizens of the captured town, having worked themselves for weeks previously into a lather of petrified hostility, moved quickly from cautious fraternity to outright celebration of their cause. Although James was only properly free to observe the 'liberating' Hanoverian troops who arrived at a later date – to hear their drums roll down from Arthur's Seat and to stare at the enormous mustachios of the Hessian Guard – 20 years afterwards he would not resist noting with an atavistic pride that, though King George's men were able to buy themselves breeches in the wynds, even with the new trews on 'you were not so stout as the bold Highlanders who went without'.

Men and women did not have to be Catholic or Tory to discover in themselves at least a grudging, exasperated respect for the Jacobite uprisings of the eighteenth century; merely Scottish. Alexander Boswell himself was one of the Edinburgh burghers who found their early distaste melted by the unexpected courtesy of those alien countrymen, and by the dignity of their generals. The Edinburgh mob which fawned with wine and bread and cheese upon the soldiers from the north in 1745 would celebrate as wildly as their counterparts in London when news arrived seven months later of the slaughter of the Highland host on the moor above Culloden House. Throwing memory to the winds, mocking the white cockades of autumn, it would sack and burn the homes of local Catholics. But Alexander Boswell did not forget, and neither – although he rarely discussed the occupation of September 1745 – did his son.

Both men spoke for the rest of their lives of Jacobism with a certain wounded deference. The Presbyterian law lord Alexander, who could be heard to mutter almost regretfully that the Young Pretender possessed 'only passive courage', told approving stories of Jacobite women in Edinburgh at services of thanksgiving after the defeat of the earlier 1715 rising, who dropped into the collection plate a halfpenny wrapped in paper which bore the words: 'Stop, good preacher; go no further! God receives no thanks for murther.' And James, whose life would be wholly changed in its course by an encounter with another Catholic insurrectionist in another coarse and rocky land, flirted with and followed for all his days the intriguing deeds of the last of the Stuart line. When Samuel Johnson slept in 1773 in the very bed at the north of the island of Skye which had once contained Charles Edward Stuart, James Boswell found his vocal chords to be drowned by emotion. The sight, he stuttered, 'struck me with such a group of ideas as it is not easy for words to describe as the mind perceives them'.

Prince Charles's army wound south into England and the

Jacobite twilight as Jamie's fifth birthday passed at the end of October, and the Boswell family returned to its usual roster. The boys spent time in the countryside of their mother's own childhood at Valleyfield and Culross on the far north bank of the inner Firth of Forth, times which would later be regarded as golden interludes of health and happiness to be regained, like paradise, only in dreams. In Edinburgh it was back to the tedious regime of inviting illness for six days a week, in often-successful attempts to avoid Mr James Mundell's private elementary school, and spending most of the seventh in the church which he had been attending since before he could understand a word that the minister said – a bad Scottish habit, he would later muse, creating as it did the contrary talent among adults for listening to a man speak for half an hour at a time without attending to a word he said.

'To confess the truth, I was badly brought up.' He learned to read by rote, accumulating phrases from the classics and grammatical discipline without enjoyment or pleasure, or even much thought. Anxious to form a library of his own, when his mother promised him a personal copy of *The Confession of Faith of the Church of Scotland* if he read it from start to finish, he skimmed it page by page – it was 'at any rate a book' – until Euphemia pronounced herself satisfied. Not a word of 'that collection of absurd unintelligibility' stayed with him.

At the age of eight, James Boswell's education, and his personal well-being, took a happier turn. His father appointed a governor, or personal domestic tutor. John Dun was a 24-year-old graduate of Edinburgh University who aspired to the ministry. Perhaps his first and most valuable piece of advice to his worried young charge was by way of clarifying the puzzling nature of heaven. Boys who behaved well in this life, said Dun, would be happy in the next. There they would hear beautiful music, acquire sublime knowledge from God, become reacquainted with all their best friends, and meet all of the great men from history books. This made better sense. Although James Boswell would become determined to render the last benefit virtually irrelevant during his mortal span, heaven seemed finally to have the edge on hell. Dun's celestial city made little mention of 24-hour psalmery.

John Dun also extended Jamie's reading. He brought into Parliament Close bound volumes of the *Spectator*, a magazine of essays and homily-tales which had been published in London by Joseph Addison and Sir Richard Steele in a whirl of creativity four decades earlier, between March 1711 and December 1714, during which period the two men, with occasional help from such as Jonathan Swift and Alexander Pope, wrote and edited some 555 issues – sometimes one a day – and set the tone and standard both of 'periodical' publishing and discursive writing for the remainder of the eighteenth century. This, surely, was more the thing. The *Spectator* was witty and elegant; the *Spectator* was written in English; the *Spectator* was secular. And, perhaps above all, the *Spectator* spoke effortlessly of another metropolis, the unparochial capital of an immensely larger country where great men met on the marbled streets and wandered arm in arm, exchanging truisms and cynical worldly quips, through placid public gardens echoing to choirs of birds. 'A kind of emporium for the whole earth,' Addison had written, '. . . in which all considerable nations have their representatives . . . sometimes I am justled among a body of Armenians; sometimes I am lost in a crowd of Jews; and sometimes make one in a crowd of Dutchmen. I am a Dane, Swede, or Frenchman at different times; or rather fancy myself like the old philosopher, who upon being asked what countryman he was, replied, that he was a citizen of the world.' What tantalising place was this to wave before a young depressive northern boy, where the food came from one country and the sauce from another, the brocade petticoats from Peru and the diamond necklaces from Hindustan? A place in which he could breathe?

Jamie was happy with John Dun, except on Sundays. Then he was reclaimed for Presbyterian Edinburgh from the vine-groves of Horace and the glittering lanes of Addison's London. Then, the minister had three sermons a day to undo Dun's benevolent version of the afterlife, and 'stern and doleful' psalms reminded the quaking child of his early terrors. Then, the evenings were spent with catechism and more psalms. On the Sabbath-day the boy was instructed, for fear of awful consequences, 'not to do my own work, speak my own words, nor think my own thoughts'. He could attempt the first but never convincingly achieve the second and third, so what horrors lay in wait for this bright, impressionable, literal-minded lad; what hideous price would be exacted for his weakness? Concentrate as he might, it was no use – his imagination fled from the dim kirk and the dour chamber walls, and 'Election and Reprobation and Irresistible Grace were to me as unknown as the systems of the votaries of Vishnu, Ishvara, and Brahma'.

In 1749, when he was nine years old, grandfather James died and Alexander Boswell succeeded to the estate at Auchinleck, and Jamie's life took another turn. From that year onward, he and his two younger brothers (John would have been six, and David in his first year) spent most of the summer in Ayrshire, only wintering with their father in Edinburgh during the months of Session.

Alexander Boswell attacked his inheritance with typical vigour. Before long, his summer house-guests were returning to Edinburgh with a story of their host which would be recounted in the town with half-approving, partly amused chuckles for a further century and more. The judge was, they said, nowhere to be seen in the hours after dawn. He had risen each day with the sun and disappeared into his policy. What was he doing there at five o'clock? Why . . . pruning his young trees. 'Employed with indefatigable pains, in every numerous and important scenes,' as the Auchinleck schoolmaster would later eulogise of his laird.

The well-being of tender hazel shoots not excluded, Alexander Boswell was a thorough, improving landowner. He entirely rebuilt the village of Auchinleck and attempted to draw weavers, shoemakers, carpenters and other craftsmen on to his feus, with legal riders which enabled him subsequently to evict 'a bad neighbour or vicious person'. He renovated and re-roofed the small parish church, and built beside it a new family mausoleum: a robust, square structure with its own doorway and vault-hatch and room beneath for some 16 coffins to be filed like index trays in the hard foundation rock. On the north wall of the mausoleum Alexander Boswell had the family arms erected: two racing hounds rampant above a helmet and escutcheon and the family motto, 'vraye foy'. True faith.

And a Scots country mile from the village kirk, hidden among birch, beech and young hazel, close by the site of the pretty tower-house built 150 years before by the first James of Auchinleck, Alexander Boswell set to erecting a new family seat. He chose a rise cleared into meadowland and invisible from all but its immediate surrounds. It stared westward over 15 miles of Lowland strath, across the hundred huddled hamlets to the blown dunes of the Ayr and Prestwick coast, and eastward it looked towards the high, lonely track to Edinburgh. The promising young architects John and Robert Adam were at that time beginning work on a new home for the neighbouring Lord Dumfries, and it seems likely – although this has never been entirely confirmed – that Alexander tempted at least one of them to Auchinleck and requested there the drawings of a modest, neo-classical Palladian mansion-house.

Auchinleck House was built over a period of at least five years, which eased its burden on the purse of the cautious Alexander Boswell. It consisted of one single rectangular block, 95 feet by 38, rising to three storeys and an attic. Viewed from east or west, it stood beneath the scudding clouds like a gorgeously assembled temple to landed security. Three layers of six well-proportioned windows faced from the doorless seaward side into the western wind, topped by a plain pediment; but at the sheltered front the main entrance was surrounded by four Corinthian pilasters in low relief. Large Grecian urns decorated each precarious corner of the high balustrade which swept around the eaves, and smaller amphorae stood guard over ten low steps below the large, glass-windowed doorway. The principal rooms were plastered and muraled from skirting-board to ceiling, and the main pediment above those flat, square columns at the front of Auchinleck House was a riot of sculpted foliage, scrolls, maces, trumpets, swords and exotic fauna. On the entablature between the columns and the pediment, directly above the main door, Alexander Boswell had engraved in Roman letters a foot high, like the dedication of a hospital or town hall, a quotation from Horace's 'Epistle to Bullatium':

QVOD PETIS HIC EST
EST VLVBRIS ANIMVS SI TE NON DEFICIT AEQVVS

What you seek is here, at Ulubrae, if contentment does not fail you. For Ulubrae, read Auchinleck. In these 'romantic shades' the young James Boswell read the Roman poets with John Dun and felt 'a classic enthusiasm'. Here Jamie and his youngest brother, David, playing in the rushes around the decaying towerhouse, took a child's vow to 'stand by the old castle of Auchinleck with heart, purse, and sword'. But contentment? Auchinleck was apparently the embodiment of the word, a place as silent and unruffled as the surface of the moon; and as boy, youth and man, James Boswell had not an hour's contentment from the place. Contentment failed him utterly, especially at Ulubrae.

But it took John Dun from him. On 9 November 1752, 11 days after Jamie's 12th birthday, Dun got his reward for steering Alexander Boswell's most difficult son through what, it was vainly hoped, had been his most difficult years. The young Dumfriesshire man was given the ministry of the thousand souls of the newly refurbished parish of Auchinleck. He stayed there for the remainder of his days, a further 42 years, marrying twice, having two daughters and a son (the last to arrive, as the product of his second marriage; he promptly, and with a relief which whistles down the years, christened the boy Alexander Boswell Dun), and finally buying a small farm in the locality before dying less than a year before James; so he and his young charge were completely separated only by a death which was, in 1752, a very long way away. But to the 12-year-old this was of no account. The years of respite were over, and he was plunged, in the Edinburgh winter of 1752, into the unforgiving regime of a new governor.

The Reverend Joseph Fergusson would be, in fact, the last all-powerful tyrant before whom Jamie Boswell was obliged to kneel, and his tenure did not last for all that long. Anyway, by 1752 the youngster knew what to expect: dogma, systematic learning, and a relentlessly unsympathetic personality. I have a friend, said Jamie one day, whom I love more than my brothers. Blockhead! cried Fergusson. Blockhead! Do you not know how affection develops? First you love your parents, then your brothers, then you spread yourself abroad on the rest of the human race! The boy returned to reading the ancients dully, comprehending hardly at all. 'He had no other idea than to make me perform a task. When I asked him questions about the poets, for instruction or amusement – and why should I not have looked for amusement? – he lost his temper and cried out with a schoolmaster's arrogance, "Come, come, keep at work, keep at work, don't interrupt the lesson. Time is flying . . ." ' Fergusson also employed an interesting, if not uncommon, means of disciplining his pupil. It was usual in schools of the eighteenth and nineteenth centuries to hang certain objects (a wooden board, a spoon, a written sign) from the necks of recalcitrant students. This punishment was imposed in Scotland, for example, upon children who were found – or merely rumoured – to have used Gaelic rather than English within school-time. Jamie Boswell could hardly have been guilty of that offence, and wooden boards with rope attached were at a premium in Parliament Close, so Joseph Fergusson compromised by draping the coal-tongs about his pupil's collar in return for insufficient achievement. Definitely the coal-tongs, Boswell would later muse, looking back at his childhood as if at some absurd, beguiling hallucination, 'not those slight things which ladies use at tea, but what you may by every chimney see'.

Predictably, the 12-year-old James Boswell fell ill. His skin erupted in a rash and he suffered fits of vomiting which were not cured by the forced consumption of cocktails of prescribed medicines. After a while, half-happy at escaping his studies even by this uncomfortable route, he developed the technique to throw up instantly whatever the visiting doctors poured down his throat. They – not altogether inaccurately – diagnosed a strange and severe nervous complaint, and he was sent to take the waters at Moffat, a tiny spa town folded in the Annandale hills 40 miles due east of Auchinleck.

Unfortunately, Joseph Fergusson went too, and proceeded to conduct himself like an ogre from the fairy tales. When Jamie was put, fidgeting, into a hydropathic tub and draped with some 'scanty covering', the governor stood glowering by, occasionally barking: 'Take care, you rogue! If we see the least disobedience to our orders, we shall proceed to instant punishment.' Jamie sat still and miserable in the tepid water. Nor was that the limit of the tutor's blackguardry. During their stay at Moffat the boy fell for a pretty young girl called MacKay, and the Reverend Fergusson mocked his tender flame in the crudest and most singular way: 'setting his teeth together and giving hard thumps on the knees of his breeches'.

Fergusson was as doomed as the ghastly green giant at the top of the beanstalk. He was quickly replaced, on the instructions of the worried Euphemia or the perceptive Alexander, by William McQuhae and by the University College of Edinburgh. James Boswell first attended university at 13 years of age. That was not unusual: he was an intelligent, accomplished child, and his father wanted him to become a lawyer. The social position of members of the legal profession in eighteenth-century Edinburgh, not to say their earning potential, was without comparison. Lawyers effectively monopolised the ruling class, the landed class, the moneyed class and – as if for good measure – the intelligentsia. Law was the sweetest occupation of the day. Landowners had long urged their younger sons to enter the Scottish Bar as a consolation prize for coming late to the inheritance queue; by the eighteenth century lairds were suggesting the same to their elder sons and heirs. Favourite daughters would be nudged away from the florid scion of a thousand acres and pointed discreetly in the direction of an unclaimed advocate. The country cousins and the town cousins became one and a whole: the gentry and provincial nobility who entered town for the season dined, drank and danced with their equals, their fellows, their friends, their relatives – the judges, the barristers and the solicitors. Of the 200 young men who qualified as writers to the signet – solicitors empowered to conduct cases at the Court of Session – in Scotland in the century between 1690 and 1789, 132 were the sons of other lawyers or landowners. Twelve, by contrast, were the seed of physicians, teachers or architects; and three the offspring of tradesmen. Little wonder that when the first street directories of Edinburgh were compiled in the 1770s citizens were listed according to a natural professional pyramid: advocates first, then their clerks, then the writers to the signet and their clerks, then the town houses of the country squires – and then the lumpen bourgeoisie, the ministers, army officers, merchants, doctors and lecturers, bundled unprotesting together in the same large but comparatively insignificant caste of low-rent, top-floor-dwelling sub-professionals. They would pass on the stairs, these groups, they would exchange affable courtesies, but in James Boswell's lifetime their aspirations were as far apart as John Dun was from the man whose name he gave his son.

It was almost a condition of rank that Alexander's first-born son and heir should go to the Bar. What else would he do? Live off his father and his name until inheritance day? Down that path, as Alexander Boswell knew well, lay debauchery, and, while Lord Auchinleck would tolerate many strange and displeasing excesses in his child, he set his face like flint against a life filled exclusively by drink and courtesans. All of Jamie's upbringing had reared him for the law. Towards the end of the eighteenth century another Scots gentleman whom James would come to know, the parliamentarian George Dempster, drew up an itinerary for his seven-year-old nephew which was guaranteed to see the boy reach his privileged majority as an advocate and a country landowner 'and as rich as his parents left him'. This education would take place mainly in Scotland so that the lad would foster a love of his native land. Between the ages of seven and 12 he would have a private tutor who would travel with him everywhere, and would also accompany him to school and help with his classes in Latin, French, writing, dancing and arithmetic. The child would summer in the country estate, where he could grasp the rudiments of riding, shooting and fishing. For three years between the ages of 13 and 16 he would study Latin, Greek, French, literature and natural history at university, followed by a further 12 months pursuing moral philosophy, history and civil law. At the age of 18 he would concentrate more thoroughly on the law, and would also travel. Upon his return from the Grand Tour, he would complete his legal instruction. It was a well-worn road, and with only slight deviations it was the road upon which James Boswell was set.

The Edinburgh University which James Boswell entered to study languages as a day student in 1753 was not yet, not quite, the academic institution whose reputation four, three, or even two decades later would be the talk of Europe and the boast of Scotland. But it was a hard-nosed school with a fierce sense of its own worth and no time at all for backsliders. Its professors, particularly in the fields of medicine and anatomy, areas of urgent concern to eighteenth-century civilisation, were ruthless in the prosecution of their research – as the occasional Edinburgh riot against grave-robbers and body-snatchers indicated. They were also at least competent and at best inspired teachers. They had to be: unlike the universities of Oxford and Cambridge, Edinburgh allowed its teaching staff no stipends. Their wage-packets were filled in strict proportion to the number of students who attended their classes and lectures.

Jamie found the university to be a form of freedom. He responded to men who, in their turn, were keen to attract and to interest him. His acute, inherited ear for languages and his voracious appetite for the literature of all ages pleased his assessors. The young Boswell would be, they assured him, a man of consequence. And he had by his side, if not on his side, the engaging character of William McQuhae. The brothers' new governor, although also a student of divinity with an eye on the Presbyterian ministry, was as different from the blackhearted 'barbarian' Joseph Fergusson, the villain of their juvenile drama, as Friar Tuck from John Knox. He was good natured and vivacious, active and ambitious, but so unclear as to whether or not God was calling the unmistakable name of McQuhae to His service that he would at one time consider joining the British Army, before due consideration of the 'uncertainties and the hazards' of military life caused him to check and turn back again 'to embrace a sure competency and live contented as a country clergyman'.

41

McQuhae was not many years older than James Boswell, and a decade afterwards the latter would be expressing a seigneurial desire to do well by his former tutor. At the age of 22, indeed, James considered 'honest McQuhae' to be one of just three real friends left to him in the world, just three like-minded souls upon whom he could unburden his heart's heavy load. But McQuhae would shortly afterwards disappear from his turbulent young life. The other two 'true friends', whom he also met first during his early years at Edinburgh University, would be parted from James Boswell only by death.

William Johnson Temple and John Johnston of Grange were his contemporaries and fellow students at a Greek class taught by one Robert Hunter, which all three boys attended at the ages of 15 or 16. Temple was the son of the mayor of the English border town of Berwick-upon-Tweed, and Johnston was the heir to a small Dumfriesshire estate. They were bound only by their constant affection for their common friend. Temple tailored a fiery Whiggish republicanism, which – although it may have amused Lord Auchinleck, had the old man ever given the boy a chance – was cut to discomfort the soft and sentimental Jamie. 'All power is derived originally from the people,' William would instruct his friend, who when they had first met was wont to match his father's loud prayers for the House of Hanover with silent supplications of his own for the good health of the Stuart dynasty. 'Kings are but the servants of the public,' the rational Temple insisted. 'A king of England has no prerogative but to do good by supplying the deficiencies of the laws, the most honourable and glorious of all prerogatives, which, whenever he shall be found again to abuse, I trust there will not be wanting other Hampdens and other Sidneys to pull the tyrant down and trample him in the dust.'

John Johnston of Grange was, however, as soft-centred a notional Jacobite as only a Lowland Scottish countryman could ever be. Loyal and easy-going, uncritical and (aside from a gloomy, commonplace inclination towards hypochondria) undemanding, he was also an impossible correspondent by virtue of his agricultural reluctance to put pen to parchment. James

Boswell himself fell somewhere between this good, slow fellow, 'who was steady to me upon all occasions', and the abrupt, opinionated, provocative, northern English vowels of William Temple. Boy and man, they would bulwark three-quarters of his adult life, unadvertised and irreplaceable; the teenagers sent by ambitious fathers to Edinburgh University who became his first, his best, and his final allies.

At the end of 1756 James Boswell fell ill again. Upon this occasion the trauma was real; the sickness truly frightening to patient, relative and friend. And its extended course did result in a kind of fatality: it somehow killed the excruciating, nervous, shamefaced boy, it exorcised the worst of the dark spirits which dictated fearful moods to all of his sentient life, and it let a new youth loose upon the world.

'Even now it does not seem clear to me.' He himself never knew what happened, only that it had happened. Puberty had caught him typically unforewarned and unprepared, unaccustomed dreams pointed him as plainly as night followed day in the direction of mortal sin and the unappeasable damnation which, it seemed suddenly to this 16-year-old, would never, ever be removed from his immediate horizon. The future, upon which at intervals – with Dun, McQuhae, Johnston and Temple, at Valleyfield and even at times in the warm harvest meadows of Auchinleck – a dim sun had seemed to shine, now looked irremediably cruel. 'My youthful desires became strong. I was horrified because of the fear that I would sin and be damned.' Should he follow the early Christians and purify his soul through contumely and physical suffering? How could he? How could a 16-year-old boy in 1750s' Edinburgh achieve the tremendous persecution meted out to Origen in the Roman world of 1,500 years before? Everything was stacked against him: his time, his family, his genes . . .

'That madness passed', and another took over. He knew, as did any educated person and most uneducated persons of the mid-eighteenth century, that a divine of the age, a latter-day St Francis, was tramping the country urging salvation through trust in Christ, offering the assurance that 'he had taken my sins, *even mine* , and saved me from the law of sin and death.' James Boswell decided to follow John Wesley into the Methodist branch of the Anglican Church.

His parents sent him once more to take the waters at Moffat. There he met and fell into intense conversation with an elderly man who believed in the transmigration of souls, and he determined to become a vegetarian, resolving himself 'to suffer everything as a martyr to humanity'. His delirium, this intense and apparently chronic state of nervous collapse, intensified. 'I imagined that I was never to get rid of it. I gave myself up as devoted to misery. I entertained a most gloomy and odd way of thinking. I was much hurt at being good for nothing in life.'

The crisis ebbed slowly. After the nadir of looking upon 'the whole human race with horror', he was at first surprised to find his mind at war with itself, torn between melancholy and mirth, and steadily mirth once more asserted itself within his daily life. Melancholy did not disappear – melancholy would never entirely be lost to James Boswell; but no more, after those months of pubescent anguish, was mirth. It passed; gradually 'I grew better and freer of my disorder'. It passed, 'I know not how'.

It passed, and in going it brought its subject alive to at least one rather ominous fact: 'I could not bear the law.' The James Boswell who got from his bed in Parliament Close one morning in 1757 to decide that he was, once more, ready to face the world, took that decision largely on the understanding that the study and later the practice of civil and criminal law in Scotland was not for him. What might take its place? 'I had been so long accustomed to consider myself as out of the world that I could not think of engaging in real life.' Clearly, it was time to put that to rights. James Boswell took to the streets of Edinburgh.

He was not an especially ugly or a handsome youth, who first swung down the Canongate. He was plump but not fat, of average height for his age and time, which is to say about five-and-a-half feet. His hair and eyes were black, his nose swept down and prominently out of rounded cheeks like a small shoehorn, and his lips were thick, red and permanently pursed. He had a short span of attention, looked constantly amused or ready to be amused, was always on the edge of speech, and when he spoke it was – unselfconsciously, in 1757 – in a moderate version of the broad Scots of his distinguished father, which Sir Henry Craik described as 'masked by such dialectical peculiarities that it was to the Englishman, to all intents and purposes, a foreign tongue'.

Such a brogue did not embarrass James Boswell in the Edinburgh wynds and taverns of the late 1750s. It was, by turns, a lively and exasperating town. The sinister, dare-devil gatherings of the early part of the century, the Demireps, the Sulphur and Horn clubs, were no more than a scandalous rumour in the town of Boswell's teens. The theatre was almost a subversive, underground activity. Just 20 years earlier the artistic entrepreneur Allan Ramsay had built a playhouse in Carrubber's Close, hard by the junction of Bridge Street and Nether Bow Port, but the clergy had instantly persuaded the magistrates to close it down. Ramsay took out an action alleging fiscal injury in the Court of Session, where it was beautifully judged that 'though he had been damaged, he had not been injured'. No theatrical show was able, for 30 years after that, to get a licence in Edinburgh. Plays were consequently performed, in such venues as the Tailor's Hall at the back of Cowgate and the Concert Hall in Canongate, under the transparent subterfuge of being small bonuses offered free of charge at the close of a legitimate and commercial musical concert. This uneasy stand-off almost collapsed in James Boswell's 17th year. On 14 December 1756 John Home, an East Lothian minister with a kenspeckle military background, presented in the Canongate his contemporary dramatic version of the improving ballad of 'Childe Maurice'. *Douglas* became the talk of Edinburgh, chiefly because of the occupation of its author. Home's presbytery promptly demanded that 'all within its bounds discourage the illegal and dangerous entertainments of the stage, and restrain those under their influence from frequenting such seminaries of vice and folly'. *Douglas* was withdrawn, Home resigned his living, and the play became a riotous success at London's Covent Garden despite the verdict of a surly critic named Samuel Johnson that there were not ten good lines in the script from prologue to curtain.

Illegal and dangerous entertainments offered in seminaries of vice and folly were just the ticket for a growing boy. James Boswell and his friends haunted the plays and the travelling players, gawped at visiting actresses, made sophisticated small-talk with itinerant actor-managers, and planned in hostelries the epic dramas of their own devising. The inns and coffee-houses of that overcrowded town were its congress halls, its offices, its market-places and its banquet-rooms. They were entirely demo-cratic centres of inebriation. Silversmiths concluded their sales over a cup of ale at John's coffee-house; workaday tradesmen wetted their bargains in the High Street wynds; magistrates tradi-tionally organised a hanging at Paxton's tavern; the Lord Provost had his guests to dinner and to supper not in his private house but at the roomier, better-victualled public bars; and the Lord High Commissioner received the members of the General Assembly of the Church of Scotland in Clerihew's or Fortune's inn. They opened with the 11.30 a.m. 'meridian' bell and suppos-edly closed when the town guard beat the 10.00 p.m. drum. From the gill-bell to the drum and beyond, Edinburgh drank, bar-gained, bickered, schemed and dreamed of a thousand futures, from the meridian to 'the noisy ten hours drum . . . gie a' to merri-ment and glee, wi' sang and glass they fley the power o' care that would harass the hour . . .'

At the end of the academic year of 1758 William Temple left Edinburgh to study law at Cambridge University. James, ever frightened by the prospect of losing a friend, begged that their relationship be maintained through the mail. It was, for a further 37 years. Boswell almost certainly started the marathon corres-pondence by writing immediately, in July, to give Temple the ominous news that he had spent some instructive time in the company of a great man, and that he had much enjoyed the expe-rience.

The philosopher David Hume had fallen on troubled times since his *Treatise On Human Nature* appeared 'stillborn from the press' in 1738 (the only good notice it received was one written anonymously by Hume himself). In 1752, however, the Faculty of Advocates in Edinburgh held out a hand to their fellow Scottish intellectual and made him their librarian. Hume cheerfully settled in among the dusty shelves, relinquished philosophical essays, and set to writing a history of England, the first volume of which was published in 1754.

At 17 years old, Boswell approached this amiable 47-year-old. He had chosen a sympathetic character. Aside from the fact that Lord Auchinleck was one of his employers, David Hume was unlikely to discourage the youth. A large and ponderous figure, the philosopher was essentially genial and thoroughly Scottish. His accent was as unrepentantly rich as that of any man; he took pleasure in referring to the inhabitants of the capital of the United Kingdom as those 'depraved barbarians who inhabit the banks of the Thames'; and he used his *History of England* as an hilarious vehicle for mischief. The Stuarts, particularly James I, had been perfect kings, argued this self-educated son of a Borders laird; the 'Glorious Revolution' of 1688, far from establishing a decent, constrained and constitutional monarchy, had actually been a step back towards the dark ages; and as for this much-vaunted 'liberty' that everyone was crowing about, that was a prize for which 'so rude a beast as an Englishman was unfitted'. David Hume was in short an emblematic Scotsman of the Union, and he was unlikely to resist the company of a young and chirpy and highly impressionable countryman.

Sadly, James was in 1758 a novice at the sport of coat-tailing celebrities, and neither he nor his target gained much from the encounter. Hume was indeed extraordinary, and discreet, and affable, and certainly full of solid learning, and he had a lot of books. He was not . . . how could the perplexed young man put it? He was not overly delicate, but he knew a lot about history, so that in conversation his guests were not only entertained but also educated.

And that was about that. Martha White, however, the pious possessor both of angelic charms and a £30,000 dowry, was certainly worth pursuing. She sang, danced, played a variety of musical instruments, and was well read. James took tea with her. They were happy days. 'My mind is in such an agreeable situation, that being refused would not be so fatal as to drive me to despair' – which was as well, for Miss White and her fortune were destined for the Earl of Elgin.

James retreated, unabashed, to a relatively undemanding and cheerfully accomplished life of study and recreation. He routinely took just two classes a day, law in the morning and Roman antiquities in the early afternoon. For the rest of the time he studied in Parliament Close, or walked through the Old Town, or met up with John Johnston at Tom's tavern – or took elocution lessons with the English actor James Love.

The vogue for such exercises in vowel-improvement is as indicative as any other aspect of eighteenth-century Edinburgh life of the city's strained, ambiguous view of itself in relation to the supposedly sophisticated south; and the fact that James Boswell, the son of a father whose accent and vocabulary might have made an Ayrshire farmhand scratch his head, took instruction in the diction of the English Court tells much of the insecurity of the time. It did much more than that, of course: it directed James away from this cramped, parochial place as surely as, but far more effectively than, his early years had pointed him at Calvinism and the law.

It could hardly do anything else. Despite the caustic insistences of such as David Hume – and, for that matter, Lord Auchinleck – that Scotland contained all that could be required by man, and that south of the Tweed lay vicious barbarisms, Edinburgh trumpeted its sense of inferiority. It was a plaintive, persistent sound, it echoed throughout the years of James Boswell's youth, and it informed the whole of the rest of his life as did no other earthly influence. The debate was not conducted so much about whether or not north Britain was a lesser place than the south, as how far lacking it was, in which areas, and how quickly and by what means could the unhappy situation be retrieved. Eminent Scottish writers such as John Home, Thomas Reid and William Robertson were known anxiously to consult their English friends concerning idiom (Robertson, in ironic counterpoint to the unashamed David Hume, while preparing his *History of Scotland*); a habit which led their colleague James Beattie gloomily to assert that Scottish scholars may as well have been writing in Latin: 'a dead language which we can understand but cannot speak. Our style smells of the lamp and we are slaves of the language, and are continually afraid of committing gross blunders.'

Even that extraordinarily diverse character Allan Ramsay, the renaissance man of eighteenth-century Edinburgh – at one moment a poet, the next a librarian, a portrait painter, a theatrical manager; whatever attracted his butterfly mind – even the ubiquitous Ramsay fell victim to the complex. His 'Select Society', which was in 1755 ambitiously retitled the 'Society for Encouraging Art, Science and Industry', changed its name again in 1761 to the 'Society for Promoting the Reading and Speaking of the English Language'. Edinburgh girls, whose quaint dialect had 30 years earlier been the subject of delighted comment from English visitors, flocked to join. When the actor Thomas Sheridan arrived in Edinburgh in the same year to deliver 12 lectures on English pronunciation at St Paul's Episcopal Church, 300 worthies packed into the building and one of the most preposterous scenes in Scottish history was performed. Sheridan was an Irishman, and he spoke like an Irishman. The clue to the way the English articulated, he told his Scots customers, lay in the alternation of weak and forcible notes – 'as "ti-tum", or "tum-ti-tum-ti". Or "ta-ta-tum-ti-tum". Come, say after me . . .' And the hallful of divines, advocates and fashionable gentlemen dutifully repeated after Sheridan, 'tum-ti-tum-ti . . . ta-ta-ta-tum', and then went back to their rooms and repeated them again, and subscribed almost to a man to the published version of Thomas Sheridan's talks on the correct use of the English language.

There were reasons, of course. Since the Union of Parliaments just half a century before, educated Scottish men and women had grown tired of mockery in London. Some of them, having altered their accents, actually changed their recognisably Caledonian surnames. Scottish politicians were weary of the condescending smiles whenever they rose to speak at Westminster; Scottish judges felt demeaned by the genuine bafflement of their colleagues in the House of Lords. Alexander Boswell himself had felt the sting. The French, he once commented, had the excellent manners not to laugh at a stranger who commits a blunder in their language, 'an absurdity that is remarkable in the English'. 'English,' his son would nonetheless pronounce, 'is much more agreeable than Scots.'

It did not end at the written and spoken word, this genuflexion to the south. Edinburgh itself, the stupendous, towering city on the rock, was a crumbling gangrenous shell to those who had seen London. In 1752 an extraordinary pamphlet was prepared by committee and published in the town. Titled *Proposals for carrying on certain Public Works in the City of Edinburgh*, this 7,500-word booklet would eventually lead to the draining of the North Loch and the creation of the magnificent New Town at its far shore, but in 1752 one of its functions was simply to point out the inadequacy of old Edinburgh, and this it did largely through unfavourable comparison with the English metropolis. London, it asserted, was a perfect place. 'We cannot fail to remark its healthful, unconfined situation, upon a large plain, gently shelving towards the Thames . . . the neatness and accommodation of its private houses; the beauty and conveniency of its numerous streets and open squares, of its buildings and bridges, its large parks and extensive walks . . . when we survey this mighty concourse of people, whom business, ambition, curiosity, or the love of pleasure, has assembled within so narrow a compass, we need no longer be astonished at that spirit of industry and improvement, which, taking its rise in the city of London, has at length spread over the greatest part of South Britain, animating every art and profession, and inspiring the whole people with the greatest ardour and emulation.'

What had Edinburgh to set beside this Shangri-La? 'One good street', with its herb, fruit and fish markets spilling across its highway, and that only accessible from the dubious Canongate; steep, narrow and dirty lanes running across its spine; the highest and most crowded housing in Europe; its refuse and sewage poured upon the banks of the North Loch . . . 'to such reasons alone, it must be imputed, that so few people of rank reside in this city; that it is rarely visited by strangers; and that so many local prejudices, and narrow notions, inconsistent

with polished manners and growing wealth, are still so obstinately retained.'

There was but one lesson to be taken from this rampant self-
abasement of the 1750s, and James Boswell took it. He spent his
late teens preparing, largely subconsciously, for the move. He
honed his accent with the roguish James Love. He listened carefully when Love advised him to keep a commonplace book, or
daily journal, and in return loaned money to the actor which
would never be repaid. He fell in love with a married actress,
made little secret of his unanswered passion, and got carted off
on an improving tour of the Northern Court Circuit with his
father and Sir David Dalrymple, Lord Hailes, a talkative acquaintance of Samuel Johnson and other luminaries of the southern
sky. But the legal processes of Perth only heightened his restless-
ness, and anyway divine providence, James would soon decide,
had seized the reins. He sponsored and produced – with money
from a weary but still indulgent father – a disastrous comedy
which was hooted off stage on its third night. He was sent to the
University of Glasgow to further his knowledge of civil law and
looked in at the lectures on moral philosophy being given by a
friend of David Hume called Adam Smith. 'A time of indisposi-
tion,' Smith told his student audience, 'is not altogether a time of
misery', and James Boswell must have nodded softly, knowingly
to himself. He encouraged with hard cash another indigent actor,
another plausible Irishman, by the name of Francis Gentleman,
to dedicate a new performance of Thomas Southerne's anti-
slavery play of 60 years earlier, *Oroonoko*, to a young man in
whom 'sense, taste, religion, and good nature' were joined. Who
was that? 'Gladly she will raise her feeble voice, nor fear to tell
that BOSWELL is her choice.' He was admitted to the Masons –
an institution detested by his father – at a Canongate lodge.

And then inevitably, in the spring of 1760, he overcame
'parental affection, ambition, interest', declared himself to be a
Roman Catholic who was about to enter a French monastery, or
– if that did not work out – a disillusioned outcast who would
seek death or glory through a commission in the Brigade of
Guards; and he fled to London.

Chapter Three

THE LAMB

. . . A Youth to Fortune and to Fame unknown.
Fair Science frown'd not on his humble birth,
And Melancholy mark'd him for her own.

THOMAS GRAY, 'ELEGY WRITTEN IN A
COUNTRY CHURCH-YARD'

It was a false dawn. Like many a teenaged runaway before and since, he soon returned: still a layman; still a civilian; but no longer a virgin.

Of the three ambitions there is no doubt which one most horrified Alexander Boswell. His son would have to discover the joys of the flesh sometime, it was of no matter, this was the eighteenth century. As for a posting in the Guards, the Boswells had never been military men, there was precious little future in such adventures and no money worth the candle, but it need not be catastrophic. Young men of family could and did leave the Guards as quickly as they had joined.

But a Catholic? He may as well have gone the whole lamb and become a monk, the effect would be the same. As a Roman Catholic, James Boswell would be debarred, under the Penal Laws which had been introduced to preserve the Glorious Revolution and the Hanoverian Order, from all inheritance, from a career in most professions, the civil services, or politics, and from all of the armed forces. He would not be able to vote, or to educate his children at any school in Great Britain. He would be liable to double taxation, and any attendance at mass would be a criminal conjoining with an illegal assembly. In England he would have been able to practise the law only as a lowly and obscure 'conveyancer in chambers'; in Scotland he would have been able to practise the law not at all, in any office, at any level, with any company.

This was what James Boswell meant by struggling against ambition and interest and overcoming those twin impostors. This was what he intended: to fly to London 'with the intention of hiding myself in some gloomy retreat to pass my life in sadness'. But they were little more than the indulgences of a confused 19-year-old, and although he would never quite shake off a residual affection for the 'regularity and ceremony' of the old Church he humoured himself with them in the spring of 1760 for as long as, and for not a moment longer than, they fitted his youthful mood.

London in 1760 was not much more hospitable to the devout Roman Catholic than was Edinburgh. In all but a few enclaves and country houses, chiefly in the north-west of England and of Scotland, Catholicism was an underground faith. There were a handful of chapels kept alive in the capital by the Catholic Embassy, and James Boswell made his way to the Bavarian Chapel and was received into communion. He also patronised a Catholic bookshop in Drury Lane and put himself up with a Catholic family. But when his new faith was confronted by its first test – a test considerably less painful than that faced by his schooldays' hero, Origen, during the persecution of Decius – it faltered, and then it fell.

His exasperated father had, from the moment of his flight, kept a careful eye on his movements. Sir David Dalrymple, the worldly young judge who had entertained young James with tales of London life on their tour of the Northern Court Circuit a year earlier, was persuaded to write to James and to the Anglican prebendary of St Paul's Cathedral, John Jortin, suggesting that they meet. On Thursday, 3 April 1760, James Boswell called on

Jortin. The divine was out, so James offered to return on the following day. Tomorrow is Good Friday, Jortin's daughter pointed out – my father will be engaged at church. Ah, said James. So it is. So he will. Saturday morning? Certainly, replied the daughter. The young visitor left Dalrymple's letter of introduction and a note of his own, and departed. 'From that time,' wrote Jortin to Dalrymple three-and-a-half weeks later, 'I have heard nothing of him. He began, I suppose, to suspect some design upon him . . . I heartily pity your good friend [Lord Auchinleck]. If his son be really sincere in his new superstition, and sober in his morals, there is some comfort in that, for surely a man may be a papist and an honest man. It is not to be expected that the son should feel much for his father's sorrows. Religious bigotry eats up natural affection, and tears asunder the dearest bonds.'

Jortin was not to know, but by the end of April James was no longer either sincere in his 'new superstition' or sober in his morals. Nor was he in much danger from religious bigotry. He had decided that he was, after all, a deist who accepted the presence of God without wishing to commit himself about the precise nature of His revelation. He had also – curiously, at about the same time – fallen into the company of Samuel Derrick and Alexander, the tenth Earl of Eglinton, and 'I gave myself up to pleasure without limit. I was in a delirium of joy.'

Eglinton was a jovial 37-year-old Ayrshire nobleman with a house just north of Hyde Park Corner who was happy, upon request, to put out feelers for his Scottish neighbour's son. He did not find what he had been warned against. Expecting a meek and troubled young man palely loitering from one subterranean chapel to the next, he discovered instead a boisterous 19-year-old intent on trawling every tavern between the Knightsbridge Turnpike and Petticoat Lane. James Boswell had, in his turn, discovered secular London. He did so through another introduction, one of his own making. Francis Gentleman, the Irish actor who had lightened his pocket in Glasgow for the sake of a few fawning lines of doggerel, pointed him in the direction of the former actor and would-be poet Samuel Derrick. This was an unsavoury man. 'After I found him out to be a little blackguard pimping dog,'

James would later insist, 'I did not know how to get rid of him.' In the April and early May of 1760, however, it is unlikely that he made much effort to do so. Derrick knew the streets, and he carried James Boswell down them.

Either Eglinton – who took quickly to his Ayrshire neighbour's son – or the 'pimping dog' Derrick escorted James to the house of the Blue Periwig on Southampton Street, between Covent Garden and the Strand, and introduced him to Miss Sally Forrester. There and then he 'first paid my addresses to the Paphian Queen'. With Sally Forrester, James Boswell 'first experienced the melting and transporting rites of Love'. Sally became his 'first Lady of Venus's Bedchamber'.

The second was Jeannie Wells of Berwick Street in Soho; the third, fourth, fifth and sixth melted into one another. The Church of Rome could not, however reassuring its solidity and however attractive its ceremony, fairly compete with Paphian queens for the affection of James Boswell. It was dropped as quickly and unrepentantly as Methodism, transubstantiation and vegetarianism. And the amused Eglinton, having routed papism more thoroughly than poor John Jortin could ever have hoped to do, continued to do his duty by Lord Auchinleck's son. James was invited into his Mayfair home, Samuel Derrick was edged out of his life, and a new and quite dazzling social milieu took his seedy place. Suddenly it was 'the circle of the great, the gay, and the ingenious'; suddenly the Jockey Club, Newmarket, and the fast company of Edward Augustus, Duke of York, a contemporary of James and heir presumptive to the throne of the 76-year-old George II. Suddenly the tipsy sophistication of men about town swapping couplets and compliments, just as Addison in the *Spectator* had suggested. 'Lord Eglinton,' James publicly versified in an excruciating burst of adolescent pomp, 'who has, you know, A little dash of whim or so; Who through a thousand scenes will range, To pick up anything that's strange, By chance a curious cub had got, On Scotia's mountains newly caught . . .' He was introduced to yet another Irishman and yet another prebendary – of York Minster, this time – who had just published in the north of England two indecorous volumes titled *Tristram Shandy*, which had prostrated chattering London at their author's feet, and James Boswell found Laurence Sterne to be a charming man, an excellent, brief companion in their dizzy whirl through the excited town.

He was liked. More than the easing of his religious woes, more than the melting joys of Sally Forrester, more even than the dash and fire of London itself, it came upon James Boswell as an epiphany to discover that wherever he poked that oddly shaped nose, it appeared to be welcomed. Eglinton liked him. The Duke of York, a young man who was hardly deprived of convivial fellowship, liked him. Even the pimping dog Samuel Derrick – who was, after all, on his way to Bath to replace Beau Nash as master of ceremonies there, and so could not be an entirely insignificant character – liked him. Sally and Jeannie liked him. They said so. Laurence Sterne laughed with him. He had at least one happy talent: at the age of 19 he was amusing company. He was witty in an erratic, hit-and-miss fashion, he would join in any conversation without fear of overstretching his limited experience, and he was duly and pleasingly deferential to his superiors. Men and women usually like a flatterer, the more so when his admiration is as clearly genuine as was the 19-year-old James Boswell's of the city and society by the Thames. And if the eulogist himself happens also to be fun, what better way is there of passing the London afternoons and nights? When he looked in a mirror he saw a plump and pot-bellied youth, a face and body which advertised his love of beef and pudding; he saw a 'large and pond'rous' head, and hair like a scarecrow. But he was liked, and liked well. Even in his self-important youngblood swank, James made people smile, made them stay, and made them want to see him again. No governors, no schools, no universities and few parents could have taught that skill.

One parent was, understandably, reaching the limits of his substantial patience. Occasionally James would surface in Mayfair and bleat that he wanted a commission in the Guards. That was why he was still in London. Not to drink hock and recite bad declamatory rhymes to the raucous laughter of the Earl of Eglinton and the Duke of York, but to become an officer. Come back to Scotland, wrote Lord Auchinleck, and we can think it over, and so in the early summer of 1760, after three months in the promised land, James took his leave of London and caught the chaise back north to Edinburgh. There Alexander Boswell took his son to see a wonderful relic of the previous century, Archibald, the Duke of Argyll, who had swept with Marlborough through the Low Countries 50 years before. How will this young man march to the fife and the timpano? 'My Lord,' growled Archibald to father and heir, 'I like your son. This boy must not be shot at for three-and-six a day.'

It was, of course, no use. The army which James desired to join did not get fired upon at all. It was an army of the night, of the raffish city night; its uniforms were frock-suits, hats adorned with golden lace, clean shirts and five-shilling stockings; its artillery was puns, chaff and epigrams; and it could only be wounded by a snub. For 70 weeks, with his age of majority creeping sluggishly near, he attempted in Edinburgh to apply himself to the study of civil law. 'But my mind, once put in ferment, could never apply itself again to solid learning. I had no inclination whatever for the civil law. I learned it very superficially. My principles became more and more confused. I held all things in contempt, and I had no idea except to get through the passing day agreeably.' Ahead of him 29 October 1761, his 21st birthday, stood like a distant flag of freedom, the border crossing of a new and friendly land. Mustering a brave smile to his face, he hobbled towards it through the long Edinburgh months. But it was hard to bear. How unjust, how cruelly wrong it seemed on every waking day. Consider, he beseeched William Temple through the mail, 'A young fellow whose happiness was always centred in London, who had at least got there, and had begun to taste its delights – getting into the Guards, being about Court, enjoying the happiness of the "beau monde" and the company of men of genius, in short everything he could wish – consider this poor fellow hauled away to the town of Edinburgh, obliged to conform to every Scotch custom, or be laughed at – "Will you hae some jeel [jam]? oh, fie! oh, fie!" – his flighty imagination quite cramped, and he obliged to study "Corpus Juris Civilis" and live in his father's strict family; is there any wonder, sir, that the unlucky dog should be somewhat fretful? Yoke a Newmarket courser to a dung-cart, and I'll lay my life on't he'll either caper or kick most confoundedly, or be as stupid and restive as an old battered post-horse.'

Wherever and whenever possible this Newmarket courser, this spiritual son of the enlightened south, set about alleviating his discontent through the re-creation in his birthplace of what he perceived to be the essence of London society. He and John Johnston established the Edinburgh equivalent of a roistering men's club at Tom's tavern. Edinburgh may not have been in much need of such an institution, but James Boswell delivered it anyway. The young men named their fraternity the Soaping Club, an enigmatic (even in the 1760s James found himself obliged to explain it to his befuddled fellow Scots) allusion to fellows 'soaping their own beard', or being in their own humour. Each, in other words, to his own.

The chief function of the Soaping Club, aside from subsidising the busy Edinburgh wine trade, was self-advertisement. Luckily a useful vehicle arrived in James Boswell's eager hands. Through his friendship with a talented contemporary called Andrew Erskine, the youngest son of a disgraced and dispossessed Jacobite earl who had risen in 1745 and fallen in 1746, James got his hands on the editorship of a collection of Scottish verse. It was a strange affair, as indicative as any of the young Boswell's ruinously persuasive manner. Erskine was a writer of ability who, thanks to his family's unfortunate circumstances (and in contrast to James's bizarre pretensions), was reluctantly obliged to make his living as a lieutenant in the 71st Foot. He communicated with, and was shyly seduced by, James Boswell. This Boswell, James informed him – half in jest and half in absolute seriousness – in 1761, 'is a most excellent man; he is of an ancient family in the west of Scotland, upon which he values himself not a little . . . His parts are bright, and his education has been good. He has travelled in post-chaises miles without number. He eats of every good dish, especially apple pie. He drinks old hock. He has a very fine temper. He is somewhat of a humorist, and a little tinctured with pride. He has a good manly countenance, and owns himself to be amorous. He has infinite vivacity, yet is observed at times to have a melancholy cast. He is rather fat than lean, rather short than tall, rather young than old . . .'

It was not a bad self-portrait, and Erskine found it irresistible. The two men colluded. In 1760 the Edinburgh bookseller Alexander Donaldson had commissioned Andrew to compile *A Collection of Original Poems by Scotch gentlemen*. It had enjoyed moderate success and a second volume was due, but Erskine's regiment called him away. James, naturally, offered his sophisticated assistance. To the contributions of John 'Douglas' Home and James 'Ossian' Macpherson he added, with justification, some small works of Andrew Erskine – and 28 products of the pen of James Boswell.

One of them will do. One of them would have done in 1761. It was an anonymous ode to Boswell and the Soaping Club. James had discovered the joy of having cake and eating it. 'B———, of Soapers the king', the second edition of *A Collection of Original Poems by other Scotch gentlemen* declared to its perplexed Edinburgh patrons, 'On Tuesdays at Tom's does appear . . .'

> And when he does talk, or does sing,
> To him ne'er a one can come near.
> For he talks with such ease and such grace,
> That all charmed to attention we sit,
> And he sings with so comic a face,
> That our sides are just ready to split.

This same B———, the upright, art-loving elders of the town were asked to appreciate, abjured snuff but drank hock, and was a pleasant, gay character who 'does women adore . . .'

> And never once means to deceive,
> He's in love with at least half a score
> If they're serious he smiles in his sleeve.
> He has all the bright fancy of youth,
> With the judgment of forty and five.
> In short, to declare the plain truth,
> There is no better fellow alive.

The second volume of the collection is about to appear, James wrote encouragingly to Erskine in December, 1761. You, he told the hapless soldier, 'make a very good figure' in the book, while Boswell himself cut 'a decent one'. In fact, it sank like a weighted corpse. A planned third volume never materialised, Donaldson's little enterprise was almost ruined, and Andrew Erskine's editorial career was destroyed. James retired to the Soaping Club, a hero for a drinking night.

His 21st birthday came and went in the late October of 1761, and to his dismay November found him bound still to the Edinburgh rock. Lord Auchinleck was adamant not so much that his eldest son should relinquish all ideas of military service but that he should complete his training in the law. To further this end, Alexander Boswell made ominous noises about putting the Auchinleck estate into trust and allowing James, by way of compensation, £100 a year.

An intricate game of family chess was being played. Alexander wanted James to be a responsible heir to Auchinleck and a lawyer with substantial earnings from outside the estate. These provisions almost exclusively required his son to live and work in Scotland, although that was an incidental rather than an essential requirement. James wanted, in time, to inherit Auchinleck and enjoyed the notion of substantial earnings, but would have preferred to make them, if at all possible, as a privileged officer in the Guards or as a member of the social intelligentsia – a writer, perhaps. Or as both. Or to matriculate to the latter after a dashing spell in the former. The Guards would be merely a passport, because mostly James wanted to be a celebrity in London. 'My fondness for the Guards,' he wrote to Andrew Erskine, who actually was in uniform, 'must appear very strange to you, who have a rooted antipathy at the glare of scarlet. But I must inform you that there is a city called London, for which I have as violent an affection as the most romantic lover ever had for his mistress. There a man may indeed soap his own beard, and enjoy whatever is to be had in this transitory state of things. Every agreeable whim may be fully indulged without censure.'

Few of their designs were negotiable. Alexander was

absolutely set on the law and equally convinced that, left to his own devices in London, James would neglect his studies and subsequently his career, with potentially disastrous consequences for the family seat. Even after Alexander's 'improvements' to the Ayrshire acreage, its annual revenue was no more than £1,500 a year, and sums like that were famously quickly dissipated. James was bored with the law, bored with Edinburgh, and convinced that if he did not get to London soon his heart would break and his chances of glittering, lifelong fame – the glory that had been, he half-seriously suggested, predicted in the skies over Edinburgh 21 years ago – would be lost in the Caledonian mist.

Few of their designs being negotiable, they hardly negotiated, and the contest devolved down to an inconclusive tactical stand-off, to shadow-boxing. James provided colourful evidence week in and week out of his discontent and his true vocation. When Thomas Sheridan arrived in Edinburgh in the summer of 1761 to deliver his lessons on how to speak proper English, James courted him violently – 'My Mentor! My Socrates!' James gambled badly and built up debts. James hungrily sought out the company of actors such as the dashing West Digges, a leading man in town with *The Beggar's Opera*, whom Lord Auchinleck would have looked upon with contempt but James considered to have 'more or as much of the deportment of a man of fashion as anybody I ever saw'. James flirted and more with married and unmarried women, and exaggerated his affairs to as many of the Edinburgh populace as cared to listen. James boasted to his friends of doses of venereal disease. James bitched at Temple when the divinity student remonstrated with his 'choice of female friends'. In January 1762 James met a 'curious young little pretty' woman named Peggy Doig. By early March he had 'made it out' with her. In between times, James studied civil law in a moody, lack-lustre, unconvincing way.

Alexander had two major sanctions left to him after his son had passed the age of 21, and he used them remorselessly. James, having signally failed to turn a penny in the theatrical and publishing worlds, needed spending money, and his father restricted its issue according to the young man's behaviour. And, perhaps above all, James needed the security of his eventual inheritance of Auchinleck. He required this not only as present collateral against his future wealth but also as a social crowbar. 'The young Laird of Auchinleck' might evoke little more than faint, quizzical interest in the Piccadilly salons ('where?'), but it was incalculably preferable to 'Master James Boswell' ('who?').

So Alexander toyed with the inheritance deeds like a big cat with a lamb. They may go into trust, they may revert to John. Goodness knows what to do with 'em. And day after stricken day, in an obstinate, mimicking mime, James toyed sulkily with the thin pleasures of Edinburgh. It could not and did not go on forever, and predictably the good-hearted, well-intentioned older man unlocked the door. Once James had passed his civil-law examinations, said Lord Auchinleck, he might go to London. That would not, ideally, represent the final stage in his education, but it would do for the moment. There would be no promises made concerning the destination of the lairdship of Auchinleck, but James might nonetheless attempt to gain a commission in the Guards. To this end, he would be furnished with an introduction to Charles Douglas, the third Duke of Queensberry, an expatriate Scot with considerable influence both at Court and in Parliament.

James Boswell passed his examinations in civil law at the end of July 1762, shortly after having been informed by 'little pretty' Peggy Doig that certain actions had resulted in material consequences. He then accepted an invitation from Henry Home, Lord Kames, one of his father's legal colleagues, to go on a tour of the southern Scottish counties. The most unusual people still enjoyed his company. Upon his return, his father paid his debts and increased his allowance to £200 a year, to be paid through a bank in six-week instalments.

'On Monday next I am to set out for London,' he wrote to Erskine on 10 November. On the morning of Monday, 15 November 1762, he rose early and went to visit John Johnston. Among other things, the two men had to finalise arrangements for the discreet care of Peggy Doig and her material consequences. Johnston, he was irritated to learn, was still in Dumfriesshire. He walked slowly back to Parliament Close, and there he had a long and affectionate conversation with his mother and father. At ten o'clock he shook hands with one and kissed the other, patted young Davy on the head, and strolled off to his London-bound chaise, armed with a list of introductions from his father and a list of useful taverns between Edinburgh and London from West Digges.

The post-chaise rattled down the long and bustling High Street, caddies and sedan-carriers stepping from its path and nodding acknowledgment as they rested by the shelved and shaded foundation stones at either side. James grinned jubilantly through the low carriage windows at familiar faces on the road. His fellow traveller on this long private hire joined him at the head of Canongate, and they continued to its foot, to the Water Gate at the end of town. There James called out for the carrier to stop. He alighted and walked up to the old Scottish royal seat of Holyroodhouse, where he bowed three times, once to the palace, once to the chapel, and once to the Scottish crown engraved in stone above the entrance. Then he looked up and beyond the buildings to the bare, brown corrie of Arthur's Seat and he bowed three times more. He returned to the chaise and – excited, emotional, satisfied, and happier than he had been for 28 months; happier possibly than he could ever remember being – instructed the coachman to whip up his horses for London.

Chapter Four

JOHN BULL AND HIS DAUGHTERS

. . . the London-lover loses himself in this swelling consciousness, delights in the idea that the town which incloses him is after all only a paved country, a state by itself. This is his condition of mind quite as much if he be an adoptive as if he be a matter-of-course son. I am by no means sure even that he need be of Anglo-Saxon race and have inherited the birthright of English speech; though on the other hand I make no doubt that these advantages minister greatly to closeness of allegiance. The great city spreads her dusky mantle over innumerable races and creeds . . .

HENRY JAMES, 'LONDON'

Eighteenth-century British highways were repaired and maintained by the parishes through which they rode, which usually meant that they were repaired only when passage over them became impossible, and that they were maintained not at all. People and horses had occasionally drowned in the pot-holes of the Great North Road. James Boswell's chaise was more fortunate; it merely broke a wheel halfway between Edinburgh and the border at Berwick-upon-Tweed. They dragged on in a new vehicle, staying in cold ale-houses, drinking muddy beer, journeying from before dawn until almost midnight. They watched the sun rise over the grey, haunted North Sea coast south of Lindisfarne Priory and the Northumbrian coastal fortresses and watched it set over Tyneside. They rolled through Durham and Doncaster to the Bell inn at Stilton, to Ermine Street and the flat and marshy pirate-lands of the Bedford Levels.

There, south of Stilton, James and his fellow traveller loaded their pistols and sat holding the weapons throughout the last two stages of the day, facing each other grimly in the dark, feigning resolution but fearful of the silent night that shuddered past their windows. Highwaymen still fed on the lonely routes north of London, villainous mounted armed robbers who frequently based themselves in the capital: drinking, eating, whoring and dealing in stolen goods at famously disreputable wine-licensed tea-gardens such as the Blue Cat in Gray's Inn Lane – a short ride from the unpoliced northern approaches to the town – or the Dog and Duck in St George's Fields, the rough parkland surrounding the Channel and Cinque Port roads half a mile south of the river, where they could be seen mounting their horses as dusk approached, stooping for a last fond kiss from the flashy women of the house before cantering tipsily away, with shrill and raucous good wishes sounding in their ears, towards the hunting grounds of Hertfordshire, Surrey and Kent. They preyed at night, and so when James reached his staging inn at Biggleswade late on Thursday 18 November, he knew that he was safe from assault. After four nights in passage, the fifth day would take him into London before the sun went down.

They saw the city first from four miles away. As the post-chaise rattled through the hamlet of Finchley to the crest of Highgate Hill, London was suddenly spread below James Boswell like a banquet. Between the twin citadels of Westminster and the squat barbican of the Tower, the churches of Christopher Wren threw up their spires to the grey November clouds, punctuating the skyline with two score and more of exclamation marks, and the dome of St Paul's Cathedral towered over them all like a vision of the east. London skirted the river for just two dog-leg miles between Westminster Bridge and Tower Hill, and the

Thames was almost as broad and busy as the urban blocks to its
north and south. James had seen the water glint before, had
watched the smoke drift from the dockside tenements across the
furled sails of three dozen men-of-war rafted in groups of five
along the wharves and stairs, had sensed from a distance the restless impulse of this infant capital of Empire, had crossed the
virgin fields within its easy, inevitable grasp – but he had not
before experienced the emotion of that day in the early winter of
1762 when he realised that London was his; that his life lay on the
Strand and the Fleet; that he was no longer a fugitive in its streets
but a part of the place, a citizen without a past of the town which
was, without question or demur, lying supine before him and
offering to be his future. He would be a Londoner. With addresses
in his pocket, charm falling from his tongue and £200 a year, he
would be a Londoner! He directed the driver to an inn at the
centre of town, an inn recommended by none other than West
Digges, leading actor, man of fashion, and friend of James
Boswell. He sang one senseless, stupid, ribald song after another,
he gave three frantic cheers, and then, half-crazed with joy, he
sang again, inventing verses and childish rhymes. And the post-
chaise hurried through the dusk, past smoking brick-kilns ringed
by huddled vagrants, past hogs feeding in filthy meadows on the
metropolitan garbage, through the low suburban shacks. From
Camden Town down Gray's Inn Lane to Holborn, Fleet Street, the
thronging crowds and yellow lamplit thoroughfares hung with
fantastic two-dimensional signs of gilt grapes and sugarloaves, of
carved and painted teapots in profile swinging from the elegant
stone shopfronts at the heart of the town, and – after a giddy farewell to his amused companion – to a wash, a shave, a dinner and
a glass of wine at the Black Lion inn.

London in 1762 was a city of immigrants, a city of dying
immigrants. Its population was about 700,000 and rising,
although nobody could say for certain that it was rising and
several were prepared to vouch that it was in terminal decline,
because, in the absence of a census, what statistics there were said
so. Every year more people died than were born in London. In
1760, an ordinary enough twelvemonth, the parish registers

showed 17,156 baptisms within the city limits and 22,001 burials. Sixty-six per cent of the burials were of children under five years of age, and the 34 per cent who ran successfully the deadly gauntlet of infancy could expect to die, of dropsy, consumption, smallpox, canker and liver-grown, between the ages of 30 and 50.

That was the diseased reality behind the 'healthful, unconfined situation' of Addison's 'emporium for the whole earth'. Londoners had a lower life-expectancy even than the people of Edinburgh. During the raging gin-drinking epidemic of the first half of the century, when the unlicensed distillation, sale and consumption of the spirit began to spread unchecked from the city (where in some districts one house in four was a gin-shop) to the English countryside, it was assuredly predicted that England was about to die, that the English people, taking their lead from London, were quite literally drinking themselves and their country into the grave. If the licensing laws of 1751 had not been introduced and had not checked the gin plague, if John Wesley had not simultaneously risen to teach the poor to value their mortal souls, those dire prognoses could have been proved unhappily accurate. As things were, although no census had been taken which could prove the fact, outside London throughout the eighteenth century many more people were being born than were dying. More people, in fact, were being born than could be sustained on the tied enclosed estates of rural England and the peasant lands of the Celtic fringes; and the excess, the disenfranchised, disinherited excess, were marching each year in their thousands towards the capital. At any given time as little as a quarter of the population of London had actually been born within its bounds. More than half came from the rest of England and Wales, and in 1762 the other quarter of the 700,000 had first seen daylight in Ireland and in Scotland and – a very few – in continental Europe.

So invisibly the city grew. The city could not feed them all, the city could not give them all employment, but the city gorged itself and grew fat on their desperate energy. Irishmen who were not busy on the stage or giving lessons in articulation worked as low-paid labourers, stonebreakers, bricklayers and publicans.

Ashkenazi Jews built a synagogue in Aldgate; Huguenots wove silk in Spitalfields; and Scottish men and women, less homogenous than any of the others – citizens, after all, of north Britain – cropped up from one end of the town to the next, as gregarious and evenly distributed between the boroughs and the social classes as Wren's churches. There was no Scottish district and no exclusively Scottish set of occupations. They were lords and duchesses, shoemakers and milliners, military men and vagrants, and as many of the Scottish women of London as those of any other origin were prostitutes.

An incalculable number of prostitutes picketed the eighteenth-century London streets. Seventy thousand, 100,000, even 200,000 . . . the estimates are wanton. In a hungry city, prostitution meant food for at least a day. As James Boswell already appreciated, London's prostitutes came in great variety, 'from the splendid Madam at fifty guineas a night, down to the civil nymph with white-thread stockings who tramps along the Strand and will resign her engaging person to your honour for a pint of wine and a shilling.' And the raped, abandoned child of the parish, with nothing else between her and a murderous or starved or syphilitic death; and the washerwoman tired of – or unable to find – 19-hour scrubbing shifts which paid her half-a-crown; and the dispossessed widow; and the girl up from the country no longer selling milk from door to door; and the actress turning a coin between scripts . . .

James found himself more permanent digs than the Black Lion inn, took in a show, and went to see how fared Sally Forrester. It was not, in fairness, that immediate. He looked up some friends of his father, a select fraction of the Scottish diaspora, drank tea with them and discussed the benefits or otherwise of the Union. He went, not for the last time, to lose himself in the theatre at Covent Garden, and by Sunday evening he found himself strolling up Southampton Street in the direction of the Blue Periwig. She was not there, and 'the people of the house were broke and dead'. Undeterred, he continued north to Berwick Street. Jeannie Wells had also disappeared. Marvelling at the flux of metropolitan life, he returned to his new lodgings at the Pall Mall home of an expatriate Scottish surgeon and wrote up his diary.

James Boswell's London journal of November 1762 to August 1763 became, after its discovery and publication two centuries later, a small literary phenomenon. That would, without any doubt, have pleased its author, for it was written to be read and appreciated by others. It was not at all a private confessional. Every week he bound the sheets together and posted them back to John Johnston in Scotland, and there is good reason to suppose that he would not have objected to a wider audience. He had already published 'The Cub at Newmarket', that execrable verse concerning himself, the Duke of York, and the Earl of Eglinton (to the horror of those two gentlemen), and had felt delight and vindication at being able to collect a 13-shilling royalty on the sheet from a London bookseller – 'Never did I set so high a value on a sum'. He was exchanging lively letters with Andrew Erskine and persuading his friend, even as he wrote them, that the correspondence should be published and put on sale. At the age of 22 James Boswell had become a natural, compulsive writer. He worked hard at his journal during those nine months in London; he shaped and crafted it, and even allowed himself some revision. When he missed a day or two he returned to them later, diligently filling out the calendar.

The result was not a casual, uncontrived and piecemeal record of the passing weeks, but the first of his significant literary works, albeit the only one not to be published in his lifetime. He even gave the journal a formal introduction, in which he coquettishly observed that 'a plan of this kind [to keep a frank and illuminative diary] was dangerous, as a man might in the openness of his heart say many things and discover [uncover] many facts that might do him great harm if the journal should fall into the hands of my enemies'. Such tantalising comments were almost deliberately designed to spur a reader to turn the page. In fact there was little or nothing in the London journal which would have reflected badly on James Boswell, or any other young man in the second half of the eighteenth century, and little to disturb the worldly reader of 200 years later. The years in between, the vast canyon of the nineteenth century across which we now strain for a glimpse of Boswell's world, were an entirely different matter, but James could not have predicted Victorian Britain and its 50 years of mincing cultural postscript.

Much of his best published work would be travel writing. That was, in the eighteenth century, already a distinguished genre. Britain was an ambitious nation, anxious to scan far horizons and dip its toes in warmer seas. Richard Hakluyt's *Voyages* was still widely read, 150 years after its first publication, and the *History of the World in Sea Voyages and Land Travels* by Hakluyt's disciple, Samuel Purchas, was on many shelves. Daniel Defoe's *Robinson Crusoe* and Jonathan Swift's *Gulliver's Travels* had been no more than travel books of the mind, fantastical variations on the theme. In the 1760s Tobias Smollett and Laurence Sterne would both set off to prepare travelogues on France and Italy, and James Bruce would begin his *Travels to Discover the Sources of the Nile*. Thomas Pennant would plan writer's tours of Wales and Scotland, John Pinkerton would start to compile a 17-volume anthology of *Voyages and Travels*, and John Hawkesworth examined *Voyages of Discovery in the Southern Hemisphere*.

The world, the Georgians knew, was a big and weird and wonderful place. James Boswell would in time contribute gloriously to their understanding of its distant, foreign mysteries. His London journal was, meanwhile, a rehearsal for the accounts of Corsica and the Highlands. It was a travel book about the capital, a well-connected Scotsman's impressions of a foreign town. And like many such volumes since – but very few before – its technique was hugely personal. The author was its hero, a flawed, *faux-naïf*, Voltairean hero, haplessly sketched through the looking-glass in a semi-comic, semi-mordant light; being hilariously conned by urchins in Whitehall; overhearing surreal conversations in coffee-houses –

1 Citizen: Pray, Doctor, what became of that patient of yours?
    Was not her skull fractured?
Physician: Yes. To pieces. However, I got her cured.
1 Citizen: Good Lord.

Enter 2 Citizen, hastily: I saw just now the Duke of Kingston
   pass this door, dressed more like a footman than a nobleman.
1 Citizen: Why, do you ever see a nobleman, dressed like
   himself, walking?
2 Citizen: He had just on a plain frock. If I had not seen the
   half of his star, I should not have known that it was him.
   But maybe you'll say a half-star is sometimes better than a
   whole moon. Eh? ha! ha! ha!
There was a hearty loud laugh.

– sallying down to the cockfight with pockets full of gingerbread
and a stout oak cudgel grasped firmly in his hand; attempting to
rise, weak with sexual frustration, from a young lady's couch,
spotting just in time his blatant erection and sitting down again
sharply; the beautiful denouement at the end of the affair . . .

The London journal is guile dressed as artlessness. Nothing
that James had written before anticipated its mastery. It was a
sudden flowering, and Boswell almost knew it. The brilliant
author of descriptive prose, of singular account, of penetrating
observation and the study of a man, or a society, or a whole world
through their mundanities, had accidentally stumbled – like a
dramatist wandering on to his own stage – into his art. 'And now,
O my journal!' he wrote in July 1763, after keeping it in London
for eight months, 'art thou not highly dignified? Shall thou not
flourish tenfold? No former solicitations or censures could tempt
me to lay thee aside . . . I have at present such an affection for this
my journal that . . . I rather encourage the idea of having it carefully laid up among the archives of Auchinleck. However, I
cannot judge fairly of it now. Some years hence I may.'

Almost incidentally, this masterpiece also provides a thorough guide to his nine months in London between November
1762 and August 1763. It was a time more of frustration than
fulfilment, of promise than reward. But promise there was. He
swallowed his disappointment at the absence of Misses Forrester
and Wells and held himself in check until the following Thursday
when, after a rebuff from another former lover, an Edinburgh

woman, he allowed himself to be picked up in the Strand and taken away from the dim oil-lamps into a murky court. She had no sheath and neither did James; they toyed with each other in the dark while she told him, and he later told his journal, and John Johnston, and posterity, that 'She wondered at my size, and said if I ever took a girl's maidenhead, I would make her squeak.' It was touch and go, but James tore himself away, gave her a shilling and fled, trembling at the thought of poxes, gonorrhoea and syphilis, into the understanding arms of the Earl of Eglinton.

Alexander Montgomerie, the tenth earl, was an able blade whose circle of acquaintance extended well beyond the privileged purlieu of his birthright. He was also a forgiving soul. Within days of James's arrival in London he had swallowed most of his fury at the young man's rash publication of 'The Cub at Newmarket', and James found himself with lodgings in Downing Street, Westminster (at that time a fashionable address, but not yet the official street of residence of ministers). The young Boswell was also precipitated into a shimmering social life. He did his best to assume that it was no more than his due.

On 26 November he dined at Eglinton's Mayfair house in the company of the young Sir James Macdonald, a genuinely distinguished scion of those remnants of the old Lordship of the Isles, the Macdonalds of Skye, who was up at Oxford University where he had somehow acquired for himself the sobriquet of 'Marcellus of the North' on account of his precocious scholarship. The two young men were contemporaries, but James would never, until Macdonald's untimely death just four years later, refer or defer to this youth with anything other than the distant awe that, in his early 20s, he reserved for elderly superiors. 'He knows a great deal,' the young Boswell's journal was shyly told of the precise, articulate, intellectually priggish Sir James, as if of David Hume or any other member of the established enlightenment upon whose door, in the November of 1762, James Boswell was nervously tapping.

On the following day Eglinton wheeled his curious protégé into an even more auspicious gathering. James's London life was quickly assuming a pattern. He walked of a Saturday morning from Downing Street up Whitehall and along the great terraced avenues of the Strand and Fleet Street into the City of London, where he breakfasted in the forenoon shadow of St Paul's Cathedral at Child's coffee-house. There he read the political sheets and chatted to (or acutely eavesdropped upon) his fellow metropolitans.

And after that he sauntered forth in search of action. He may have called upon a putative military contact with a view to furthering that commission in the Guards, or gone in search of William Temple, who had graduated in law from Cambridge and practised in London's Inner Temple before family crises called him back to Northumberland.

On the late morning of 27 November James ambled down to Eglinton's. To his delight, the peer poured them both into a coach bound for Covent Garden. There, Eglinton told James to wait in Bedford's coffee-house until called for. After a few minutes the new manager of Covent Garden Theatre, the celebrated actor John Beard, appeared at Bedford's and escorted James into the theatre, up a substantial staircase, into a room with a gridiron fixed into the stucco ceiling where a dozen or more men were deployed around a large table. At the head of the gathering the First Lord of the Admiralty and one of George III's principal secretaries of state, John Montagu, the fourth Earl of Sandwich, sat beneath a canopy, above which was scripted in large golden letters the words 'Beef and Liberty'.

Eglinton had introduced his protégé to one of the last dinners of the Sublime Society of the Beefsteaks before its riotously brilliant members imploded and tore their individual reputations, and consequently their social gatherings, to shreds. James Boswell was fed only beefsteak, had wine and punch poured down his willing throat, listened to the songs and repartee, and looked about that room with the eyes of a young man whose horizons seemed suddenly – more suddenly than even his brash optimism had ever dared to assume – without end.

As well as Sandwich, Beard and Eglinton (who solicitously sat James at his own side), there was the actor and playwright William Havard. There was the famous Lieutenant-Colonel John

West of the Guards, the Earl de la Warr, the veteran of Dettingen, the soldier-politician who would three years later become a general of horse. And loud and sly and sharp and abrasive and exuding the damn-your-eyes confidence which led them to walk together, laughing, past the shadow of the traitors' gallows into official ignominy and popular worship – which brought their fellows, including Sandwich, Havard, Eglinton and West, to fear or to detest or to mourn for them, and brought the London mob surging through the streets to protest their exile – there sat in the Beefsteak Club on 27 November 1762 the beetle-browed twins of political nightmare: John Wilkes and Charles Churchill.

'Mr Churchill the poet, Mr Wilkes the author of the *North Briton*,' James deferentially, coyly introduced this duo to his journal. Churchill, at 31 years old, was indeed a satirical poet whose verses on the contemporary theatre had led many actors and actresses – including William Havard – to contemplate an early retirement. Charles Churchill was also an ordained minister of the Church of England who would, a year later, famously desert his wife for a 15-year-old girl whose furious father would be curtly informed not to fret – he would 'have done with her in about ten days'. Wilkes and he were fellow members of darker societies than the Beefsteak Club. Both had been introduced by Francis Dashwood (a former chancellor of the exchequer and future Baron Le Despencer) to the Monks of Medmenham Abbey, or Hellfire Club, which Dashwood had launched for various profane and rather silly purposes in 1755. Sandwich, their present chairman and First Lord of the Admiralty, was also a member of this amusing fraternity, whose chief delight was the practice in lambent Thames-side moonlight of the black mass. One such ceremony at Medmenham had recently been hilariously disrupted by Wilkes – who was incapable of taking anything, even diabolism, very seriously – releasing into its centre a live baboon decked out in the traditional insignia of Satan.

John Wilkes had become the Member of Parliament for Aylesbury in 1757, at a cost of £11,000. In June 1762 – just six months before their late lunch above Covent Garden Theatre in the wondering presence of James Boswell – Wilkes and Churchill had determined to express their common genius through a pamphlet titled the *North Briton*. Within five more months issue number 45 of the *North Briton* would excite the country into its first great seditious publishing scandal, would lead Eglinton to despair of the terrible two, Dashwood to lose them from his black masses, and Sandwich to screech at Wilkes that he would die 'either of the pox or on the gallows'; to which Wilkes sagaciously bowed his head across a seething House of Commons and replied, 'That depends, my Lord, on whether I embrace your mistress or your principles.' Interestingly, in the askant perspectives of the mid-eighteenth century, following this dispute, following Wilkes's imprisonment in the Tower of London and subsequent exile, it was George III's secretary of state, the fourth Earl of Sandwich, who would be expelled from the Sublime Society of the Beefsteaks, and not John Wilkes. Charles Churchill would soon be dead. As James Boswell surveyed this large, full-jowled, heavy-drinking wit, the satirist would see almost precisely two more years of mercurial dissolution before succumbing to a fever while visiting the exiled Wilkes in Boulogne. Like Wilkes (and like, in time, the adult James Boswell), he was a more honourable and decent man than his preferred image suggested: he left annuities both to his abandoned wife and to the girl that he had, rather than send back spoiled to her father within ten days, lived with for the rest of his brief time. 'Life to the last enjoyed,' read the line on his Dover gravestone, 'here Churchill lies.' John Wilkes took his friend's papers and travelled on, along roads which would intersect at momentous milestones with those taken by the plump, nervous, alert young man whom he had briefly glimpsed on the afternoon of 27 November 1762.

As Eglinton had anticipated – if not intended – James Boswell was abashed by this company. Timidly, the young man sought refuge in conversation with his mentor.

'I am now,' offered James in reference to his earlier London sojourn, and in part apology for the offensive publication of 'The Cub at Newmarket', 'a little wiser.'

'Not so much as you think,' replied Eglinton. James was deceiving himself. His brash disregard for others, his imprudent, youthful egotism, were still his greatest faults. Eglinton knew his Boswell. 'The little advance you have made in prudence appears very great, as it is so much before what you was formerly.'

James, squinting around that devastating dining-table, agreed. He needed a bit more diffidence, he suggested. And . . . he was sorry about the distress caused by 'The Cub at Newmarket'. He had not realised that dedicating the published sheet of verse to the Duke of York without that gentleman's permission would create such outrage. Perhaps Eglinton could arrange a reunion? Wearily, wonderingly, the good Alexander neither shook nor nodded his head, but half-assented, half-accepted that such a thing could happen and looked from his strange young companion to the rest of the Sublime Society and to the charging of the tankards. He did not so much as laugh. I like you, he assured James instead, as well as ever. 'Nobody can be more agreeable company to him,' was James Boswell's confident conclusion to his journal, and to John Johnston in poor old, dull old Lowland Scotland.

They left at seven in the evening. James strolled before bed to the Royal Opera House and saw there King George III and Queen Charlotte leave for St James's Palace, where the Guards were drawn up beneath the stars, splendidly erect and ordered in the courtyard. A choice of lives lay before him, amply illustrated in the affairs of that November day and night, but he could not yet distinguish between the two.

As Eglinton had guessed, and had kindly attempted to assuage with his insistence of continued affection, but as James insistently denied to all, to his journal, and to himself, after the heady descent of that first afternoon he had trodden his London streets in a steadily growing anguish of uncertainty.

He was worried about money, at one point deciding to leave Downing Street for cheaper rooms until his landlord knocked his rent down to £300 a year. He was unsure of his reputation and standing, even with Eglinton, with Thomas Sheridan (whom he had rediscovered in the capital), and with the disturbingly unfathomable Sir James Macdonald. His calling card, left at stately doors, was not always acknowledged. Temple was nowhere to be found for reassurance, and John Johnston, that slack correspondent, could only be contacted through the mail. Nobody was falling over themselves to offer him a commission in the Guards, or even to suggest that he might be suited to such a post. In early December the Duke of Queensberry arrived back in London. After two snubs, James achieved an audience with the old man. Queensberry was blunt. He would find it, he said, 'very difficult' to place James in the Guards. James's disappointment was not noticeably tempered by the fact that at a dinner party on the very next night a serving soldier 'made us shudder' with tales of battle and dreadful wounds – 'really, these things are not to be talked of, for in cold blood they shock one prodigiously'.

James had also heard from John Johnston at the end of November that he was the father of a boy through Peggy Doig. The child would be baptised on 14 December, with Johnston as godfather, and christened Charles after the executed Charles I. He was then handed over to a foster mother. James oscillated between a guilty rejection of and a seriously sentimental attraction to his first son. He insisted that Charles be allowed the surname Boswell – 'I am not ashamed of him' – and that his own younger brother Davy could see him. In the months to come he would allow himself maudlin dreams of overseeing Charles's education and future career from afar, like some wistful, benevolent spirit. (The fact that not a hint of any of this was confided to his journal at the time is a clear indication that the possibility of its publication was on his mind.) But he never saw the child, and he would not be given the chance to guide him anonymously through schooling and into a fitting profession.

And, to cap it all, he was unsure of his nationality. No matter how brightly their nobler representatives might adorn the upper reaches of society, or how bravely and persistently their soldiers were even then advancing the cause of British dominion, Scots were not altogether popular with the lumpen Londoner in 1762. For centuries they (unlike, for instance, most of the Irish) had been regarded as foreigners, and as frequently hostile foreigners.

The Union of Parliaments a mere 55 years earlier had eased a millennium of enmity hardly at all, to the south as much as to the north of the border. And then, in 1745, came the Jacobite rising which the infant James had observed from within the walls of his own home town. Just 17 years before James cantered through Highgate to find his new life in London, the city had enjoyed a positive orgy of panic. Thousands of barbarian troops, wild men speaking only Scottish Gaelic and conforming to the semi-paganism of the old rites, were camped beneath bridges and in barns no further north than Derby. Derby! One hundred short miles from St Paul's, and St James's, and the Blue Periwig, sharpening their knives and uttering incomprehensible oaths . . .

The London mob, as it was conveniently characterised, was not susceptible to the finer distinctions of Scottish political, religious and social life. Those barbarians had been Scottish, they had put the fear of death itself into the heart of a fragile metropolis, and for that their whole race would not easily be forgiven. It said much for the sophistication of the newly unionised Court and Parliament that in 1761, a mere 15 years after the Battle of Culloden, a Scottish politician of Jacobite origins, John Stuart, the third Earl of Bute, should have been allowed to become the chief minister at Westminster. But to the mob (and to much of the parliamentary opposition, including John Wilkes) Bute's rise to power in the early 1760s was evidence not of a mature partnership between the two traditions but of the sequestration of their very government by a sinister Scottish cabal.

The results, as James Boswell entered London for the second time, flared up in occasional bright and unforgiving forms. Effigies of Bute were burned in the street, and the chief minister himself – having once been attacked – hired a personal bodyguard of butchers and prize-fighters. The actor David Garrick ceased playing the part of Macbeth in tartan, so that he and his colleagues could hope to leave the Drury Lane Theatre with their persons intact.

They were niggling cries rather than deafening howls of racism. A Scotsman such as Eglinton could tread his blithe way from home to ballroom to club to theatre and be affected hardly at all. But James Boswell had been just two-and-a-half weeks back in the city of his dreams before the image of his countrymen dealt him, and his faltering confidence, a sorry blow.

He had gone to Covent Garden to see a new comic opera. The theatre was a balm to James: he loved it deeply, and all who came with it, from actors and actresses and stoutly charismatic managers to the baying, bawdy, critical masses of the pits. During his first fortnight in London in 1762 he attended virtually every new performance, which meant an almost daily spin to the Garden or to Drury Lane. The theatre was a cerebral home to him, a place both of familiarity and escape from daily concerns. He thought he knew the London theatre.

On that night early in December two officers of a Highland regiment entered Covent Garden Theatre just as the overture began. The crowd in the upper gallery responded instantly to this distinctive flash of colour. A chant went up of 'No Scots! No Scots! Out with them!' and an ugly hissing filled the hall. Apples rained down on the officers. James jumped upon the pit benches and yelled back, 'Damn you, you rascals!' And, briefly, his heart filled with an atavistic hatred of the English. 'I wished from my soul that the Union was broke and that we might give them another Bannockburn.'

He went to join the Scots officers, who commented laconically that they had just got back from capturing Havana on behalf of the British people (the Caribbean port had fallen in August). 'And this is the thanks that we get . . . if I had a grup o yin or twa o the tamd rascals I sud let them ken what they're about.'

But the abuse died out as quickly as it had begun. The mob simply, and typically, grew bored with the easy distraction and ran out of apples. James regained his bench, forgot his righteous Caledonian fury, and all present enjoyed the performance. The residue, for James Boswell, was a distant, sickly unease which troubled the pit of his stomach throughout the following days and weeks, and would not finally be dispersed for three more decades of his curious struggle for the heart, the soul, and the acknowledgment of the capital of England. Could he be disliked by the people of this town, purely because of his birthplace?

Could he fail here, for no reason other than the fact that he was a child of Edinburgh and Ayrshire? Addison had not mentioned this. They surely could not . . . surely he could not . . .

A few days later he was given the opportunity to share a Scottish view of London with a countryman. James Macpherson and James Boswell had a great deal in common. Each wanted the city at his feet. To Boswell, in December 1762, it seemed that Macpherson was as successful a guide as any to fulfilling that ambition. They were almost contemporaries. James Macpherson had been born in 1736 in Badenoch in the central Scottish Highlands. After comparatively undistinguished studies at Aberdeen and Edinburgh universities (he spent the winter of 1755–56 at the latter, but the paths of the confident, galumphing 19-year-old man and the shy, secluded, sickly 15-year-old boy did not cross) he returned to Badenoch to teach at a village school.

Even in the middle of the eighteenth century Badenoch was on the outskirts of the Scottish Gaidhealtachd, and Macpherson, despite being the son of a poor tenant farmer, was never fluent in the Gaelic language. But he could not be entirely ignorant of the old tongue, of its traditional tales, its songs and legends, and its velvet-gloved hold on the hearts of all Highland Scots. In 1759 he met the minister-turned-playwright John Home at that bourne to which all bourgeois Scots returned, the spa town of Moffat. The two discussed Gaelic folklore; Home expressed an interest in reading some; Macpherson agreed to provide a translation of sorts; and in June 1760 a thin volume of the Badenoch teacher's offerings was published in Edinburgh, titled *Fragments of Ancient Poetry collected in the Highlands of Scotland and translated from the Galic* [sic] *or Erse Language* .

This was tantalising material to those Scots who were anxious to prove, in the years of cultural timidity which succeeded the Union, that their own country had a heritage at least as old and rich as that of the Saxon. Macpherson was persuaded to travel west, deep into the Gaelic fastnesses, in search of more material. He did so and returned with extended sections of verse which, on the particular advice of David Hume, he took to be printed and published in London at the end of 1761. Inadvisably, the modest 'fragments' of 1760 assumed, by 1761, colossal pretensions. For half a guinea the discerning southern reader could now obtain *Fingal, an Ancient Epic Poem, in Six Books; together with several other Poems, composed by Ossian, the son of Fingal. Translated from the Galic Language by James Macpherson* – and the Ossian controversy, which divided literary Britain for half a century and more, which persuaded Samuel Johnson to hunt for the fraudulent Macpherson on the streets of London with a large stick, which inspired Napoleone, Goethe, at least one president of the United States of America, William Wordsworth and arguably the whole of the rest of the Romantic Movement, was born.

The poems of the ancient Gaelic bard Ossian, as passed down through the generations by his descendants in the mysterious Hebridean gloaming before being uncovered, rendered into English and delivered to a grateful world by James Macpherson, were ripe material. Macpherson had serious poetical ambitions of his own, he was familiar with the works of Homer, and most of his Georgian readers (excepting, for the moment, the significant figure of Samuel Johnson) found themselves thrilling to accounts of sons of Erin who appeared 'like a ridge of rocks on the coast; when mariners, on shores unknown, are trembling at veering winds . . .' A thousand ghosts shrieked, groans of the people spread over the hills, Fergus rushed forward with feet of the wind, and 'Fingal' sold in its thousands. By the time that James Boswell shared a table in a London coffee-house with the large-limbed, plain-faced James Macpherson, the latter was a very rich young Scot indeed, and *Temora, an Ancient Epic Poem, in eight books, together with several other Poems, composed by Ossian, the son of Fingal* was already in preparation.

James believed at that time in Macpherson and in the authenticity of his source material. It was almost a totem of his Scottishness to do so. In later years some Scots – including James and David Hume – would become deeply sceptical of Macpherson's claims; and Englishmen such as Wordsworth would find themselves rapturous in praise of the Ossianic charms. But the Ossian debate was in 1762 a chamber divided by

Hadrian's Wall. To James Boswell, upon first sight James Macpherson was 'a man of great genius and an honest Scotch Highlander'.

And a man, he might have added, to be emulated. They talked of women and of their wonderful availability in this city. Women as fine as ever were created. Women for a guinea! What a preparation it was for marriage, to be able to sample so many of them before settling into domestic satisfaction. 'Why do you live in London?' another acquaintance once asked James Macpherson. 'You cannot be that fond of John Bull.' 'Sir,' he replied, 'I hate John Bull, but I love his daughters.'

Macpherson was talking from experience; Boswell mostly through wistful fantasy. Terrified of London's famously pernicious strains of venereal disease, and genuinely anxious not to smear or disappoint in exile the fond memory of his good father and mother, James had determined after his initial frustrated search for Sally and Jeannie and that close-run thing with a girl of the street that his first sexual experience back in London would be an uncommercial exchange. He had consequently remained reluctantly celibate. It was a disheartening experience, on top of his other woes. It affected him in the most unsatisfactory manner. One Sunday, during holy service, he found himself assaulted by persistent, stirring sexual fantasies; and the next – at which he had determined to be good – he unfortunately found himself sharing a congregation with the sensationally beautiful 24-year-old Duchess of Grafton, who 'attracted my eyes rather too much'.

And then he met Louisa Lewis, and his second visit to London came truly alive. Just as he had glumly resigned himself to being 'a single man for the whole winter', his attention to the theatre paid off. Louisa Lewis was an actress whose last engagement at Covent Garden had closed in October. Tall, 24 years old, with languid eyes, a good sense of dress, humour and vivacity, it seems that Louisa – a married woman separated from a 'harsh, disagreeable' husband – spotted James at least as quickly as he had noticed her. Certainly, when he called at her rooms in the middle of December (the very day, in fact, of Charles Boswell's baptism in Edinburgh) James found her to be in a condition of 'pleasing undress'. They talked modestly, and arranged a further assignment.

At this second meeting a young man, whom Louisa introduced as her brother, sat with them. 'I could have wished him at the Bay of Honduras,' pondered James. Louisa mused on the unfairness of those who assumed that, because a man and a woman enjoyed each other's company, something more sinister was underway. After some delicate conversational interplay on the subjects of love, manners, passion, and how much better the French were at these things, Louisa commented demurely and without apparent cause that some fellow had recently offered her £50 for unknown reasons, but had fled when her brother appeared. James left, after several hours, with knitted brow.

On the next afternoon he returned and told Louisa that he was falling in love with her. 'You are welcome here as often as you please,' Louisa assured him. James repeated his devotion two days later, adding as a precautionary measure that he had a moderate allowance and was obliged to live economically. Then he made his way to a bookshop on Russell Street owned by one Thomas Davies, whom he knew to be acquainted with Samuel Johnson, and after a while James admitted that he would like to meet the great lexicographer. 'Dine with me on Christmas Day,' suggested Davies. 'You shall see him.'

The next day Louisa's brother sat with them again as they drank tea, and the day after that James hurried round immediately after breakfast. Louisa was, she declared, in no state of mind to see him or any other human being, as she had just been badly let down by a great friend who had promised a trifling loan but had defaulted on the offer, and now she despaired of the entire human race.

What, wondered James, is a trifling loan? He called together his nerve and asked her. 'Only two guineas, Sir.' Overcome with relief, he pulled out two guineas, gave them to her, told her that her credit was good with him as far as a full ten guineas, and immediately regretted it. They kissed and parted.

Three days before Christmas their conversation crept round to religious intolerance of extra-marital affairs. Both agreed that while Roman Catholicism had much to be said for it, the faith was not for them. James sat close to Louisa, exclaimed suddenly that he was miserable and stupid and would immediately leave, got to his feet, observed a shaming erection and sat down again. 'I adore you,' he concluded. Come back on Friday, said Louisa. He did, and she took the opportunity of their Christmas Eve meeting to insist that an elevation of their friendship such as James so obviously desired would spoil a pleasant relationship – 'Instead of visiting me as you do now, you would find a discontented, unhappy creature.'

James's social life, not to say his ambition to see military service, was suffering. Eglinton left pained cards at his door, wondering at his sudden inexplicable absences. He went to dinner with Thomas Davies on Christmas Day, and observed with only mild disappointment that Dr Samuel Johnson was unable to join the party but chatted instead with 'a curious, odd, pedantic fellow' named Oliver Goldsmith (whose most celebrated works lay several years beyond that Christmas Day). They disputed the merits of Shakespeare (Boswell for, Goldsmith against) and agreed that the absent Samuel Johnson was a fine talent. Thomas Davies added that the doctor was also the best of companions.

Enough of that. On Boxing Day he assured the besieged Louisa Lewis that his happiness depended entirely upon her. He was, she replied, running a great risk. James shrugged off the comment. She asked for a week. If, by the first day of January 1763, James Boswell still felt for her, 'she would then make me blessed'. James returned to his rooms to find a letter from the Duke of Queensberry which insisted that he would never get into the Guards, 'and therefore the best advice I can give you is to turn your thoughts some other way'.

He celebrated New Year's Day by breakfasting at Child's (it was a Saturday), striding around to Louisa's rooms, pressing her to him, fondling her and demanding his verbally contracted dues. Come back tomorrow, she said, sighing sweetly, at three in the afternoon. He did so, barred the door from the inside, led Louisa 'all fluttering' into her bedroom, and gaped in dismay as she slipped from under him, ran out, intercepted the landlady on the landing, and admitted instead her brother to the room. 'Oh dear,' she said, 'how hard this is.'

There was apparently nothing for it other than a room for the night at an inn. Saturday night, then, it must be, said Louisa, as she would not be called upon to act at the playhouse on a Sunday. James thought hard before pacing over to the Black Lion inn off Fleet Street, where he had spent his first night in London all of those long winter weeks before, and booking a room for his 'absent wife'. On Friday Louisa called off their tryst due to 'Nature's periodic effects'. They agreed on the following Wednesday. James perambulated through the town for a day or two with his veins glowing and his mind 'agitated with felicity'.

On Wednesday he engaged in deep, ferocious debate with Thomas Sheridan on the qualities of the actor David Garrick before meeting Louisa at eight o'clock in the Covent Garden piazzas, hiring a hackney, making for the Black Lion and booking in there as 'Mr Digges'. While Louisa prepared, with the help of a maid of the inn, for bed, James strolled in the cold yard. Then they made love throughout the night. She hoped that his affection 'would not be altogether transient'.

Four days later they made love again, at her rooms. 'I felt,' James admitted to himself, 'a degree of coldness for her.' One or two of her mannerisms, he had not previously noticed, were unpleasantly affected.

Forty-eight hours after that James was shown at least part of Louisa Lewis's reasons for procrastination, of the risk that he had been obscurely warned against. His coldness was offset by a familiar, unpleasantly ominous heat in the groin. He dismissed it initially from his mind, got into another fierce argument with Sheridan, this time concerning a piece of his own writing which Sheridan disliked, walked from Hyde Park Corner to the Whitechapel Turnpike with Andrew Erskine, who was about to be discharged by the military, and another exiled Scottish friend, the MP for Forfar and Fife, George Dempster, watched from the top of London Bridge as shoals of floating ice crashed into each other on the Thames, drank warm, spiced wine at an East End public house, and returned home to undress and discover with sorrow and distress that 'too, too plain was Signor Gonorrhoea'.

With pride and penis smarting unendurably, James confronted Louisa. She denied being the agent of his infection and hoped, as they parted, to be allowed in future to enquire after his health and well-being. 'I fancy it will be needless for some weeks,' he replied archly. Two weeks later he wrote to ask her to return the loan of two guineas, as a contribution to his surgeon's fee. Seven days after that a sealed packet, unaddressed and containing no written note, arrived at Downing Street. James opened it and two guineas fell out. He briefly 'felt a strange kind of mixed confusion'. But he pulled himself together. The brief Jacobean farce was over. It had run an amusing course, left its central figure dazed but content and its audience (John Johnston) laughing merrily, and enlivened what could have been a desperate winter. James Boswell recollected his mission on earth, and set off once more in pursuit of his brilliant career.

There was much to pursue, even with swollen testicles. The Guards were slipping relentlessly out of reach, but 'how easily and cleverly do I write just now! . . . words come skipping to me like lambs upon Moffat Hill'. And as spring came slowly to London and his disease ebbed, even a career at the Scottish Bar appeared strangely, newly attractive, coupled with the lairdship of Auchinleck, an agreeable wife, and a sideline literary career . . . after, perhaps, a run through the Low Countries, France and Italy . . . or possibly a melancholic exiled life called to him once again, in Spain or in the southern Romance lands. Would his father finance it?

And in the meantime there was gorgeous London, soirées with Elizabeth Percy at Northumberland House, Eglinton's gay company and gloriously abandoned domestic life, the japes of his young friends. London – spoiled only, perhaps, by the occasional intrusion of a coarse, embarrassing Glasgow accent at an uncouth dinner table, an accent which had no place in the world of the upwardly mobile young native of north Britain and which was pointedly to be avoided – London still held its sumptuous arms out wide to a young man of affairs. James Boswell was, as March turned into the April of 1763, no clearer as to his future, but far happier in his uncertainty.

Early in April William Temple returned to London carrying the distressing news that his father's bankruptcy had obliged him to give up the law. He was hoping to enter the clergy. On the 12th of that month Andrew Erskine and James received from the printers the first copies of an exquisitely arrogant piece of vanity publishing: their collected letters to each other from their Edinburgh days. Despite the fact that James reviewed it himself in the *London Chronicle* – 'Upon the whole, we would recommend this collection as a book of true genius, from the authors of which we may expect many future agreeable productions' – *Letters between the Honourable Andrew Erskine and James Boswell Esq.* left literary London almost unmoved. It could never have been otherwise. James had, once more, labelled himself a celebrity in advance of the fact. Nobody had been able to teach this 22-year-old, although Eglinton had tried, that the achievements come first and the collected miscellania follow.

On 23 April James left London to visit James Macdonald in Oxford. As a consequence, he missed, possibly for the first time since encountering the two men at their Sublime Society, an issue of Wilkes's and Churchill's *North Briton*. The 45th edition of the sheet was published on that day. It stated that part of the recent king's speech to the House of Commons had been 'the most abandoned instance of ministerial effrontery ever attempted to be imposed on mankind', and suggested that George III may have been prevailed upon by his ministers and other advisers to tell deliberate lies to Parliament.

While James Boswell wandered miserably about dreary Oxford, wining and dining with Macdonald's stunningly erudite friends and pining for the city, for the coffee-houses, whores, pimping waiters and scandalous gossip, back in London the law officers were advising King George that Wilkes and Churchill were guilty of seditious libel, and the *North Briton*'s printers were being apprehended because, unfortunately for them, theirs were the only names on the publication and consequently only they could be issued with a warrant (it was a common omission before

April 1763; but a rare one after that date). James arrived back in London on 26 April, violently and unaccountably depressed by his time spent away from the place, and for several days he moped from friend to sympathetic friend while the agencies of the law caught up with John Wilkes, bundled him off to the Tower of London, ransacked his house and confiscated his private papers.

On 3 May James came alive to the momentous scandal which was threatening to engulf many of his friends and acquaintances (Wilkes, Churchill, Sandwich, and even Eglinton as one of their drinking associates and also one of George III's closest advisers) and which had thrown the state into constitutional crisis (the article in the *North Briton* had been unsigned, and Wilkes, although admittedly the journal's publisher, was a Member of Parliament and therefore entitled to certain loose and dubious privileges). Wilkes was due to be taken from the Tower to make a common plea at the Bar. James trudged down to watch but missed the whole episode – Wilkes, refusing to put up bail, was quickly returned to jail – and consoled himself by wandering on to Newgate Prison and gazing at two prisoners who were due to be executed on the following day: a man for highway robbery and a woman for common household theft.

The travails of John Wilkes slipped from James Boswell's mind. He made the grave error of travelling on the following day to the north-westerly reach of civilised London, to Tyburn Tree, for the hanging day. On this public holiday – one of eight offered in the course of the year to the London journeymen – coach-makers, frame-makers, tailors and all of the scattered free-masonry of industrial London downed tools and thronged through the streets, greedy for the incomparable thrill of the most basic sport of all, to the turnpike corner of Tyburn Road and Tyburn Lane, where the bricks and mortar ended and the enormous gallows loomed over rancid fields fit only for pigs and lapped by ditches of swill and sewerage. James watched, across the heads of an enormous crowd, this terrible ending of the lives of Paul Lewis and Hannah Diego, heard the satisfied hoarse sigh of the masses as the rope snapped taut, and 'I was most deeply shocked, and thrown into a very deep melancholy'.

A part of James Boswell's future career was informed on that day. For three nights afterwards he could not sleep alone. He fled from Tyburn to the Earl of Eglinton in Mayfair, and the sympathetic older man attempted to entertain and console him. But James would not be distracted and was inconsolable. He returned to Downing Street, where he lay beneath his blankets consumed by depression, and then rose in the night and crossed the town to share a distressed bed with Andrew Erskine. George Dempster and Erskine walked him briskly through London on the next day, and he slept with Dempster that night. The next morning Dempster insisted that he get his blood moving by dancing around the room. They heard that Wilkes had been released from the Tower under parliamentary privilege and that a crowd – the same mob which James had stood behind at Tyburn Tree – had cheered him to his home, chanting in a curious echo of the Sublime Society's golden motto: 'Wilkes and Liberty!' James went once more to Downing Street, was yet again 'haunted with frightful imaginations', and made his way back to Erskine's bed. Two days later, a Sunday, still anguished, he stepped slowly from an Anglican chapel into a nearby Roman Catholic chapel, and he steadily, sadly wondered. His composure returned like a creeping winter's dawn.

A week later James won himself a breakfast engagement with the leading actor of the day. David Garrick, a native of Hereford, had become, at the age of 18, one of the first pupils at a school established near Lichfield by Samuel Johnson in 1735. Teacher and pupil became good friends (Johnson was just eight years older than Garrick), and in 1737 they had left together to find their fame in London. Garrick's success as an actor was almost instant and entirely extraordinary. Having conquered both Drury Lane and Covent Garden theatres, he became the actor-manager of Drury Lane in 1747. He was 46 years old when he first breakfasted with Boswell in 1763, he was easily the most popular entertainer in Great Britain, and he had achieved the unlikely feat of riding this wave to fame while making hardly an enemy in the land. In common with most of the rest of the country, James Boswell was helplessly charmed by this stylish and considerate man.

Two days later, on the evening of Monday 16 May, irritated at being unable to reclaim a small debt from an old acquaintance, James walked to Thomas Davies's bookshop in Russell Street. He sat in the back room drinking tea with Davies and his wife when, at about seven o'clock, a huge, badly dressed man with rheumy eyes and a nervous tic playing on his fleshy, pock-marked face, slouched into the shop.

Davies grinned knowingly at James. 'This is Mr Boswell . . .' the bookseller said to the newcomer.

James lost his nerve. 'Don't tell where I come from,' he hissed.

'. . . from Scotland,' concluded Thomas Davies happily.

'Mr Johnson,' protested James, 'I do indeed come from Scotland, but I cannot help it . . .'

Everybody expected a rejoinder from Samuel Johnson, particularly Samuel Johnson himself. 'That, Sir,' replied the deep, bastard accent of southern Staffordshire, the dialectical confluence of five counties, where midland and north country and the western marches met, 'I find, is what a very great many of your countrymen cannot help.' It was not especially good, but it was enough.

Johnson, a childless widower, enjoyed the company of younger men, and James had for two years been collecting celebrities as his father collected coins. Each man's interest was quite unclouded. Johnson liked to be listened to and to be reassured, by the attention of others, of his genius; James wanted to learn from the great how to be great – and possibly to have greatness attach itself to him by association, like a taste for wine and good clothes. But, if anything, the need of the 53-year-old Johnson was more urgent than that of James Boswell. Johnson was concerned, in 1763, that his career was behind him. He had exceeded the average lifespan of his time, and almost all of his noted published works – his idiosyncratic and epochal *Dictionary of the English Language*, his *Life of Savage*, his romance *Rasselas*, his two ponderous failed periodicals – lay in the past. Most of his contemporaries assumed that his acceptance in the previous July of a pension of £300 a year from the government of the Earl of Bute signified little more or less than the capitulation of the independent spirit of Samuel Johnson to the numbing imminence of senility. Those contemporaries had good reason for such cynicism: the younger Johnson's dictionary definition of a pension had read: 'An allowance made to anyone without an equivalent. In England it is generally understood to mean pay given to a state hireling for treason to his country.' This matter of a pension had led to a further embarrassment. When he learned, shortly after accepting his own £300 per annum, that the actor-turned-elocutionist Thomas Sheridan was also to get £200 from the Civil List, Johnson could not resist quipping – in open, spiteful company – 'Then it is time for me to give up mine.' The sentence inevitably made its poisonous way to the pompous Sheridan, and the two men never exchanged another word in each other's presence, preferring instead to jibe through second and third parties. Sheridan had wasted no time in telling an innocent such as James Boswell that Mr Samuel Johnson was a disgraceful hypocrite with bearish manners (Johnson would be pursued in old age by comparisons with the family Ursidae) and a bad character; and one of Johnson's first instructions to James was that Sheridan's current oratorical tour of Bath was destined to fail, as 'ridicule has gone down before him'.

There could only be one winner in the battle for this particular young heart and mind. Thomas Sheridan was a low rung on the ladder to fame; Samuel Johnson was up among the eaves. James left Davies's bookshop that May evening with a sense of achievement. He had not particularly liked Samuel Johnson. He – a well-groomed young immigrant – had found his appearance to be surprisingly repellent, his voice uncouth, and his dogmatism disagreeable. In all of those hostile impressions he was, without doubt, correct, and certainly not alone. But James was also accurate in discerning immense knowledge and substantial powers of expression, coupled with a native good humour and a quality that not many had thought to attribute to Samuel Johnson: worthiness. He was patently a decent man. 'I shall,' commented James auspiciously to his journal, 'mark what I remember of his conversation.'

A week later James achieved an almost perfect day. Aside from his own anonymously entered review, his and Erskine's

'Letters' had been favourably noticed in one other outlet. The *Public Advertiser* had published a few pleasant comments by the freelance wit Bonnell Thornton, who had now written to say that Mr Boswell was invited to call on him. James wasted no time in going round. He had exchanged no more than a few pleasantries with the 'lively and odd' Thornton when three more visitors were announced. John Wilkes, Charles Churchill and another doomed and deadly soul, the poet and editor Robert Lloyd, entered the room. Wilkes and Churchill had forgotten the young man from the previous year's meeting of the Beefsteak Society, but upon reintroduction 'the London Geniuses . . . were very civil to me'. Wilkes, indeed, held out an open invitation to James to visit his George Street home. John Wilkes was, at that time, striking back against his persecutors, and legal action was being instituted in his name against the offending ministers. James Boswell found himself, as at the Sublime Society of the Beefsteaks, to be suddenly quite out of his depth. His residual Edinburgh primness – the same flushed bourgeois propriety, in fact, which had had him responding with dismay to Johnson's tone, dress, and posture – started back, blinking, from the noisy, intimate profanities of this reckless company. Wilkes, Churchill, Lloyd, and now even the urbane Thornton made a social grace of outrage. They played off each other's fantastic imagination like a diabolical, well-rehearsed madrigal. James felt privileged but far from comfortable. The antidote, he felt, as he made his polite excuses and left, was a visit to his new friend Samuel Johnson. Had he not suggested, in a throwaway comment in Davies's shop, that the best treatment for Wilkes would be not prosecution but a ducking at the hands of a parcel of footmen?

There were people with Johnson too, scattered around his bookish, slovenly Inner Temple chambers, but they were orderly types who soon rose to take their leave. James respectfully did the same, and Johnson turned to him.

'Nay,' he said, 'don't go away.'

Surprised, James stammered that he did not want to intrude.

'I am obliged to any man,' said Johnson deliberately, 'who visits me.'

The philosopher talked, of morality and motives and madness and religion, and James Boswell listened and looked at this curious oracle in his rusty brown old suit of clothes, his shrivelled unpowdered wig too small for his massive cranium, his loose shirt-neck and breeches, his wrinkled stockings and unbuckled shoes. Everything about Samuel Johnson was ill-fitting and undone, it seemed, except his mind.

Their friendship developed slowly and pleasurably, through incidental and intentional meetings with days and weeks between them. It was a remarkable relationship, both because of the 30-year difference in their ages and because of Johnson's supposed (rather than actual) antipathy to Scotland and the Scots, and in the hothouse of London society it was, of course, remarked upon. 'Who is this Scotch cur at Johnson's heels?' some forgotten soul asked Oliver Goldsmith.

'He is not a cur,' said Goldsmith. 'He is only a burr. Tom Davies flung him at Johnson in sport, and he has the faculty of sticking.'

Goldsmith's comment, routinely thrown into the chattering mainstream of Georgian England, would become the authorised version of events, if only because it sounded clever, was an ingeniously plausible metaphor, and it contained a rhyme. Those qualities alone did not, as Goldsmith knew well enough, qualify it to be the truth. James Boswell never adhered unrequested to Samuel Johnson's person, and in the summer of 1763 he had still too much of a young man's life to lead, he had still too many pretty young things to leer at across gilded drawing-rooms, too many whores to seek out afterwards, too much wine to drink with the Earl of Eglinton, too much sauntering to do about the Covent Garden piazzas on the arms of Erskine and Dempster, too many plays to see, too many people to accost about the faded prospect of a commission in the Guards . . . He saw Samuel Johnson when time and patience allowed, and more often than not they met as a result of the older man's initiative. James Boswell was still, three years after first captivating the Earl of Eglinton, an easy young man to like.

Early in June James's feckless gallivanting, as it was increasingly seen from the stern eyries of Edinburgh and Auchinleck, was reined remorselessly in. By an extraordinary mischance, some of James's earlier journals had fallen into the hands of Reverend George Reid, the minister at Ochiltree in Ayrshire. James could hardly have anticipated this: he had sent those particular sheets to his hapless old mentor William McQuhae, as he was presently sending his current journal to John Johnston. As part of his own preparations for the clergy McQuhae happened to go and stay with Reverend Reid, who promptly stumbled upon James's uninhibited confessions. Ochiltree Manse lay less than a mile from Auchinleck House, and Reid inevitably told James's father of his son's bizarre predilection for describing his most outlandish thoughts and adventures on vellum and mailing them around the country. Almost immediately after that, Alexander Boswell had received word of an odd collection of letters between James and his friend called Erskine, which would have been bad enough kept private, but which they had seemingly had printed and put on sale to the general public!

The results were almost catastrophic. 'I had determined to abandon you,' wrote Alexander to his son and heir, 'to free myself as much as possible from sharing your ignominy . . . But I have been so much importuned by your excellent mother, the partaker of my distresses and shame on your account, again to write to you.'

Alexander then inserted the knife. Had James considered, wondered his father, how preposterous a figure he must cut in London, where he had chosen 'to live in dependence upon strangers in another country . . . from whom you have nothing to expect but fair words. They have their relations to provide, their political connections to keep up, and must look on one who comes from Scotland as an idle person to have no right share of their bounty; in the same way that we here would never think of bestowing anything upon a vaguing [idling] Englishman except a dinner or a supper.'

James had, his father insisted, a clear choice to make, and the fantasy of the Guards was no longer an acceptable part of that choice – 'I never declared positively against any kind of life except that of dissipation and vice, and as a consequence against your going into the Guards.' He could continue with his legal studies, for which he had 'showed as much genius for it when you applied as any ever I knew', or he could join a marching regiment. A fighting regiment. One that might be called upon at any time to exchange musket fire with Spaniards and Frenchmen, to lose blood on continental fields. 'If you set up in the character of my eldest son,' thundered Lord Auchinleck, 'you may expect regard and respect, but in the style of a vagrant must meet with the reverse . . . it is better to snuff a candle out than leave it to stink in a socket.'

The game, for the moment, was up. Characteristically, James looked on the bright side, congratulated himself on not having been entirely dispossessed, and confided in friends his delight at being once more in healthy, constructive communication with his father. But the die had been cast. Between a career in the law and a career in a fighting unit of the British army there was, for James Boswell, no choice. It was determined that he should travel to Holland – a common practice among Scottish law students, given the similarities between the Dutch legal system and their own: Alexander Boswell and his father before him had studied at Leyden, and Sir David Dalrymple at Utrecht – and following an admissible period there, he might be allowed to visit France and certain other northern European states. James talked with Dempster and Erskine about his prospects and intentions. 'I said I wanted to get rid of folly and to acquire sensible habits. They laughed.'

Samuel Johnson was more comforting. 'Your father,' he said, 'has been attempting to make the man of you at 20 which you will be at 30,' adding that James had, nonetheless, had a lucky escape from the Guards, and that the lot of a Scottish laird was an honourable and important inheritance. 'I think,' he added, 'your breaking off idle connections by going abroad is a matter of importance.'

By the end of June the glass was running thin. James's destiny, so recently taken with confidence into his own young hands, had

'I love the young dogs of this age . . .' The 24-year-old James Boswell, portrayed in Rome in 1765 by George Willison (Scottish National Portrait Gallery)

The city on the rock: Edinburgh in the 1750s, seen from its rural environs (Edinburgh Central Libraries)

Walls towering like cliff-faces – the Old Town of Edinburgh

'What you seek is here, at Ulubrae.' Auchinleck House

'There is a city called London, for which I have as violent an affection as the most romantic lover ever had for his mistress'

'A huge, badly dressed man with rheumy eyes.' Samuel
Johnson by Joshua Reynolds (The National Portrait Gallery)

'Wilkes and Liberty!'
John Wilkes, by Hogarth

'Where mountains ripped across
the skyline like a howl frozen in
mid-air' – the island of Corsica,
by Edward Lear

TOP LEFT: *'I was, for the rest of my life, set free from a slavish timidity in the presence of great men, for where shall I find a man greater than [Pasquale] Paoli?'*

TOP RIGHT: *'One of the most remarkable masks upon this occasion.'* James Boswell in the costume of an 'armed Corsican chief'

LEFT: *'If ever a man had his full choice in a wife, I would have it in her.'* Margaret Boswell, née Montgomerie

The middle-aged Boswell in an etching taken from a sketch by Bennet Langton

The old castle at Inverness and the bridge over the River Ness in the eighteenth century

The great biographer. James Boswell, in 1793, sketched by George Dance

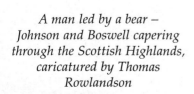

A man led by a bear – Johnson and Boswell capering through the Scottish Highlands, caricatured by Thomas Rowlandson

been as firmly removed from them. The older members of his family had decided that Utrecht was to be his destination. Could it not be anywhere . . . gayer? pleaded James weakly. No, came back the advice. 'Utrecht!' he told William Temple. 'Utrecht!' You can always move on if the place proves impossibly gloomy, his friend unconvincingly replied.

All that remained was to make the best of the disappearing days. James booked a room at the Mitre tavern in Fleet Street and threw a condemned man's last supper, inviting Johnson, Goldsmith and Tom Davies, and listening agog as Goldsmith argued – apropos the Wilkes affair – that it was certainly possible for a constitutional monarch to be at fault, while Johnson replied that the agents of the king, rather than the king himself, must in Britain always be held accountable.

He roamed the city with a weighty heart. He was due to depart for Holland on 6 August, and on the morning of 19 July James entered St Paul's Cathedral, climbed up to the Whispering Gallery and out on to the open cupola dome. He gazed over the roofscape, south across the smoky Thames and north to the verdant hills of Hampstead and Highgate, and he urged himself to feel his old passion for this place, he dredged his soul for a vestige of the intoxication of eight months earlier. But nothing came. It was as though his heart had necessarily hardened itself against the agony of departure. He stood in bleak and silent emptiness above the town, seeing there no more than bricks, and tiles, and narrow streets leading each to the other and thinning, finally, out of sight.

He dined again and again with Johnson, as if the old man's endless proselytising could somehow shore up his soul against the cold months of exile. Johnson welcomed James. He liked young people, he said – as much to himself as to his eager listener – 'Because in the first place, I don't like to think myself turning old. In the next place, young acquaintances must last longest, if they do last; and in the next place, young men have more virtue than old men. They have more generous sentiments in every respect. I love the young dogs of this age: they have more wit and humour and knowledge of life than we had.' They talked on, across a cluttered table at the Turk's Head coffee-house. The name of the young Sir James Macdonald came up, and Johnson said that he had a mind to visit the Western Isles of Scotland and would go there with James upon his return unless a better companion came forward in the meantime, which Johnson thought hardly possible.

'There are few people I take to as much as you,' he told James gravely.

James muttered maudlin sentiments about having to leave England, and the big, bullish, honest Staffordshire accent urged him to be cheerful: 'My dear Boswell! I should be very unhappy at parting, did I think we were not to meet again.'

Day after day they met, as the dreaded sailing date approached. With a week to go, they took a boat down the Thames to Greenwich. James went prepared. Upon arrival, he took a sheet of paper from his pocket and read some lines from Johnson's poem 'London':

> On Thames's banks in silent thought we stood,
> Where Greenwich smiles upon the silver flood;
> Struck with the seat which gave Eliza birth,
> We kneel, and kiss the consecrated earth.

James then genuflected on the shore of the silent waterway. When they returned that evening to the city Johnson announced: 'I must see thee out of England. I will accompany you to Harwich.' The next day was a Sunday, and James continued his spiritual explorations by attending a meeting of Quakers in Lombard Street. To his surprise, the speakers included a woman, which strange news he conveyed to Johnson later in the day. 'A woman's preaching,' rumbled Samuel, 'is like a dog's walking on his hinder legs. It is not done well, but you are surprised to find it done at all.'

On 1 August James went to the apprentice watermen's boat race for the Doggett's Coat and Badge, and strolling back down the Strand he hired his last whore in London for the forseeable future: an officer's daughter from Gibraltar. The last days passed as a weary dream, hungover with stupid, feverish sensations, and on 4 August he told his poor abused journal that his mind was 'gloomy and dejected at the thoughts of leaving London'.

James then committed himself to the care of his merciful creator, and on the morning of 5 August the two men boarded the Harwich stage-coach. They stopped overnight in Colchester, with Johnson fulminating endlessly about the misunderstood Spanish Inquisition and the virtues of eating well. At one point, late into the night, a moth fluttered suicidally around the candle on their table-top and fell, scorched and dead, to the floor. 'That creature,' said Johnson in a 'solemn but quiet tone', 'was its own tormentor, and I believe its name was Boswell.'

They arrived in Harwich on the evening of the following day. James's baggage was put aboard the packet-boat *Prince of Wales* and they went to dine at an inn. Then they walked together to the beach, embraced and agreed to correspond.

'I hope, Sir, you will not forget me in my absence,' said James.

'Nay,' replied Johnson, 'it is more likely you should forget me, than that I should forget you.'

James stood at the stern of the *Prince of Wales* for a long time as the packet lurched out into the North Sea, staring back at the large impassive creature who planted himself patiently on the coastline of England and shifted his weight on the sands from one foot to the other so that his giant frame rolled from side to side as if he bestrode an invisible rocker. And then the figure turned and shambled back up the beach towards Harwich. His heavy hunched shoulders were lost in the spray and the western evening light and the grey masonry of the port. James turned away and pondered on the unimaginable Netherlands, and was violently sick.

Chapter Five

A FEELING HEART

I pity the man who can travel from Dan to Beersheba, and cry, 'tis all barren.

LAURENCE STERNE, *A SENTIMENTAL JOURNEY*

'Utrecht seeming at first very dull to me,' he would later write, 'after the animated scenes of London, my spirits were grievously affected.' In fact, melancholia had fallen on him like an Arctic winter before the *Prince of Wales* put into Helvoetsluys, and it would lift hardly at all for ten pitiless months.

James Boswell hated Holland. It was nothing personal: he could put no good reason to it. He liked the Dutch – or rather, he liked the idea of the Dutch: he appreciated their tolerant solidity, he found their education worth while, he knew that large parts of what Holland was meant to do for him were extremely praiseworthy, he fully understood his parents' motives in sending him to this place, and he did his very best to live up to all of it. And in the process he was driven to distraction.

It was not intended to be that way. Lord Auchinleck had increased his son's personal allowance by 20 per cent, to £60 a quarter, for the duration of his stay in a town which was far less expensive than London. He had been directed towards the eminent professor of civil law Mynheer Christian-Heinrich Trotz and the classical scholar Abraham Gronovius. He had introductions to good Dutch and exiled British families.

And he had the very best of intentions. The young James Boswell may have been an entirely receptive agent of eighteenth-century moneyed male morality in matters such as the hiring of whores and the wholesale consumption of port and watered wine, but he recognised, as did most of the thoughtful minds of his age, that a rounded and responsible life required more than flirtations with depravity. Given his background, he could hardly know otherwise. The difficulty lay in granting his better intentions dominion over his base satisfactions. Utrecht – whose stolid Dutch Calvinism inevitably gave the good fairy the highest ground that she was ever to occupy in her struggle for James's adult soul – became a battleground for the two.

In the middle of October, after two anguished months, James sat down in his lodgings and prepared for himself an 'Inviolable Plan' of behaviour, 'to be read over frequently'. It was an exercise – neither his first nor his last – in self-analysis and a brave attempt to come to terms through the written word with what had seemed, for eight or nine weeks, to be an intolerable lot. His depression had been of a startling severity. His first evening in Utrecht had been spent alone in his rooms in Cathedral Square, picking at food while the bells of the cathedral tower rang out a sombre hourly psalm.

'A deep melancholy seized on me,' he wrote to John Johnston. 'I groaned with the idea of living all winter in so shocking a place. I thought myself old and wretched and forlorn. I was worse and worse next day. All the horrid ideas that you can imagine recurred upon me.'

William Temple received a similar cry of despair: 'I have been melancholy to the most shocking and most tormenting degree . . . I was sunk altogether. My mind was filled with the blackest ideas, and all my powers of reason forsook me. Would you believe it? I ran frantic up and down the streets, crying out, bursting into tears, and groaning from my innermost heart. Oh, good God! what have I endured . . . !

'I cannot read. My mind is destroyed by dissipation. But is not dissipation better than melancholy? Oh, surely, anything is better than this . . . I am terrified that my father will impute all this to mere idleness and love of pleasure . . . I would fain return to London and shelter myself in obscurity . . . Oh, my friend! what shall I do?'

George Dempster happened to be at the time in Paris, and James wrote to him there. They were unable to meet, but Dempster – who had, upon hearing in London of James's Dutch proposals, warned him that anybody who had found Oxford tedious was unlikely to be much cheered by Utrecht – wrote to advise him to 'consider Holland as the dark watery passage which leads to an enchanted and brilliant grotto', and above all not to let the poor, lack-lustre but sensitive Dutch see what he thought of their provinces. William Temple also responded instantly, telling James to lose himself in work and not to disappoint his father – 'he is a sensible, good man, and has nothing more at heart than your welfare.'

And so James worked. He set himself a demanding schedule of Latin instruction, daily French composition, some Greek of an afternoon, the preparation of regular verses ('Ten lines a day I task myself to write, Be fancy clouded, or be fancy bright'), orderly personal memoranda, and his journal, as well as classes and lectures. The only subversive distraction available in Utrecht, he observed, was the game of billiards, and so James resolved to avoid it. And by 15 October he considered himself to have conquered melancholia. He had written (rather too weightily and with a strained, nervous, hyper-conviction to his tone) to tell his solicitous friends of this considerable achievement, and he took out his pen to prepare the Inviolable Plan.

Inviolable Plans, particularly when written by James Boswell, were made to be violated, for which posterity has reason to be grateful. The remarkable thing was that so many of those good resolutions were kept for so long. And the self-portrait, for a lonely and miserable man just 14 days short of his 23rd birthday, was passably honest. 'You have got an excellent heart and bright parts,' James reassured himself. 'You are born to a respectable station in life. You are bound to do the duties of a *Laird* of Auchinleck. For some years past you have been idle, dissipated, absurd and unhappy. Let those years be thought of no more. You are now determined to form yourself into a man . . . This is a great era in your life; for from this time you fairly set out upon solid principles to be a man.'

The Inviolable Plan was thus intended to mark James's passage into adulthood. It did not, of course. Like many men, James Boswell would not learn until middle-age that the announcement of an accomplishment was wholly different from its achievement. As he had in London assumed celebrity before the fact, so in Utrecht he wished maturity upon himself. The former would arrive in time, full and merited; but large segments of the qualities that he and his father both vaguely identified as being essential to a complete and rounded male of the species – most notably a kind of stern solidity and sense of station, which he affected in his youth with comical results and in later life with a discernible reluctance – would remain endearingly absent from James until his dying breath. He was trying, however.

'Your worthy father has the greatest affection for you,' the Plan continued, 'and has suffered much from your follies. You are now resolved to make reparation by a rational and prudent conduct . . . You have an admirable plan before you. You are to return to Scotland, be one of the Faculty of Advocates, have constant occupation, and a prospect of being in Parliament, or having a gown. You can live quite independent and go to London every year; and you can pass some months at Auchinleck, doing good to your tenants and living hospitably with your neighbours, beautifying your estate, rearing family, and piously preparing for immortal felicity.'

And he must stop talking so much: 'For some time be excessively careful against rattling, though cheerful to listen to others. What may be innocent to others is a fault to you till you attain more command of yourself. Temperance is very necessary for you, so never indulge your appetites without restraint . . . Exercise must never be neglected . . . Never indulge the sarcastical Scotch humour. Be not jocular and free . . . Return with redoubled vigour to the field of propriety . . . yield not to whims, nor ever be rash.'

These interesting attempts to convert himself overnight into a middle-aged burgher of the Flemish plains attracted the interest and support of Lord Auchinleck, who wrote and urged his son to study Dutch cow-byres, as they had 'a contrivance for making their dung no way offensive', a method which the excellent Alexander had noticed in his own Dutch days but had since quite forgotten. Luckily, on or around his 23rd birthday, James met Belle de Zuylen.

It was lucky because without a serious, extended infatuation with an intelligent, independent and absorbing young woman, his time in Utrecht could have become seriously distraught, and without the civilising influence of one who expected of her suitors the highest possible standards of dignity, wit, and good behaviour, James could easily have sunk rapidly from the Olympian moral heights of the Inviolable Plan into their degenerate antipodes. Isabella van Tuyll, Belle de Zuylen, 'Zelide' to her carefully chosen circle of intimates, made Utrecht almost interesting.

James Boswell performed much the same function for her. Zelide was also just turned 23 years old, she was at least as vivacious as the old James – whom the new James was trying to disinherit – had been, she was certainly prettier than he was handsome, she was of an old, rich and distinguished family, she was in love with at least one other man (which she never disguised from James), and she also thought that Utrecht was one of the most boring places in Europe. For the next eight months they performed a chaste, flirtatious minuet around each other, and then they parted. It might not have been, as it turned out to be, for ever. They would come perilously close to pledging marriage through the mail – a marriage based on nostalgia – in the years beyond Utrecht, when James had discovered that even literary fame did not deliver all that life could offer; but if he was willing, she was always the more sane. In the winter, spring and early summer of 1764 James and Zelide probably got as close as ever would have been possible, and in so doing they kept alive a spark of youth in a stifling place.

Without Zelide, James had just his letters. Dempster wrote to say that Wilkes was continuing down the noisy road to hell, having been condemned by most of the House of Commons, having been seriously injured in a duel, and having celebrated by publishing a blasphemous poem ('An Essay on Woman'). His 'most affectionate servant' Samuel Johnson wrote to tell him: 'Resolve, and keep your resolution; choose, and pursue your choice.' And Alexander Boswell fondly imagined that on top of James's studies 'you'll too in Holland probably acquire a taste for gardening and send me home some instruction about it. In my last I put a query about a Dutch cow-house or byre which I suppose you'll solve me in . . .'

But with Zelide, Utrecht had parties and other social gatherings, Utrecht had a mischievous young lady to irritate and tease and tantalise the self-conscious Boswell, the young 'Baron' Auchinleck, who was, he once announced unrequested to all in her company who cared to listen, on occasion both firm and fair to his shuddering tenantry as their behaviour required. With Zelide, James Boswell decided before 1763 was out, Utrecht was actually 'agreeable'.

She was even available to sympathise with a personal tragedy which, for obvious reasons, could not fully be explained to her. On 8 March 1764, the morning after a night during which he thought he saw two beams of light appear at and then vanish inexplicably from his bedroom window, James received a letter from John Johnston telling him that his 16-month-old illegitimate son, Charles, had died. 'Alas,' he wrote, 'what is the world?'

> I weep for him whom I have never seen.
> For in my heart the warm affection dwelt,
> For I a father's tender fondness felt . . .

He did not at first mourn extravagantly, but he moped for the first human loss of his young life. His disquiet was obvious, and as if to test Zelide's qualities as a partner in sorrow as well as in joy, he told her that a dear friend had died. Could she 'be company to the distressed?'

'Yes,' she replied, but shortly afterwards James was offended to see her laughing in the presence of other friends. 'What a world is this!' On the next Sunday James attended mass. Within a week it seemed that the worst of his sadness had passed, but when, 21 days after receiving the news, his 'black foe' returned, he attempted to exorcise it in a fierce, dramatic ritual. He walked to the outskirts of Utrecht, gazed up at the cross atop the Gothic cathedral tower, drew his sword, fell to his knees, and swore that if death came then it was ordained, and it would not diminish him. Later he climbed to the top of the tower and gazed silently out over the flat, expansive countryside.

But the foe came back again, urged on by the vague, unaccustomed grief of Charles's death and by stultifying Utrecht, and alleviated only temporarily by tea and gossip and cards and fantasies about a mythic future with Zelide. He broke with an earlier resolution and played two games of billiards. The game took his mind from the pressing moment, and so he played again. He studied relentlessly. He wrote back to Johnston after a month, thanking his friend for the kindness he had shown to Charles and for his 'melancholy news . . . It has affected me more than you could have imagined . . . I had formed many agreeable plans for the young Charles. All is now wrapped in darkness. All is gone.'

The fact that those 'agreeable plans' had not, in the space of 16 months, involved James setting eyes on the child was not pointed out by John Johnston. There was no reason. By the standards of wealthy young men fathering children through young women of no account in the eighteenth century, James Boswell had behaved well. He had sent money to all concerned, seen to a baptism, a nurse and a doctor, and passed on his surname. Only the type of man whom James too often claimed himself to be – a truly religious, sensitive, honourable and upright soul – would have behaved better, and that by not fathering the boy in the first place. The mourning which James permitted himself throughout the March and April of 1764 was to a large degree indulgent and was certainly confused with a broader sadness at his circumstances, but it reflected, nonetheless, a loss: even if it was little more than the loss of a future dalliance with playful, painless paternity which he had promised himself in consolation for the unhappy accident with Peggy Doig; even if it was merely distress at the abrupt cancellation by thoughtless fate of a young man's fancy. It was real enough while it lasted, this occasionally tearful sorrow, real enough to infect a letter to his father and cause Lord Auchinleck to write back anxiously, forgetting cow-sheds for the moment, but recommending that James fight depression and 'acquire a taste for planting and gardening'.

James had, as spring came round, diversions other than pruning on his mind, diversions which Zelide was clearly never going to provide in advance of some impossibly remote wedding ceremony. Not since the night of 1 August , after the Doggett's Coat and Badge river race back in London, had he . . . 'Think,' he urged himself, 'if God really forbids girls.' By May he was resolved: 'Go to Amsterdam and try Dutch girl Friday, and see what moderate Venus will do.'

In truth, James had been under a bombardment of advice from different quarters as to how to cure his depression; advice as varied as his father's gardening hints, suggestions that he take a cold bath first thing in the day, that he seek more sensual pleasure from life, that he live temperately and take exercise, and that he abandon his rational attachment to stifling moral logicians such as Samuel Johnson.

He had decided to attempt a remedy of his own. He visited Zelide and her family, quipped gaily with them about her marriage prospects, urged her laughingly to jump at the first amiable baron to come along (she cheerfully agreed to do so), and assured her that he personally would not marry her even if her dowry was a throne. James then caught the night boat up the Amsterdam Rijn canal to the Dutch capital, and went in search of wine and women. The claret was no problem, but the girl was a disaster. He found himself repelled by her and by the brothel, he had no prophylactic and dare not risk disease, and he left accusing himself of possessing 'the low scruples of an Edinburgh divine'. After a brief round of some of his father's acquaintances, James strolled again through 'mean brothels in dirty lanes', but he went no further. He then returned, tired, dishevelled and confused, down the canal to Utrecht.

On 4 June James received two letters. One was from an extraordinary family friend, George Keith, the Earl Marischal of Scotland. A sly, wise and wrinkled survivor of virtually all that the eighteenth century could throw at a man, Keith should never have seen his 70th year, let alone enter it as a friend of Lord Auchinleck, Voltaire, Rousseau, and the London Court. In 1764, he was hastening back to Potsdam at the request of his old employer, Frederick the Great of Prussia. Keith had, after all, at the age of 22 commanded the Jacobite cavalry of the Old Pretender in the uprising of 1715. He had subsequently invaded Great Britain at the head of a Spanish force through Loch Duich in north-western Scotland in 1719, and escaped the resultant shambolic rout at the battle of Glen Shiel (which left hundreds of Castilians shivering on Highland mountainsides in the middle of a Scottish winter). He found exile first, for 20 years, in Valencia, and later in Paris, where he was employed by the Prussian diplomatic service, and in Switzerland where he became the governor of the autonomous principality of Neuchâtel and, as a consequence, the sympathetic overlord of that district's most celebrated inhabitant, the haunted Jean-Jacques Rousseau. He was mysteriously pardoned by the British in 1759, presumably for secret services rendered and because he had signally failed to support the Young Pretender in 1745, which left him free to repossess his Scottish properties and roam the courts and stately homes of all Europe, dabbling richly in intrigue and fine living, and generously able to offer to the indigent sons of Scots abroad – as he did to James Boswell that June – the occasional shared coach between Utrecht and Berlin.

The second came from George Dempster. The solution to James's woes, he skittishly opined, was to: 'Avoid all company in general, and all kinds of reading, whether law, history, morality, poetry, or politics. Never roger any woman, eat but once a day, and that of one dish. Tailors are thieves all Europe over, so make up no clothes. Avoid travelling, either by land or by water, but leave Utrecht as fast as possible.'

The last was superfluous. James despatched a complimentary 45 bottles of port to his erstwhile tutor Abraham Gronovius and engaged a French- and German-speaking Swiss servant from Berne named Jacob Hanni. He wrote to William Temple: 'Let me rejoice thee, for the joy of thy friend is fully thine. In a day or two I am to set out for Berlin.' He exchanged capricious farewells with Zelide, each of them denying with competitive vehemence (and, in the end, on her part with perfect honesty and on his with unconscious truth) that their feelings for each other had anything to do with true love, and on 18 June he set out in a coach and four with George Keith and his companion, a strange, darkly silent lady, into the Rhinelands of the eastern United Netherlands and the western German States.

And his transformation was instant and complete. As they rolled from the barely reclaimed flatlands into the Sauerland hills, the Earl Marischal rumbled elegantly on in favour of the Spaniards and the Scottish Highlanders, abusing with great percipience the British government for 'taking their clothes from them and extirpating their language' as punishment for the 1745 uprising, and James listened enthralled as Keith argued that such measures would destroy the best militia in the world instead of allying them to Britain. He slept well, if roughly, he ate and drank with relish, he toyed with the inadvisable notion of pressing his sexual favours upon Keith's odd female companion (who was by estranged marriage a Sardinian but by birth a Turk, and James correctly surmised that he might never again have the chance to make love to a Turk). He wrote light-headed, ridiculous, pompous letters to Zelide back in Utrecht, advising her as a man of substance and quality that her 'libertine sentiments' did her no favours in the necessary hunt for a husband (not that he, James, should be for a moment considered as quarry in that chase), and he got out of his bed in the morning 'fresh as a roe on the braes of Lochaber'.

His contentment astonished him. 'I am now, Temple,' he wrote to his friend from Berlin, 'really happy . . . What a gloomy winter did I pass at Utrecht! Did I not speculate till I was firmly persuaded that all terrestrial occupations and amusements could not compose felicity? Did I not imagine myself doomed to unceasing melancholy? . . . And yet, my friend, I am now as sound and as happy as a mortal can be. How comes this? Merely because I have had more exercise and variety of conversation . . . While my blood stagnated in the fogs of Utrecht and my sullen mind beheld the whole creation with horror – while my imagination ranged over the face of the earth, considered all that could be seen and all that could be done and concluded that all was dismal – had I been told that by being drawn some hundreds of miles in a certain machine, seeing another assemblage of houses and some more of those miserable two-legged animals called human, hearing them talk, capering with them to the sound of an instrument of music, and pouring now and then into my stomach a certain liquid . . . had I been told that by doing thus I should feel myself a happy man . . . I should most certainly have treated him who told me so as a great philosopher treats a very ignorant fellow.'

There was no going back. Not even the Earl Marischal could gain James an introduction to Frederick the Great, who thereby achieved the distinction of becoming the only celebrated figure of his time to be sought after by James Boswell and successfully resist his company. It was a small disappointment, but there was no going back. There was Voltaire to seek out, and Rousseau. The lime and lemon groves of Italy and France lay on the warm southern horizon, the antique cultures and modern women of the luscious Mediterranean were almost within reach. There was no going back to another dour northern winter. It had been Lord Auchinleck's understanding – and intention – that James would return to Utrecht after his summer fling in the German States. His coach and four was no more than a day's ride from the Dutch border before such a thing had become utterly unthinkable. To return would be deliberately to relinquish happiness, and James would never ever again voluntarily give up the delights of life. There was a brief struggle through the mail which ended when Alexander Boswell astutely recognised his son's determination and extended both his assent and – more crucially – his largesse. James would go to Italy. James would travel in popish lands. James would even, if he so wished, visit the lair of the Beast of Rome. James accepted from George Keith a brief introduction to 'Monsieur Rousseau' and left Potsdam with a song in his heart.

So Jacob Hanni and his master, the young Baron Auchinleck, the benevolent tyrant of the Ayrshire vales, moved on from town to town. They made a pretty pair. The Swiss had, he confided, left Holland in the wake of an attempted seduction by a young army officer. Hanni, not himself being of 'Italian taste', had resisted the man's advances and proposals that they live together until one extraordinary day when the officer finally exclaimed, 'I am not what you think me', ripped open his own tunic at the breast, and proved himself to be a young woman. After that, the genteel, kindly Swiss decided, it was time to do the decent thing and leave the Dutch provinces. Boswell liked Hanni. He was as much companion as servant, he was alert, sober, active and generous, and he had made it perfectly clear that he would fight for his master if required to do so. The fact that Hanni, one of the most attractively cynical characters of James's youthful acquaintance, also liked his employer for much of the time says much for the heir to Auchinleck. Before he left Holland, James had dismissed his manservant there with a reference. He then asked the man to give him a reference in return. Jacob Hanni's predecessor had proceeded to point out a variety of faults, such as an offensive lack of punctuality, a propensity for overwork and for keeping late nights, and negligence concerning his personal effects, before solemnly concluding that James Boswell had a good and a noble heart which deserved the protection of the Lord. 'I shall never,' he added, 'forget Monsieur.' This was the master inherited by the independent Jacob Hanni. Hanni held less modern views on the relationship between employer and employee, and he would later use what freedom of expression he felt to be his due to castigate James Boswell for being too free and easy with the serving classes, but he would also, in the months to come, care for his exasperating master well enough to see him safely through the most hostile lands in the Europe of their time.

One piece of good luck followed the other. On a September

morning in Berlin a pregnant chocolate-seller entered James's inn. Within minutes he had elicited the welcome news that her husband was a soldier in Potsdam, they were in his bed, and a year's chastity had finally ended. He consoled himself that 'a soldier's wife is no wife' and sent her off, determined no longer to abuse his own desires – 'Divine Being! Pardon the errors of a weak mortal.'

He erred again within days, with a street-girl, and 24 hours after that, in Stralau, it briefly seemed that the Divine Being had decided against one pardon too many. In the course of a drunken dinner he insulted the entire French nation in the presence of a French officer who had actually paid for the fare, and who replied by calling James a scoundrel.

The word struck him like a 'blow on the heart'. This was serious indeed, mortally serious. It was a duelling matter. James instantly sobered up and continued with his meal, thankful for the eating and thinking time being allowed to him over the meat and vegetables, feeling the pregnant tension around the table and the flickering watchful eyes of his fellow guests, and fancying that he heard his ancestors calling on him faintly across the long-dead centuries to honour the name of Auchinleck. But a duel with a serving soldier would effectively be suicide, and no family's name, least of all their own, had been worth a death to any of the Boswells since the instructive example set by Thomas in 1513. James filled up a bumper of hock, extended it to the Frenchman, and offered an apology. It was accepted. James stood on his dignity for the remainder of the evening, but sank back into his lodgings weak and whistling with relief. Lord Eglinton would have nodded knowingly. James had broken a commandment of the Inviolable Plan – the one against rattling – with almost fatal consequences. That loose tongue, so quaint in Mayfair, so exhilarating to Samuel Johnson, so diverting to Zelide, so entertaining to most of his friends, could yet have been the death of him.

They meandered slowly south through the courts and the taverns of Saxony, Hesse-Kassel and Mainz – James dallying expensively with the pick-pocket girls of Dresden, James observing the students of Halle in their college library and thanking

God for his own deliverance from that condition – and as November came to a close they crossed the border into Switzerland where the young River Rhine flowed down amid a hundred snow-capped peaks from Basel.

James was rapidly reading *La Nouvelle Heloise* and *Emile*. When they reached Berne Jacob was given a week's furlough in his native town, and James continued on to the shores of Lake Neuchâtel. There, at a hamlet called Motiers, he booked into an inn and sat calmly down and wrote a letter introducing himself to the famous recluse of the village.

'I have heard, Sir,' he told Jean-Jacques Rousseau, 'that you are very difficult, that you have refused the visits of several people of the first distinction. For that, Sir, I respect you the more. If you admitted all those who from vanity wished to be able to say, "I have seen him," your house would no longer be the retreat of exquisite genius or elevated piety, and I should not be striving so eagerly to be received into it.'

It was a breathtaking belletristic performance. The writer presented himself, he continued, 'as a man of singular merit, as a man with a feeling heart, a lively but melancholy spirit. Ah, if all that I have suffered did not give me singular merit in the eyes of Monsieur Rousseau, why was I made as I am? Why did he write as he had written?' James anticipated his prospective host's request for credentials and insisted that they should be unnecessary when two such minds met (he had, in fact, forgotten to bring the letter of introduction from the Earl Marischal). He threw in a couple of slick references to *La Nouvelle Heloise*, concluded 'Open your door, then, Sir, to a man who dares to tell you that he deserves to enter it', sent the letter off by hand to Rousseau's house, and went for a short walk in the snow and the pines and the rock-strewn riverside wilderness, in the clear cold afternoon air.

On 3 December 1764 Jean-Jacques Rousseau was at the apex of his creative powers and of his fame, and trembling on the edge of despair. He was 52 years old and had published, all within the previous three years, *La Nouvelle Heloise*, *Emile*, and *Le Contrat Social*. The scandalised response to *Emile* in particular had led to him running for cover for months between France and his native Switzerland. He holed up finally in Motiers, part of Neuchâtel, which was governed by George Keith, a man with long personal experience of the tribulations and requirements of exiles, who guaranteed his liberty and as much peace of mind as would ever be enjoyed by this frightened genius ('the goodness, the lovable virtues, the gentle philosophy of that venerable old man,' Rousseau would later write of Keith). He was in physical pain for much of the time due to a chronic urethral condition, and although he did not know it, he was about to become the victim of a withering and terribly destructive personal attack by his aging literary rival and fellow resident of Switzerland, and successor on James Boswell's visiting list, Voltaire.

Struck by the innocent presumption of the introductory letter and inclined towards Scots through his experience of George Keith, even if he did not actually suspect that this latest apparition came directly from the Earl Marischal, he agreed to see James Boswell. When he returned to the inn from his walk, James was handed a card which informed him that M. Rousseau was ill and in pain and not fit to receive anybody, but he nonetheless could not resist Mr Boswell, albeit for a short time. James was met at the street door by Rousseau's mistress, Thérèse Le Vasseur, to whom he was instantly attracted. They went up gloomy stairs and into a kitchen, and there before him was a slightly built man with black hair and large, worried brown eyes and exquisite features, dressed in the kaftan which he wore whenever possible, to put no pressure on his urethral duct and to facilitate the number of times that he had to urinate.

'Many, many thanks,' said James, asking how fared Rousseau.

He was ill, very ill, replied the great man, but had no time for doctors. He was oppressed on all sides but had no intention, at present, of responding. They talked of George Keith – 'my protector, my father; I would venture to say, my friend . . . the only man on earth to whom I owe an obligation,' said Rousseau. They agreed that the French were a contemptible lot, but, added Rousseau, 'You will find great souls in Spain.'

Fancying that some of the groundwork here had already been laid by the Earl Marischal, James put in, 'And in the mountains of Scotland. But since our cursed union, ah –'

'You undid yourselves,' said Jean-Jacques Rousseau.

They talked of kings and countries and liberty, and inevitably a subject dawned which would divert the course of James Boswell's life. In August the French monarchy had signed a treaty with the failing Genoese Republic, agreeing to garrison against insurgency the five main coastal defensive towns of the island of Corsica, which had been a Genoese colony for the previous 200 years.

Corsica had been a *cause célèbre* among enlightened westerners for ten years, and James had been vaguely aware of its condition for most of his sentient life – 'As long as I can remember any thing, I have heard of "the malcontents of Corsica, with Paoli at their head",' he would say later. The reality of the Corsican uprising was apparently straightforward, and complicated only by the internal tensions which seethed beneath its surface. After several decades of ragged, clannish guerrilla warfare against their bankrupt Genoese governors, the Corsicans had in 1755 invited the son of an exiled patrician family, the 30-year-old Pasquale Paoli, back from Naples to announce himself the head of an independent Corsican state. Paoli seized his moment with élan. He formed a national assembly, drew up a liberal constitution, crushed revolts from Genoese-backed malcontents, built a small navy, founded printing presses and a newspaper, constructed a mint, opened up mines, started an arms factory, instituted agricultural improvements and reforms, cleverly negotiated a papal presence in Corsica (although his was a secular state), and enforced a visibly fair and open code of civil and criminal law which did much to reduce the terrible traditional incidence of death by vendetta which, at the height of Genoese rule, was killing as many as 900 men a year in an island whose total population numbered less than 200,000. Even as James Boswell met with Rousseau that December, Paoli was about to establish a university in his central island capital of Corte.

It quickly became apparent that Genoa alone could not keep its fractious charge within the fold of the European imperial establishment. By 1764 Paoli's inspired roughneck military had harried the Italians quite out of the mountainous interior and had them locked impotently within their coastal fortresses. The mercantile Genoese were frantically petitioning the French for assistance and a possible sale of this dubious asset, while the Corsicans had felt secure enough to build for themselves an independent entrepot at Isola Rossa on the north coast, not much further than a cannon-shot from the Genoese redoubts of Calvi, Algajola and San Fiorenzo.

The western world was, on the whole, pleased by these developments. Some other powers delighted in this bucking of their imperial rivals, while visionaries saw in Pasquale Paoli's endeavours the exciting possibility of a new type of civilised society: the small but independent republican nation-state. Tributes flooded to Paoli from most areas of Europe outside Genoa and the interested, vulpine Parisian court. Joseph of Austria applauded him; with publicity that James could not have ignored, Frederick the Great sent from Potsdam a sword engraved with the words 'Patria, libertas'. Voltaire announced that 'Europe regarded him as the legislator and the defender of his Fatherland . . . the Corsicans were seized with a violent enthusiasm for liberty and their General redoubled that passion until it became a species of fury.' His name became a symbol of resistance against imperial oppression even in the discontented colonies of British Upper America. And Jean-Jacques Rousseau wrote in *Le Contrat Social* in 1762: 'There is still in Europe a country capable of being given laws, and that is Corsica. The valour and persistence with which that brave people has regained and defended its liberty well deserves that some wise man should teach it how to preserve what it has won.'

One of Paoli's brasher lieutenants, Matteo Buttafuoco, took this to be a veiled promise by the great philosopher and wrote to Rousseau asking him to frame a constitution for the independent Corsica. Paoli himself, upon hearing of the invitation, was not entirely pleased, but he could hardly pursue it with a rejection of

Rousseau's help, and so he simply issued an invitation to Jean-Jacques to come and live among the Corsicans and help the people as he saw best. Life in such a wilderness garden might have been prescriptible for *Emile*, but Rousseau himself shied from it, and the project – as Paoli had secretly hoped – withered on the vine; although before he died Jean-Jacques Rousseau wrote but failed to publish a Projected Constitution for Corsica. It never reached Buttafuoco, Paoli, or Corsica. It was not put into print until 1861, when its interest to most people was, sadly, no more than academic.

But in the winter of 1764 the invitation had only recently arrived in Motiers. Rousseau was flattered and interested, and he mentioned this notional constitution to James Boswell. Will you write it? wondered James.

'It exceeds my power,' he said, 'but not my zeal.'

After 90 minutes James broached another important issue. What did Rousseau think of him, James Boswell? 'Do you not find that I answer to the description I gave you of myself?'

'It is too early for me to judge,' replied his host cautiously. 'But all appearances are in your favour.'

Fine. 'I shall take the honour of returning tomorrow,' concluded James, picking up his lace-lined hat.

'Oh,' said Rousseau hastily, 'as to that, I can't tell.'

I shall be in the village anyway, said James.

'I am overwhelmed with visits from idle people,' said Jean-Jacques. It was pointed but useless.

'And how do they spend their time?' inquired James with genuine curiosity.

'In paying compliments.'

James got up to leave and Rousseau followed him out of the door just as he was making his fulsome farewells.

'What,' said James, 'you are coming further?'

'I am not coming with you,' replied Rousseau testily, and probably in need of the toilet. 'I am going for a walk in the passage. Goodbye.'

Their conversation was conducted in French, and Rousseau may have said, 'au revoir'. That was certainly James's interpretation: he returned on the following evening to find Rousseau temporarily happy to discourse on the subject of useful and useless professions. No son of the house of Rousseau, for instance, would be allowed to become a wig-maker, 'for so long as Nature continues to provide us with hair, the profession of wig-making must always be full of uncertainty'.

This cheering interlude did not last for long. The subject of the proud and noble Scots insinuated itself once more into their discussion, and Rousseau took the opportunity to say: 'I love the Scots; not because my Lord Marischal is one of them but because he praises them. *You* are irksome to me. It's my nature. I cannot help it.'

'Do not stand on ceremony with me,' allowed James pointlessly.

'Go away,' said Rousseau.

James went away, and returned the next morning.

'My dear Sir,' said Rousseau, 'I am sorry not to be able to talk with you as I would wish.'

James dismissed this irrelevancy and got the conversation going with a full confession of his youthful conversion to Catholicism. Rousseau was engaged despite himself. 'What folly!' he concluded when James had finished.

'But tell me sincerely,' continued James, fixing the philosopher with what he imagined to be a penetrating gaze, 'are you a Christian?'

'Yes. I pique myself on being one . . . I am weak; there may be things beyond my reach.'

'How can I be happy?' beseeched James.

'Do good,' suggested Rousseau. 'You will cancel all the debt of evil.'

'Will you, Sir, assume direction of me?'

'I cannot,' said Rousseau. 'I can be responsible only for myself.'

'But I shall come back.'

'I don't promise to see you. I am in pain. I need a chamber-pot every minute.'

'Yes,' said James, 'you will see me.'

And he did. James left Motiers that evening and rode to Neuchâtel, where he was reunited with Jacob Hanni. Nine days later he returned to Motiers and knocked, unannounced, on Rousseau's door. Thérèse Le Vasseur admitted him, warning that the philosopher was extremely ill. He was, but seemed touched at Boswell's return and advised his visitor that if he returned that afternoon he could put his watch on the table and stay until its minute hand had passed across a quarter-hour.

'Twenty minutes,' haggled James.

Rousseau laughed painfully. 'Be off with you!'

They talked for more than 20 minutes in the afternoon, of James's vexed relationship with his father and of his plans to join the Scottish Bar. James had, he finally confessed as if to a lover, 'a great desire to share a meal with you.'

Jean-Jacques Rousseau was almost broken, almost seduced. 'Well, if you are not greedy,' he consented, 'will you dine here tomorrow? But I give you fair warning, you will find yourself badly off.'

'No, I shall not be badly off.'

'Come then at noon; it will give us time to talk.'

And so at midday on 15 December 1764, James Boswell consummated his relationship with the philosopher-king of his time. He told Rousseau of Samuel Johnson, and Rousseau listened carefully before concluding: 'I should like that man. I should respect him. I would not disturb his principles if I could. I should like to see him, but from a distance, for fear he might maul me.'

They drank red and white wines and ate beef and veal and cabbage, turnip and carrot, cold pork and pickled trout, pears and chestnuts. 'You are so simple,' flattered James. 'I had expected to find you quite different from this, the Great Rousseau . . . enthroned and talking with a grave authority.'

'Uttering oracles?' laughed the host.

'Yes, and that I should be much in awe of you,' lied James. 'Yesterday,' he continued auspiciously, 'I thought of asking a favour of you, to give me credentials as your ambassador to the Corsicans. Will you make me His Excellency? Are you in need of an ambassador? I offer you my services: Mr Boswell,

Ambassador Extraordinary of Monsieur Rousseau to the Isle of Corsica.'

'Perhaps,' said Rousseau, 'you would rather be king of Corsica?'

'Not I. It exceeds my powers.' Then James stood from the table and bowed low. 'All the same, I can now say, "I have refused a crown".'

They talked of cats, which James admitted to disliking, prompting Rousseau to assert that that displayed a despotic character, 'because the cat is free and will never consent to become a slave'. They discussed Voltaire, and Rousseau became agitated and told James that it was time for him to go.

'Not yet,' said James. 'I will leave at three o'clock. I have still five and twenty minutes.'

'But I can't give you five and twenty minutes.'

'I will give you even more than that,' said James.

Rousseau was more than equal to such banter. 'What! Of my own time? All the kings on earth cannot give me my own time.'

Slowly Rousseau and Thérèse edged James towards the door of the room, and there Rousseau looked fondly on the young man, asked him to take a letter for him to Parma, and embraced him – only partly with relief – at the edge of final departure. 'Goodbye,' he said. 'You are a fine fellow.'

It was not an idle compliment. In the letter which he trusted James to take to Italy he introduced the bearer to the recipient by saying: 'I think you will both be grateful to me for bringing you together. In the first letter he wrote to me, he told me that he was a man 'of singular merit'. I was curious to see a man who spoke of himself in such a fashion, and I found that he had told me the truth. In his youth he got his head confused with a smattering of harsh Calvinist theology, and he still retains, because of it, a troubled soul and gloomy notions . . . He is a convalescent whom the least relapse will infallibly destroy. I should have been interested in him even if he had not been recommended to me by Lord Marischal.'

'You have shown me great goodness,' said James. 'But I deserved it.'

'Yes. You are malicious; but 'tis a pleasant malice, a malice I don't dislike. Write and tell me how you are.'

James tore a hair from his head and handed it to Rousseau. 'There are points,' Jean-Jacques replied, clearly moved, 'at which our souls are bound.'

'I shall live to the end of my days!' cried James, half-quoting *Emile*.

At the street door Thérèse Le Vasseur bade an affectionate farewell to the man whom, she had previously told her master, 'has an honest face'. James asked this small, neat, attractive woman if she would like a gift from Geneva.

'A garnet necklace,' she suggested. They shook hands, and he strode, welling with emotion, back to his inn. He sincerely intended to revisit Jean-Jacques Rousseau in the hazy years ahead. His 'au revoir' to Thérèse would be, however, more quickly, more fully, and more unexpectedly realised.

Nothing, now, was beyond James Boswell; none of his ambitions need lie fallow. Not only London but Europe – which was as good as to say the world – was ready to answer its door to him. He travelled south to Geneva and on Christmas Eve took a coach to nearby Ferney, where he walked through the front doors of the chateau belonging to François Marie Arouet, whose pen-name was Voltaire.

James had leaped from one Alpine peak to the next. Rousseau and Voltaire straddled the world of eighteenth-century philosophy and literature like Tritons; no other writer approached them in stature; they faced no threat other than that which one posed to the other. And in December 1764, that threat was significant enough. As James walked through the portals of the Swiss country-house, its owner had just completed, and was gleefully awaiting the publication of, a despicable leaflet which stated that Jean-Jacques Rousseau's urethral complaint was actually chronic venereal disease and that he had mistreated his children, Thérèse Le Vasseur and Thérèse's mother – all of the scurrilous libels, in fact, which attached themselves to Rousseau's name for the remainder of his life and for two centuries afterwards, which sent him almost mad, which led to his small retreat being stoned by a gullible Swiss mob, and which drove him once more into a restless search for peace and freedom in some corner of the shrinking world.

James Boswell strode gregariously into this psychological war zone with an innocent beam on his face and his hand held out to both men, sublimely blind to the hatred in their eyes, innocent of the fact that greatness could drag at its heels such ugly jealousies, and deaf to the cannon exploding all around him. It was the extraordinary passage of the artless native son, and it would not end in Switzerland. It was only just beginning in the Alps.

The old slanderer, like his target, was unprepared for this single-minded, guileless intruder, this grinning, well-intentioned Visigoth. A couple of footmen saw James in, and he peremptorily despatched one of them to announce him to Monsieur Voltaire. He was getting the hang of this. The man returned, however, to say that Voltaire was both in bed and extremely annoyed at the disturbance. James simply held his ground in the visiting-room and finally the eldritch appeared, eyes twinkling malevolently out of a pinched and vicious face.

Anxious once more to test the reputation of his homeland against continental genius, James talked of Scotland. Voltaire admitted that Scottish books were well prepared, but they both agreed that Scottish painting was inferior. This was, said Voltaire, due to the climate. 'It's hard to paint when your feet are cold.' James mentioned his vague plans to visit the Hebrides with Samuel Johnson. 'Very well,' said Voltaire, 'but I shall remain here.' He was getting the measure of his peculiar guest. 'You will,' he added, 'allow me to stay here?' He fed James, who then returned to Geneva and promptly wrote back to Ferney, asking to be allowed to spend a night under Voltaire's roof.

Voltaire agreed, and on 27 December, the very date of the publication of that ruinous attack on Rousseau, James found himself in a mixed winter gathering around the fire at Ferney. He was fed alone, like a tamed animal at a table, and later Voltaire engaged him in debate. Or rather, led James on a roller-coaster from one sally to the next.

'I'll tell you why we like Shakespeare,' offered James.

'Because you have no taste.'

'But, Sir –'

'All Europe is against you. So you are wrong . . .'

And on, and on, to Milton, British comedy ('A great deal of wit, a great deal of plot, and a great deal of bawdy-houses'), and the poems of Macpherson's 'Ossian' ('The Homer of Scotland,' pronounced the old Frenchman). And two days later James left with the scalp of another eminence hanging proudly from his belt. Back in Geneva, he posted a garnet necklace to Thérèse Le Vasseur and wrote to Jean-Jacques Rousseau. 'I have been with Monsieur de Voltaire,' said James. 'His conversation is the most brilliant I have ever heard.' Remarkably, Rousseau would still in the months ahead see fit to help his erstwhile visitor.

James and Jacob Hanni followed the winter sun southwards into Italy in the New Year of 1765. A libidinous wave overwhelmed him as he crossed the Italian border. He had been convinced for some time, in common with many of his countrymen, that society ladies south of the Alps offered the grandest opportunity on the Tour for a free and blameless sexual vacation. Unlike some of his countrymen, however, James Boswell took this to mean that all common niceties were cast aside in the Italian states in the carefree rush to bed. What James consequently saw in himself as open, manly ardour was seen by the Italians, as it would have been seen in Edinburgh or Utrecht, as crass behaviour. He embarrassed his hosts, he caused signora after signorina to turn from him with wide-eyed astonishment on her face, and his sexual fervour was left, as ever, to find its satisfaction on the streets.

He was in a confusion of high spirits. Rejected and mortified in Turin by an older woman whom he had supposed would be grateful for his offer of a lark between the sheets, he fled to a public hanging. He saw the victim stood high on a ladder, saw the crucifix waved under his nose, and saw the ladder whipped away and the hangman press with his feet from above on the dying man's shoulders and strangle him. James was distraught with a mixture of thwarted passion and the agony of naked murder, and he went into a candle-lit church and prayed. He felt 'raging love – gloomy horror – grand devotion. The horror indeed I only *should* have felt.'

Eastward along the River Po he went, in search of everything and nothing in particular, to Milan, Piacenza and Parma, and south across the Apennines to Rome where, as he was about to pass through the customs post of that city state, James caught sight of a familiar slim and haughty figure.

Wilkes! John Wilkes! Just six weeks earlier James had been told that they were both in Turin. He had sent Wilkes his card, and even caught sight of him at the opera, but no meeting had resulted. And now in Rome . . . the same John Wilkes! But a different James Boswell to the shy young man that Wilkes had hardly noticed at the Sublime Society of the Beefsteaks two years earlier, or the diffident, nervous character who had fled from Bonnell Thornton's house; or the Boswell whom Wilkes had half-avoided in Turin. This new James Boswell pounced on Wilkes amid a crowd of Romans, seized him, hugged him, and arranged a café meeting for that very day. This James Boswell was loud and confident and welcoming as if he, not Wilkes, was the man of affairs, the lad about Europe, the accomplished renegade, the citizen of the world, the accomplice of the good and the great and the powerful. This James Boswell had an itinerary of his own, and John Wilkes felt suddenly, unexpectedly pleased to be on it.

It was also a slightly different Wilkes. A year earlier the aging rapscallion had finally had his parliamentary privileges (which included his immunity from prosecution) stripped from him, and he had seen the remaining issues of the *North Briton* number 45 ominously handed over to the public hangman for incineration. He had then been badly wounded in a duel – as James knew through George Dempster's letters – and had fled to France. While in exile he had been expelled from the House of Commons, found guilty of libel, and outlawed from Great Britain. And at the end of 1764, just two months earlier, his dear young friend and partner-in-outrage, Charles Churchill, had died, virtually in Wilkes's arms, at Boulogne.

They fell together like separated twins. Before Wilkes could help himself, he was telling James that he, Boswell, would have been in all of Britain the man best qualified to reply in print to his, Wilkes's, admittedly intemperate attacks on Scotland and the Scots, if only Boswell would trouble his fine mind with politics. '*Such* compliments,' glowed James.

In February they left, within days of each other, for Naples, and there for three weeks they cavorted up and down the slopes of Vesuvius, they drank and dined together, they sought a villa for Wilkes to let. Day after day they talked, as only exiles can, of the men and the politics and the country they had left behind, of London and Edinburgh and even – on Boswell's part – with fondness of Auchinleck.

'If we were to die here,' wondered Boswell, 'how would they write of us!'

It was not a question, but Wilkes was fiercely proud of his strong residual popularity among the mob who had chanted, and would chant again, 'Wilkes and Liberty!' 'If I died and you lived,' he assured James, 'by the Lord, a Middlesex jury would bring you in guilty of my murder.' They talked, understandably, of duels, and Wilkes said that after one such encounter his mother had reproached him for rushing into the providence of his Maker.

'I've always been in it,' replied Wilkes.

'And into eternity.'

'Where have I been all this time?'

'When Wilkes and I sat together,' James would later say, 'each glass of wine produced a flash of wit, like gunpowder thrown into the fire – puff! puff!' Towards the end of March they separated over a last supper. 'You are engraved on my heart,' said Wilkes to Boswell at the end of the night.

A month later he wrote from Naples: 'I thank you . . . for the many agreeable hours you favoured me with here. You have made me know halcyon days in my exile, and you ought not to be surprised at my cheerfulness and gaiety, for you inspired them . . . You are a singular man. What you told Rousseau of yourself is exactly true . . . *Cura ut valeas, et nos ames, et tibi persuadas te a me fraterne amari.*'

Look after yourself, continue to love me, and be persuaded

that I love you as a brother . . . James Boswell was, as he occasionally found time to remind himself, irresistible to other men.

If not always to women. James headed north again from Rome to Venice in the fresh company of another young Scot on the loose, John Stuart, Lord Mountstuart (Mountstuart was actually none other than the son of Wilkes's bitterest enemy, the chief minister Lord Bute; James Boswell cast an indiscriminate net), and all the time disquieting thoughts of Zelide grappled in his mind with visions of the street-girls who had, once more, left him with a bout of gonorrhoea, and of mature Italian women. In Florence and Siena he developed liaisons with two married ladies, Porzia Sansedoni and Girolama 'Moma' Piccolomini. The first proved fruitless, the second was consummated. But then he fled. She was in her late thirties, she had three children and her husband was the mayor of Siena, but worse, much worse: Moma actually liked James Boswell and showed signs of wishing to extend their relationship. She realised his liveliest fantasies of the women of the deep south, and as she did so he woke up. Life was no fantasy. Life meant promises and lies and complications and staying out of the way of mayors in strange cities. The Italian summer was gone. He rose one late September's day in Siena and remembered another commitment to another place. He told Moma that he must leave. 'You go to greater and greater happiness,' she said, 'but you leave me here to go continually from bad to worse; for after a few years my youth will be gone.' James looked at her sadly, and sadness turned into desire, and they went to bed for a final time. On the following morning James Boswell and Jacob Hanni left for Lucca and for the Tuscan port of Leghorn.

In May James had written from Rome to Jean-Jacques Rousseau asking for a letter of introduction to the Corsican nationalists. 'I cannot restrain myself,' he said, 'from paying a visit to those brave islanders who have done so much for their independence, and who have chosen M. Rousseau as their legislator.' Without such an introduction, he added, he would go anyway, although 'it would be singular if they hang me as a spy. If you care for me, Sir, then write me immediately. This is too romantic a project for me to forgo. I am serious.'

The embattled Rousseau had spared the time to respond almost at once. 'Go directly,' he said, 'to M. Pascal Paoli, General of the Nation, you may in the same manner show him this letter, and as I know the nobleness of his character, I am sure you will be very well pleased at your reception . . . You need no other recommendation to these gentlemen but your own merit, the Corsicans being naturally so courteous and hospitable that all strangers who come among them are made welcome and caressed.'

Since that correspondence, as James wrote to Rousseau from Lucca early in October, 'my life slipped away in a delicious dream'. One dream had evaporated, and it was time to drift into the next. He travelled down the coast from Lucca, by way of Pisa, to Livorno, the main port to Corsica outside the Genoese Republic and, in neutral Tuscany, a haven for exiled Corsicans. There he booked into a pensione and made tactful enquiries about sailing into any part of the island other than the chief ports, such as Bastia, which were occupied by French and Genoese troops. He was told that he could in a few days take a merchant vessel to a remote part of the northerly tip of Corsica. He visited in Livorno the commander of the British Mediterranean Fleet, Commodore Thomas Harrison, and obtained a document which was intended to assure Barbary pirates that he was a British citizen ('I hope,' said Harrison pleasantly, 'that it shall be of no use to you . . .'); and Count Antonio Rivarola, a Corsican who in the web of Latin politics had become the Sardinian consul at Livorno, who gave James several introductory letters to his fellow islanders.

So he whiled away the days until six o'clock in the morning of 11 October 1765, when he was woken by two Corsicans hammering on his door to say that his ship would sail in two hours' time. They had, in fact, been ready to leave on a favourable wind during the previous night, but had courteously allowed their foreign supercargo his sleep. While Jacob gathered their belongings together, James sat down by lamplight and wrote again to Rousseau:

'I have received your letter, illustrious philosopher. I see that you do not forget me . . . At present, I account myself, my petty pleasures and petty anxieties, as nothing. In half an hour I embark for Corsica. I am going directly to the territories of Paoli. The worthy Count Rivarola has given me recommendations in plenty. I am all vigour, all nobility. If I perish on this expedition, think of your Spanish Scot with affection, and we shall meet in the paradise of imaginative souls. If I return safely, you will have a valuable account. I cannot write. I shall be able to speak. Death is nothing to me.'

Then James Boswell and Jacob Hanni walked in the thin morning sunlight down to the Livorno harbourside, where they were rowed in a lighter out to a Corsican barque which was flying the Tuscan flag in those dangerous seas, and they set sail on a gentle autumn breeze for Cap Corse.

Chapter Six

SEAS OF MILK AND SHIPS OF AMBER

. . . he fell into one of the strangest conceits that ever entered the head of any madman; which was, that he thought it expedient and necessary, as well as for the advancement of his own reputation, as for the public good, that he should commence knight-errant, and wander through the world, with his horse and arms, in quest of adventures, and to put in practice whatever he had read to have been practised by knights-errant; redressing all kinds of grievances, and exposing himself to danger on all occasions; that by accomplishing such enterprises he might acquire eternal fame and renown.

MIGUEL DE CERVANTES, *DON QUIXOTE*

They sailed on a calm Ligurian Sea for two days and a night. The barque's owner was Corsican; the ship carried a company of six Corsican sailors, as well as Boswell, Hanni, and two Corsican merchants; its function was to transport Corsican wine to Livorno; but its master was a Tuscan, for the same reason that its mast flew the Tuscan flag: any Corsican vessel in those waters at that time was liable to be blown out of the sea by the vengeful Genoese fleet. The Tuscan ensign was a familiar flag of convenience in the eighteenth century. Just a few years earlier,

French merchants had used it frequently to attempt to evade the blockading British navy.

They ate bread and cold tongue and rice. One of the sailors strummed on his *cetra* and James and Jacob accompanied him with their flutes, and when the sun slid into the western sea the ship's small company fell to its knees and sang the *Ave Maria*, as was then the custom among sailors throughout the Catholic Mediterranean Sea. They slept on mattresses laid on provision chests beneath a sail slung crudely over four chairs, and Jacob Hanni was moved by the gentle rituals and the sea and the stars, and he hoped that the voyage would be a long one. What wind there was had dropped so far that on the following day James Boswell helped to row, and as the barque rounded the northern tip of Cap Corse, the peninsula which pointed from the fist of Corsica like an accusing finger at Genoa, the sailors assured him that he would receive great hospitality in their country, 'but if I attempted to debauch any of their women I might expect instant death'. At seven o'clock in the evening of 12 October the boat slipped quietly round the sun-washed rocks of Capo Bianco and entered a small harbour ringed by elegant granite houses. At the end of the jetty was a stocky, round defensive tower. On top of the high wooded hillside above the town two more towers stood proud against the darkening sky. The barque docked, and James stepped out into Centuri-Port.

As James Boswell had wandered innocently through the scatter-shot of the war between Rousseau and Voltaire, so he would thread a passage through the treacheries and blood-feuds of Corsica like a man in another dimension. As innocent and optimistic as Quixote or Candide, he wished to see only what he had led himself to expect – which, in James's case, was the noble Corsican savage at war with the iniquities of the modern world. Corsica was not like that – Corsica was riven by the different ambitions of opposing clans and their chiefs – but he was a young man in search of a cause, and that cause must be unblemished. His myopia became his best defence in that ruthless place; his transparent trust, his hopeless gullibility, his blind faith took him to his goal and back again as surely and safely as an apostle.

He had been advised by the equally innocent Rousseau to visit the one Corsican other than Pasquale Paoli whose name was familiar to the philosopher: Matteo Buttafuoco of Vescovato, near Bastia, who had first written to request a guiding hand on the constitution. By the autumn of 1765, when James made landfall in Corsica, Buttafuoco was already a traitor. He had gone over to the French, whose injection of new military power would, he correctly perceived, prove to be irresistible. His betrayal would become evident within a year, but that October Buttafuoco was already dealing secretly with the French command in Bastia.

In order to circumnavigate that very command, James had avoided Bastia, and so he would avoid – for the moment – Matteo Buttafuoco. Hanni and Boswell were given an armed baggage-carrier in Centuri-Port and directed southwards out of the town, up a gently contoured lane through vine and olive groves, through *macchia* of scented myrtle, thyme and fennel, from whose depths gun-strewn Corsicans occasionally appeared like brigands in the dusk, and James recited to himself, more fittingly than he knew, some lines from Ariosto:

> Together through dark woods and winding ways
> They walk, nor on their heart suspicion preys . . .

There was fortunately no need for suspicion of his earliest Corsican hosts. Antonio Antonetti of Morosiglia was a thorough-bred nationalist who fed James, took him to church, and sent him south, armed with a letter of introduction to the next village, along a terrifying cliffside track 500 feet above the sea, the black rocks and sudden death. At Pino he found himself so well regaled by Damiano Tomasi that he temporarily forgot himself and shouted for more wine 'with the tone which one uses in calling to the waiters at a tavern'. Signora Tomasi looked him calmly in the face and rebuked: 'Una cosa dopo un'altra, Signor.' One thing after another, Mr Boswell. At Canari he stayed in his first convent, and gained his first experience of the Franciscans of the island, whose evangelical cult of righteous poverty had led them into denunciations of property and the devilish vanities of feudalism

– denunciations which so offended Rome that Corsican monks were occasionally denounced as heretics, but which bound them more securely to the egalitarian hearts of their fellow islanders than any bejewelled pontiff from the louche palaces of Italy and France. The vestigial Calvinist buried deep inside James Boswell was also impressed: 'I soon learned to repair to my dormitory as naturally as if I had been a friar for seven years . . . A little experience of the serenity and peace of mind to be found in convents would be of use to temper the fire of men of the world.'

They wandered south past the black sands of Nonza, past a towering monastery where a fundamentalist brotherhood founded by a companion of St Francis had found refuge for two centuries from papal condemnations. They saw the badlands of the Desert des Agriates shining palely in the west and the foot-hills of the colossal interior mountains sliding towards the sky. They were among roadless, lawless, insular foreign wastes, and James Boswell's heart was lifted up to the hills. They hired two women to carry their belongings, and they entered through the civic gates of Patrimonio, where the captain of the guard sternly demanded to know their nationality. James Boswell's Caledonian pride, a fickle animal at the best of times, deserted him.

'Inglese,' he replied. It was an entirely mistaken attempt to impress. The captain, no Barbary pirate in need of a reference from Commodore Harrison, looked at him seriously and then said, in a tone between regret and upbraiding, 'The English; they were once our friends; but they are so no more'.

Hanni and Boswell moved slowly on and into the mountains, towards Corte: the nucleus of the vast web of pathways which traversed an island where stagecoaches were utterly unknown; the town sequestered amid vicious sierras where no Genoese dared to tread; Pasquale Paoli's Corsican seat of power. They stayed in Oletta with Count Nicholas Rivarola, the brother of the consul in Livorno and son of a liberationist from a former time who was by 1765 extremely celebrated and quite dead. They visited the independent Corsican mint at Morato, and James took specimens of silver and copper coins and was told that soon, when this terrible war was won, there would be gold currency struck in Paoli's land. They hired ponies, small horses, mules and donkeys, all with simple cords instead of bridles around their necks, and they climbed through chestnut forests over great divides and down through valleys formed when primitive deities took cleavers to the naked rock. They came finally to a vast bowl among forbidding peaks, at the very centre of which a fortified citadel rose impertinently from its crag, and grey, small-windowed houses built into each other tumbled down towards the lonely plain.

Pasquale Paoli was not in Corte. James and Jacob were received in his place by Signor Boccheciampe, the duplicitous leader of a clan whose every member would be expelled from Corsica within a few years because of their anti-Paolist activities and covert support for the French, who was at that time disguising himself most effectively as a loyal member of Paoli's Supreme Council. Paoli, they were told, was in the deep south of the island, holding a *sindicato*, a series of legal hearings, at a village named Sollacaro.

They rested before travelling on. They saw the university and they climbed up into the castle where, in a tiny corner turret, the Corsicans kept their detested national hangman in abject conditions. A proud people who believed that the spilling of blood with a knife or a gun was, in the appropriate circumstances, not only necessary but honourable, cathartic and redeeming, they nonetheless could not stomach the notion of hanging people after a slow and steady process of law. When Pasquale Paoli had instituted such a process of law, with its logical, ultimate penalty of the gallows, not one single Corsican could be prevailed upon to tie the noose, although Paoli attempted to quell his people's unease by guaranteeing that each death sentence would be carried out within 24 hours of its resolution, thereby making it marginally more hot-blooded a killing. Eventually a Sicilian had arrived and announced, 'My grandfather was a hangman, my father was a hangman. I have been a hangman myself, and am willing to continue so.' He was given the job, a miserable bed in a cramped room in a distant tower high above Corte, and just enough food to survive. Nobody would so much as speak to him. If he dared to show his grimy face in Corte, backs were turned to it and doors shut at its approach. 'I went up and looked at him,' wrote James Boswell, 'and a more dirty, rueful spectacle I never beheld. He seemed sensible of his situation, and held down his head like an abhorred outcast.' The Sicilian would be replaced, within a few weeks of James's departure, by the only Corsican found willing to do his job: one who was under a sentence of death and had been given the unenviable choice of being executed or executioner. His appointment was widely regarded among Corsicans as a national disgrace.

On his second day in Corte James decided to get himself issued with a Corsican passport. He was taken to the house of Grand Chancellor Massesi, who immediately ordered his secretary to make out the document. While the man was doing so (in the name of 'Giacomo Bouswel di Nazione Inglese'), Massesi instructed his endearing son to run and fetch the great seal of Paoli's kingdom. 'I thought myself,' said James delightedly, 'sitting in the house of a Cincinnatus.' Three years later young Matteo Massesi would be found to be colluding with the French. Some of his incriminating captured correspondence with the invaders contained the clear implication that his father, the grand chancellor, would also be extremely happy to entertain French sovereignty over Corsica. Matteo, the child who entranced Boswell, was executed by the successor to that hideous Sicilian hangman at the command of Pasquale Paoli's courts; his father, the Cincinnatus of Corte, was, in the absence of conclusive evidence, merely deprived of his office.

The seal was stamped on the rarest and most curious European passport of its time, and with the commendations of the Generale e Supremo Consiglio di Stato del Regno di Corsica sitting comfortably in a satchel beside those of Commodore Harrison, Jean-Jacques Rousseau and Count Rivarola, James and Jacob set off once more with a gourd of wine, a string of pomegranates, and two Corsican guides.

He may never have been happier, before or afterwards, while in a condition of enforced celibacy. After an hour or two on muleback in the thickets and meadows of the Corsican interior, James jumped down to walk alongside his Corsican guides, 'doing just what I saw them do'. They threw stones at chestnut trees and ate the fruit which showered down, they lay by rushing brooks and drank, and James imagined himself to be a noble savage for a day, one of 'the primitive race of men' who ran about the heavenly woodland beneath those incomparable shoulders of rock, eating when they wished and drinking when they wished and knowing not and caring not what the rest of the world thought or felt or did. 'I was,' he would write, 'in great health and spirits, and fully able to enter into the ideas of the brave rude men whom I found in all quarters.'

He was also travelling away from the zones of treachery, away from the insidious affairs of state and from the glib and worldly merchants of the coast, away from the sly sons of colonialism and into the simple heartland of Paolist support. In the profuse and colourful collage of the central mountains sturdy black-haired fellows, who had never seen a Genoese tax-collector and never met, let alone considered dealing with, an officer of the French monarchy, looked him in the eye and said what they thought:

'Inglese! They are barbarians! They don't believe in the Great God.'

'Scusi, Signor,' replied James, laughing. 'We do believe in God, and in Jesus Christ too.'

'And in the Pope?'

'No.'

'Why?'

'Because we are too far off.'

'Too far off! Why, Sicily is as far off as England. Yet in Sicily they believe in the Pope.'

'We,' said James decisively, 'are ten times farther off than Sicily.'

'Aha,' said his interlocutor, retiring satisfied and leaving James to wonder 'whether any of the learned reasonings of our Protestant divines would have had so good an effect'.

They entered Sollacaro suddenly, crossing a final ridgeway

out of the interior mountains and finding themselves in a cluster of houses high above a broad valley which swept down to the sea. They rode through the village and met a detachment of the General's guard. James left Jacob Hanni with his guides and went on to Paoli's house. He was shown into a room, and there, standing alone, elegantly clothed in green and gold trews and waistcoat, was a tall, well-built 41-year-old man with blunt, open features and large, intelligent, sympathetic eyes, and the unnaturally fair complexion of a Latin man of family.

James handed over his letters from Rivarola and Rousseau. Paoli looked at them politely, and then the most celebrated guerrilla statesman of his day set to studying James Boswell's face. It was a trying time. For several minutes James, unsure as to what to say next, walked about stuttering obsequiously while Pasquale Paoli 'looked at me, with a steadfast, keen and penetrating eye, as if he searched my very soul'. The problem did not, in fact, lie in James Boswell's appearance, or in his references, or even in his soul. It lay in his extraordinary habit of noting down conversations as they were taking place.

'He came,' Paoli explained to a common acquaintance 17 years later, 'to my country, and he fetched me some letters recommending him; but I was of the belief he might be an impostor, and I supposed, in my mind, he was an espy; for I look away from him, and in a moment I look to him again, and I behold his tablets. Oh! he was to the work of writing down all I say! Indeed I was angry.'

As unaware as ever of the impact of his indiscretions on other people – indifferent as only a born biographer could be to the dangers of recording, without permission and before his very eyes, the words of a man whom the heads of two empires and a good number of his own countrymen would dearly have liked to see dead – James's keenly honed defensive mechanism, the unlikely survival device which the gauche youth had somehow slowly developed in Edinburgh, London, Utrecht, Motiers, Geneva, Rome and Siena to see him safely through such awkward social occasions, came heroically to his rescue. He stopped writing for an instant and charmed Pasquale Paoli into believing that the whole misunderstanding had been the Corsican's fault.

'Sir,' he said, 'I am upon my travels, and have lately visited Rome. I am come from seeing the ruins of one brave and free people: I now see the rise of another.'

James was not to know it (although he might have guessed), but he was speaking as one classicist to another. Paoli melted. 'Soon,' he would fondly reflect two decades later, 'I discover he was no impostor and no espy; and I only find I was myself the monster he had come to discern. Oh – he is a very good man; I love him indeed; so cheerful! so gay! so pleasant!'

At the time the General merely commented modestly that Corsica had no chance of extending its jurisdiction, as Rome had done, over half the globe. But it may be a very happy country.

And so it began, the week that led to William Pitt the Elder thundering one of the most celebrated lines about liberty in British political history, that led to Horatio Nelson losing the sight of his right eye, that brought about one of the briefest and least celebrated chapters of British colonialism, and that changed irrevocably the lives of James Boswell and Pasquale Paoli.

James was lodged in a decaying sixteenth-century mansion-house at the foot of the escarpment below Sollacaro, which belonged to the absent Antonio Colonna of the famous Istria clan, one of the older schools of Corsican nobility and one which had also proven itself to be less than wholehearted in support of Paoli's revolution. Wind and rain forced their way into his bedroom, but his spirits were unquenchable. He was woken of a morning with drinking chocolate served on a silver salver adorned with the Corsican arms; he rode out from Sollacaro on the General's horse, 'with rich furniture of crimson velvet, with broad gold lace, and had my guards marching along with me'; he hunted in the parkland below Paoli's temporary seat, along the valley of the Tavaro where rabbits and wild boar ran and mega-lithic statue-menhirs glowered at each other in the *macchia*. He became friendly with Paoli's two priests, his personal secretary, Father Guelfucci, and his aide-de-camp, Abbé Rostini. Most of the travelling Court and virtually all of the villagers assumed

James to be a British ambassador (although Paoli knew better), and he revelled in the status. He was in a unique place, at a unique time, in unique company, and 'every day I felt myself happier'.

And whenever possible, usually at mealtimes when Paoli laid out a table for ten or 20, he engaged his host in conversation. He heard Paoli on the advantages of guerrilla warfare – 'every single man is as a regiment himself' – and of his unwillingness to take a post as governor of Corsica under another country's rule – 'to accept of the highest offices under a foreign power would be to serve'. It would prove to be prescient comment. Pasquale Paoli in later years would attempt to govern Corsica on behalf of two other governments, and would find himself finally unable to countenance either of them. James saw in his library copies of Pope, *Gulliver's Travels*, and – extraordinarily – some tattered copies of his own childhood friend, the *Spectator*.

The 'ambasciadore Inglese' had a Corsican costume made: a jacket with the emblem of independent Corsica stitched to its breast, that extraordinarily distinctive design which Paoli's men carried before them into pitched battle and Paoli's small fleet flew unflinchingly in Genoese waters – the Moor's head in profile with a white headband loosely tied at the nape of his neck and thereafter fluttering free; a crude set of leggings and a waistcoat; and a feathered hat with the words 'Viva la Liberta' embroidered on its band. He wandered about in those clothes with a gift of Paoli's pistols stuck in his belt and rifles slung across his back, 'with an air of true satisfaction'. At night he sat outside beneath the stars with the other men, lying on the ground among large mongrel hunting dogs, listening to haunting Corsican melodies of love and loss and exile and death, and hearing stories of martial valour. Prevailed upon to offer a British tune to the gathering, he at first played one or two Scottish airs – 'Gilderoy', 'The Lass of Patie's Mill', and 'Corn Rigs are Bonny' – on his flute. The Corsicans pronounced themselves charmed by what James himself admitted to be appalling performances (which means that the sound must have been truly dreadful; he had only bought the flute in Germany, where the noted amateur flautist

Frederick the Great had popularised the instrument, and he would never master it), and so James quickly prepared an impromptu Italian translation of a song which David Garrick had recently made enormously popular in London. 'Cuore di quercia . . .' he sang, '. . . hearts of oak are our ships, hearts of oak are our men . . .' and the unlikely band of Corsican nobility, peasants, guerrillas, priests and statesmen erupted into delighted applause. 'Bravo, Inglese, bravo . . .'

James's new-found role as ambassador occasionally went to his head. What about, he suggested to Paoli, an alliance between Great Britain and Corsica? The General deflated him gently. 'The less assistance we have from allies, the greater our glory.' He also reminded James of the British government's recent reference to his people as 'the rebels of Corsica' – the same utterance, much resented in the island, which had so annoyed the captain of guards in Patrimonio. 'Rebels! I did not expect that from Great Britain.'

What, then, can I do? pleaded James.

'Only undeceive your Court. Tell them what you have seen here. They will be curious to ask you. A man come from Corsica will be like a man come from the Antipodes.'

Inevitably, their conversation came round to the subject of James Boswell and his private concerns. Even when least affected by it, as in this exhilarating place, James could not escape the demon melancholia. To understand it, he felt, might be to conquer it, and he would seek any help in understanding it.

'I told him,' he would later write, 'I had rendered my mind a *camera obscura*, that in the very heat of youth I felt the *non est tanti*, the *omnia vanitas* ["all is vanity"] of one who has exhausted all the sweets of being, and is weary with dull repetition.'

'All this,' said his host, 'is melancholy . . . But let us leave these disputes to the idle. I hold always firm one great object. I never feel a moment of despondency.'

The realisation that a character from romantic fiction such as Pasquale Paoli actually existed was, considered James, 'of more service to me than all I had been able to draw from books, from conversation, or from the exertions of my own mind . . . [he]

appeared like the ideas we are taught in the schools to form of things which may exist, but do not; of seas of milk, and ships of amber. But I saw my highest idea realised in Paoli.'

This was not sycophancy. It was an idea whose proper time would actually come much later to James Boswell: the idea that human character and its expression was the brightest bloom of history and the one best worth anatomising. His interest in what cultivated the finest minds of the enlightenment had been developing since the 1750s and those early, hesitant meetings with the likes of David Hume. That interest would be harvested to the benefit of all subsequent generations and all English literature in the years which lay ahead. It merely flowered on a hilltop in the deep south of the island of Corsica, in circumstances of such extraordinary drama that he knew even at the time that, should he return safely to Great Britain, he would arrive home as a changed man. He would be, enviably, the first northern European to have spent time in the famous man's camp. And he would be, thanks to the previous 18 months, and thanks in particular to the self-respect which he had gained by accomplishing such an arduous and dangerous mission by himself, on his own initiative, an adult, at least in reputation. But, most of all, he would return to Britain with new horizons. 'It was wonderful how much Corsica had done for me,' he told Paoli many years afterwards, 'how far I had got in the world by having been there. I had got upon a rock in Corsica and jumped into the middle of life.'

Day after day, fully aware of the future possibilities, he transcribed the General's contemplations, either in his tolerant company or afterwards, down in the draughty mansion-house. He learned that Paoli benefited from second sight, a common Corsican phenomenon, as well as one that James would later encounter – in a remarkably similar form – in equally lonely and mountainous areas of his own native land. 'I can give you no clear explanation of it,' said Paoli. 'I only tell you facts. Sometimes I have been mistaken, but in general these visions have been proved true.' He observed the six mountain dogs who kept guard over Paoli day and night, and he thought of the dogs of Telemachus and Patroclus in Homer's *Odyssey*.

Attracted by the life of a mock-ambassador, James mentioned to Paoli the possible advantages of a fully accredited life in the diplomatic. Paoli agreed that it would be agreeable employment for a year or two. 'In that situation,' he said, 'a man will insensibly attain to a greater knowledge of men and manners, and a more perfect acquaintance with the politics of Europe. He will be promoted according to the returns which he makes to his court.'

After six full days and seven nights, on the morning of his 25th birthday, 29 October 1765, James Boswell left Sollacaro and his formative years behind. He was suffering from a severe cold brought on by his wet and windy accommodation, and it seems likely that Paoli suggested that he stay and rest for a while: certainly the General later rebuked him for departing so quickly and bringing a fever on himself. But he must be away. There was a world outside, waiting to be told not only of Pasquale Paoli but also of the new and exciting James Boswell.

'Remember that I am your friend, and write to me,' said Paoli as they parted, stressing that it was now safe for him to travel back to Italy through Bastia, as the Corsicans had negotiated a hesitant truce with the French, and giving him a commendation to the French commander, Louis Marbeuf. James said that when Paoli himself wrote, he hoped that he would do so not only as a soldier but as a philosopher and man of letters. Paoli took James's hand. 'As a friend,' he repeated.

Deeply moved – so moved that he later considered that the notes he had taken down afterwards about this parting were too emotional to be allowed into print – James, and Jacob, and two Corsican guides, and a large, swarthy priest, and a mastiff called Jachone which Paoli had given to James as a guard-dog for Auchinleck, set off like an unlikely pilgrim caravan back north along the mountain tracks.

'From having known intimately so exalted a character,' he would conclude, 'my sentiments of human nature were raised, while, by a sort of contagion, I felt an honest ardour to distinguish myself and be useful, as far as my situation and abilities would allow; and I was, for the rest of my life, set free from a slavish timidity in the presence of great men, for where shall I find a man greater than Paoli?'

He celebrated his birthday on the back of a nag between Sollacaro and the main Corsican port of Ajaccio, shivering violently with fever while the jovial priest tried to lift his spirits by singing comic songs about the devil and the Genoese. He stayed with a Paolist family in Ajaccio and then unwisely set off again, drawn back to the printing presses of northern Europe. The weather worsened. Jacob Hanni complained of bad meals and hard beds and swore that once he had returned to the mountains of Switzerland, 'I will see who shall prevail with me to quit them.' The Corsican guides, like the priest, tried to cheer their charges by telling of how, if two Genoese could be got exactly in a line of rifle fire, it was possible to shoot them both in the head with one bullet. Rather than raise James's stricken spirits, the story unnerved him, and he insisted from there on that the storyteller walk in front. James added further to the tension by insulting him ferociously when they briefly lost their way. And the poor dog, Jachone, which James found impossible to like, was either neglected or kicked on its way. It would run off later, in France, and never see Auchinleck.

He fell into the arms of the fathers at the convent of Corte. They put him to bed and kept him there for several days. Two surgeons were assigned to attend to him, and Grand Chancellor Massesi and a more faithful servant of the Paolist regime, Padre Mariani, the rector of the university, visited his pallet. He wondered at the ecumenical instincts of his Franciscan hosts – 'I was not in the least looked upon as a heretic. Difference of faith was forgotten in hospitality.'

After a week's convalescence he left, still sick but more anxious than ever to head northwards for Bastia. He journeyed along the sides of vast valleys, past the wooded hills of Morosaglia, where Pasquale Paoli had been born, past a stone packhorse bridge which spanned the River Golo where the great crouched dragon's back of Monte Cinto ripped across the skyline like a howl frozen in mid-air and where, in the unimaginable months ahead, Paoli's dream of a fully independent republic of

Corsica would finally be shattered on a lazy afternoon in spring. On the second night, James and Hanni stopped in Vescovato, where James took the opportunity to look up Rousseau's correspondent, the ambitious and duplicitous Matteo Buttafuoco. Buttafuoco produced Rousseau's response to the request for a constitution, and James diligently offered another small favour to history by copying it down. The very idea of writing such a constitution for Corsica, Rousseau had written, 'elevates my soul and transports me. I should esteem the rest of my days very nobly, very virtuously, and very happily employed . . . if I could render these sad remains of any advantage to your brave countrymen.' Then Hanni and Boswell and Buttafuoco rode side by side into Bastia, where without a blush the Corsican introduced his guests to the Comte de Marbeuf: the French military commander in Corsica and the future colonial governor of the island; the man who would finally demonstrate that all of the elevated thoughts of Jean-Jacques Rousseau, James Boswell and Pasquale Paoli counted for nothing beside the brute power of a European imperial force; and the man who, as no small consequence, ensured that Napoleone Buonaparte was, despite his name and progeny, born a Frenchman.

It was a civilised rendezvous. It could hardly have been otherwise, in those years before total warfare when even enemy officers dined and drank together away from the battlefield and tipped their hats in polite acknowledgment from either side of the belching cannonade. There was a truce and there were treaties to be haggled over, and even Paoli himself was at that time anxious to stress that his quarrel was not with Paris but with the Genoese. And James was, as he frankly admitted, not unhappy to return to health among the drapes and dinner-services of a French colonial drawing-room. The life of a noble savage had been interesting, but 'It was like passing at once from a rude and early age to a polished modern age; from the mountains of Corsica to the banks of the Seine.'

The dizzy, weak and white-faced James was put in a warm bed in a warm room, given books to read and denied visitors by his indulgent host, fed *bouillons* by trained servants, and only gradually allowed back into stressful society – where he promptly met a woman from Cumberland who had taken up with a French *picquet* when Charles Edward Stuart's army marched through Penrith in 1745 and 20 years later found herself married to him and transported to barracks in Bastia. 'So Venus wills . . .' he mused.

And there, in the Comte's luxurious Bastia chateau, while the 'worthy, openhearted' Marbeuf flattered him with rumours of his true diplomatic initiative as a servant of George III in Corsica – ever his Achilles heel in that place – the trusting Boswell found himself too easily lulled. 'The French seemed to agree very well with the Corsicans,' he considered, while in another land Rousseau was raging at the iniquities of Paris. '. . . M. de Marbeuf appeared to conduct himself with the greatest prudence and moderation. He told me that he wished to preserve peace in Corsica . . . Perhaps, indeed, the residence of the French in Corsica has, upon the whole, been an advantage to the patriots. There have been markets twice a week at the frontiers of each garrison town . . .'

He broke with these reflections to write a valedictory letter to Pasquale Paoli, and then, on 20 November, the innocent abroad began his journey home by taking ship from Bastia to Genoa.

Chapter Seven

CORSICAN BOSWELL

Two voices are there; one is of the sea,
One of the mountains; each a mighty Voice:
In both from age to age thou didst rejoice,
They were thy chosen music, Liberty!

WILLIAM WORDSWORTH,
'NATIONAL INDEPENDENCE AND LIBERTY'

Our spies, said the Genoese politician Signor Gheradi at a dinner party shortly after Boswell's arrival in his city, were watching you throughout your time in Corsica.

I was just a simple traveller, protested James.

Signor Gheradi shook his head. I can even tell you what you were wearing, he added. While travelling you were in clothes of scarlet and gold, but at the Supreme Council in Corte you appeared all in black. It was – unsurprisingly, given hindsight into the true nature of many of Pasquale Paoli's supporters – true; and James Boswell shivered with delight. It was time to make hay.

Early in January 1766, some idiosyncratic items of news began to appear in the *London Chronicle*, that willing journal of self-advertisement in which Boswell had earlier reviewed his own collection of letters. 'About the middle of October,' the

147

Chronicle informed its readers, 'Mr Boswell, a Scots gentleman upon his travels over Europe, sailed from the port of Leghorn for the island of Corsica . . . and went above a hundred miles into the territories of the malcontents, as they were formerly called, but must now have the title of the nation . . . he was received by [Paoli] with every mark of distinction, was lodged in a palace of the noble house of Colonna, and whenever he chose to make a little tour, was attended by a detachment of guards. He passed ten or twelve days with General de Paoli, dined and supped with him constantly, and was every day in private conference with him for some hours. Mr Boswell gave it out in Leghorn that he went to Corsica merely for curiosity, but the politicians of Italy think that they can see more important reasons for his visiting that island. The Genoese have been not a little alarmed by it, and having received very early intimation of Mr Boswell's having sailed from Leghorn, they procured constant intelligence of his motions during the whole time of his stay in the island . . . People in this part of the world are curious to know what will really be the consequence of Mr Boswell's tour to Corsica.'

James Boswell, gentleman spy, shady diplomat, blade on the loose, *homme mysterieux*, knew the potential for self-promotion when it gave him bed and board. The despatches – all sent from France as he wound his homeward way – continued, week after week throughout January and February, sketching a retrospective of his six weeks (or, to adopt the inventive mathematics that he himself employed while calculating for the public prints his time spent with Paoli, three months) in Corsica. They were not entirely devoted to spinning a fascinating web of romantic subterfuge about the mission and the personage of James Boswell. The justice of the Corsican cause and the stupidity of the Genoese were trumpeted throughout. The Genoese, suggested one article, 'are at last come to believe themselves that the Corsicans are like the anthropophagi – the most terrible of barbarians. To a Genoese gentleman who asked, with much earnestness, what Paoli was like, he replied that he was like the astonishing beast in the Revelations, with seven heads and ten horns, full of eyes before and behind . . .'

But two days later the *Chronicle*'s readers learned again of their anonymous hero, the dark figure whose name was on all lips and was scattered liberally throughout the gazettes of Europe: 'Mr Boswell, a Scots gentleman, who has been in Corsica. It was at first rumoured that he was a desperate adventurer, whose real name was McDonald, and who had served during the last war in North America; but it has since appeared that he is a gentleman of fortune upon his travels, a friend of the celebrated John James Rousseau . . .'

The *London Chronicle*'s readership was large, but it hardly extended outside the capital. It was Boswell's misfortune that the reports were picked up in Edinburgh and reprinted in the Scottish press, and that Lord Auchinleck consequently allowed himself the full-blooded tantrum that he had hitherto been spared for the best part of two years.

James had returned to continental Europe to find, waiting like watch-dogs on the shore, a series of letters from his father. They did not make pretty reading. Auchinleck had been seriously ill, and was concerned to see his first son before death. 'Inexcusable neglect,' the correspondence fulminated, '. . . I don't know whether you are still with Lord Mountstuart or not; I have been informed that Lord was to come straight home from Italy. If so, I think you should return with him . . . Your conduct astonishes and amazes me . . .' It was inevitable that the old man would learn within weeks, from one source or another, of his heir's unlicensed jaunt to Sollacaro. The desperate adventurer packed up his things and hurried home to face parental wrath before his spending money was cut off.

He went north through Marseilles to Lyons, losing Jacob Hanni at the former and the dog, Jachone, somewhere north of the latter, from where he wrote again to Jean-Jacques Rousseau, who had fled from Motiers after the stoning of his house which had followed Voltaire's slanders and made his desperate way to Berne, Strasbourg, Paris and, finally, England. The visit to Corsica, Boswell told the harried philosopher, 'has done me a wonderful amount of good . . . Paoli has given a temper to my soul which it will never lose. I am no longer the tender, anxious

149

being who complained to you in your Val de Travers. I am a man. I think for myself.'

James arrived in Paris to discover through the boat-mail that his father had quite recovered and had experienced another swift paternal change of mood. He was relieved to find his son returned in apparent health from a long and worrying silence and granted him leave to dally for a few weeks in the French capital. The stay of execution was brief but welcome: John Wilkes was in town.

Paoli, said Wilkes in a superior tone, offered me a regiment!

James, finally, was man enough to deal equably with all of this. 'You must know, Sir, that there are no regiments in Corsica.'

'Oh. An equivalent . . . a command,' the great parliamentarian spluttered. 'It was offered me in Naples . . .' and they laughed together, two Georgian filibusters alive and well and at large in France. 'I wonder you could leave it,' continued Wilkes of the island of Corsica. 'As I passed by it in a tartane, I pulled off my hat and drank his health.'

Boswell called later on another Englishman abroad in Paris, the writer and politician Horace Walpole. Walpole disliked James by reputation, tried to avoid him, failed, disliked him even more upon sight, and was to continue disliking and criticising him until 1797, when Horace Walpole died. There was more to this unusual animosity than a surface resentment of an old talent for the young. In 1736 a bizarre Westphalian named Theodor von Neuhof had landed in Corsica from North Africa, wearing a scarlet silk kaftan, Moorish trousers and yellow shoes. He also carried with him guns, ammunition, money and the promise of more. He wanted, in return for this largesse, to be crowned king of an independent Corsica. Von Neuhof's 'reign' lasted for seven months before he fled the island, having grown too fond of summary denunciation and execution for his subjects' taste, and fetched up in England, where he died in a London poorhouse. Forgotten by most and remembered only with hilarity by a few outside Corsica (including Voltaire, who was inspired by the tale to write *Candide*), von Neuhof had just one champion in Britain. Horace Walpole had decided that the Westphalian adventurer was an heroic figure, and upon von Neuhof's death he had actually erected a plaque to his memory in Soho. And here was James Boswell arriving impertinently from Corsica and spouting to all Paris about a new leader, a better leader than the great Theodor. It was calculated to make a man purse his lips and frown. Walpole did, however, do James Boswell one large favour. He may have done it generously or unwittingly, he may have spoken the words openly or through clenched teeth, we will never know. But he did advise the younger man to write a book about Corsica, 'as there are no authentic accounts'.

Towards the end of January the island of Corsica was, however briefly, dispelled from his thoughts. James received a letter from his father saying that his mother had died. It was quite unexpected. While Alexander had himself been ailing, Euphemia had complained of slight rheumatics. She had requested some medical assistance, had developed a fever, and had then deteriorated with the helpless, alarming speed common to the times until, early in the morning of 11 January, she had turned to Alexander, said weakly that she wished to be with Christ rather than with her family, turned away and fell asleep forever. She was 48 years old. 'I have lost,' wrote Alexander heartbreakingly to his eldest son, 'my friend, my adviser and assistant in everything . . . it will occur to you how much I need your assistance . . . Do not disquiet yourself about the money you have spent; if you turn out in the way I expect, I shall never grudge these expenses . . . Farewell, my dear Jamie, may God bless and preserve you.'

With his mother as the first and entirely unexpected occupant of the new family vault in Auchinleck village, James wandered through Paris in a passing daze. Whenever he felt saddened by her death, he remembered heaven and her attachment to the authorities in that place, and he cheered up for a moment. At other times he would idly picture Euphemia alive and pleasantly project his absent mind to the loving welcome home which was due to her wandering son, and he would then come round with a physical start. He was in this state of nervous agitation when he received word of the arrival in Paris of Thérèse Le Vasseur, Rousseau's mistress, on her way to join her master in England.

He did not intend what happened next; nor did he know, at that age, always to expect the unexpected. On the last day of January he stayed up all night before departing Paris for the Dover packet, writing letters and occasionally crying out in alarm that it was not possible that his mother was dead. He left on the same coach as Thérèse, and within two nights they were sharing a bed. It was even more fraught an affair than was usual for James Boswell. He fluctuated between alarming impotence – arguably brought on by the very thought of taking such liberties with Jean-Jacques Rousseau's paramour as much as by the lingering pathos of his mother's death; although there is evidence that his actual virility did not always live up to expectations – and rampant enthusiasm. But he tried again, successfully, and recovered himself sufficiently to remind Thérèse of her extreme good fortune in having found a Scotsman in her bed. And after 12 days they reached Dover. 'Yesterday,' read a notice in the *London Chronicle* of 15 February 1766, 'James Boswell, Esquire, arrived in town from his travels.'

He deposited Thérèse with Rousseau in Chiswick, where he found his former hero – a worried man at the best of times and not well suited to exile among a people whose language he could barely speak and whose climate was detestable – to be old and weak and lodged in a shop, and altogether not quite so interesting as he recalled, and he fled instantly to Fleet Street and knocked on the door of Samuel Johnson.

It had been two-and-a-half years since that sea-blown evening parting at Harwich. Johnson stood at his doorway and held his arms out wide; Boswell dropped to his knees and asked to be blessed. Anna Williams, the sightless caretaker of Johnson's house, muttered something about being glad to have him back and quickly left, whereupon Johnson hugged Boswell to him and grumbled, 'I hope we shall pass many years of regard.'

He gave himself a final month in London, and he used it well. He knew what he had to do with his life; he knew that in his 26th year, with his father ailing and his mother dead, with his Grand

Tour behind him and all of the acquaintances made that should see him through his days, the reckoning time had come.

Wilkes bids me not to be a lawyer, he told Johnson, as I should be excelled by plodding blockheads.

'In the formal and statutory practice of law,' said Johnson, 'a plodding blockhead may succeed, but in the equitable part of it a plodding blockhead can never succeed.'

'I fear I shall not be a good advocate.'

'No man is a good advocate at first; and perhaps in seven years you will not be so good a lawyer as your father, and perhaps never. But it is better to be a tolerable lawyer than no lawyer.'

In the meantime, and quickly before Edinburgh and Auchinleck enveloped him for countless tedious months to come, there were Corsican affairs to pursue. He wrote to William Pitt, the first Earl of Chatham, the most powerful ex-governmental political force of the hour, suggesting that the gout-tortured and mentally dubious old statesman might be interested in hearing of Boswell's meeting with Signor Paoli. I am flattered, replied Pitt, but I am not in office. Try a secretary of state.

'Sir,' responded Boswell, 'Mr Pitt will always be the prime minister of the brave, the secretary of freedom and of spirit; and I hope that I may with propriety talk to him of the views of the illustrious Paoli.'

Finally, Boswell was able to stroll across to the house in Bond Street where Chatham was residing with the Duke of Grafton. A clutter of other lords was in evidence, but they were shortly cleared away and the two men got down to business.

'I cannot properly receive,' announced Pitt, 'communications from General de Paoli, for I am a privy councillor, and have taken an oath to hear nothing from any foreign power that may concern Great Britain without declaring it to the king and council . . . [as well as which] I am now just a private member of parliament . . . I resigned, and ever since I have known no more of what has been doing in the cabinet than the most remote man in the kingdom. I know not what Corsica has been able to receive by way of France. I –'

'Sir,' put in Boswell, 'the General – Paoli – felt severely: to be given into the bargain that poor Corsica should be considered as nothing.'

Strange indeed, thought Pitt, that an island in so strategically strong a position should be considered as nothing. 'How are their harbours?'

'One or two excellent, with some expense,' replied James Boswell, marine engineer.

That was of consequence. 'We have no such place in Italy.'

'General de Paoli said –' attempted Boswell.

'Sir! You'll remember my situation!'

They talked of a letter from Paoli to Pitt which had either been intercepted or had gone astray, and the politician was somehow disturbed by this. As Boswell prepared to leave, the passion of the William Pitt of yore stirred in his 58-year-old breast, and his visitor received a short, thrilling personal sample of the oratory which had once hypnotised a nation. The long, stern face turned to James Boswell, and none of the incipient madness was there, and briefly this was much, much more than a tired, grumpy, proper old man with one leg on a gout-stool. The first Earl of Chatham thundered, without prompts or rehearsal, 'Sir, I should be sorry that in any corner of the world, however distant or however small, it should be suspected that I could ever be indifferent to the cause of liberty.'

Naturally, James had arrived back in London with no clear plan as to what action the British government should take concerning Corsica's war of independence from Genoa and the collateral Genoese willingness to sell its colonial outposts to Louis XV. He was vaguely interested in some form of intervention, but the nature of that intervention eluded him. It was not only a question of whether or not Great Britain should once more go to war with France on the advice of an Edinburgh judge's son and his Catholic republican friends. Wiser and more experienced heads, such as that of William Pitt, knew that Britain had once before intervened in Corsican affairs and had gained scant reward for it. In 1743, indeed, they had paraded Theodor von Neuhof off the north coast of Corsica in a British warship, but the post-Neuhof and pre-Paolist patriots had simply ignored the ridiculous Westphalian. British vessels had twice dutifully bombarded Bastia later in the 1740s but gained no discernible advantage. 'Liberty' was indeed a British war-cry in colonies other than its own, but this Corsica was truly an imperialist's graveyard, an obstinate, impenetrable place. Useful Mediterranean harbours it may have had, but the unspoken consensus of informed British political opinion of the island at the time of James Boswell's return was: good luck to the French, and anybody else who dares to collect taxes there.

It was, in other words, a perfect ideological vehicle for Boswell. He could bang the drum of freedom without fear of open contradiction and with the certainty of receiving uncritical mobbish support from the literate classes; and he could be assured of being able to go on banging it for years – until, in fact, he grew tired or the drum burst – because nothing whatever would be done by the British authorities, either to support or to undermine his vaunted freedom-fighters.

And for almost 30 years that was exactly the case. The powder-store did eventually blow, and all of the accumulated propaganda of the years did finally have its effect. But by then it was almost too late to embarrass James Boswell by requiring that his roseate recollections of the homeland of an uncorrupted race be focused into a sharp administrative scheme. Almost, but not entirely, too late.

Boswell left William Pitt and Samuel Johnson and took the coach back to Edinburgh and to Auchinleck, where his father had assembled several piles of garish red stone with the intention that his son should exploit the experience of his travels by designing Italianate outbuildings attached to the classical, pearl-grey Palladian façade of Auchinleck House. His son did so, to gruesome effect.

He had been a long time away, and it appeared that his duty and his career would now ensure that he spent a long time at home. James was admitted to the Scottish Faculty of Advocates in July, launched his modest career in the law, and began to prepare a book on Corsica. 'He often talked to me of marriage,' he would find himself writing of the pristine bachelor Pasquale Paoli, 'told me licentious pleasures were delusive and transient, that I should never be truly happy till I was married, and that he hoped to have a letter from me soon after my return home, acquainting him that I had followed his advice, and was convinced from experience that he was in the right.'

He exchanged pleasantly regretful letters with Moma back in Siena; he enjoyed transient licentious pleasures with the gardener's daughter at Auchinleck; he went to Moffat to take the waters for the first time since his childhood and courted a Miss Moffat there. He looked as keenly as a farmer at a mart at Catherine Blair, at the distantly related Elizabeth Bosville, and at the Irish girl Mary Anne Boyd; he wrote to Zelide in Holland and he lazily scoured the remainder of polite Scottish society; but no answer to Paoli's kind prescription presented itself, other than the Auchinleck gardener's daughter – who was, he confessed to William Temple, so accomplished in bed that he could do worse than call the banns with her.

He passed his time with diligence. He wrote more semifictional paragraphs for the *London Chronicle* on the subject of Corsica, he practised the law, and for the first time in his life he began to drink seriously. Previous to his becoming an advocate, James Boswell's routine alcoholic refreshment had been modest quantities of negus, or diluted wine. Back on the rutted, staggering Royal Mile of Edinburgh, seduced by the song of the meridian bell, drawn into meetings in taverns which lasted throughout and lost in pleasurable talk the long wet afternoons, which drowned the tedium which otherwise would have conquered all, then he began for the first time to drink heavily and undiluted, and to get drunk, and to experience hangovers. 'I have given a great deal too much in to that habit,' he wrote apologetically to William Temple, 'which still prevails in Scotland.'

Old friends were taking their own ways. Temple himself married in the July of 1767, and all that Boswell had, it seemed, was a long, slow book on Corsica and the gardener's daughter. The pregnant gardener's daughter. Another embarrassment hastily, if not guiltily, to be paid off and forgotten. It was wholly unsatisfactory, to his father, to his friends, and to James himself. Desperately, he trawled from one polite female acquaintance to the next, and one after the other rejected this over-anxious, over-eager young suitor. 'Marriage,' he wrote fretfully to William Temple, 'is like to lose me a friend.' A life of bachelordom, deserted in gloomy middle-age by his former accomplices, did not exactly loom, but it threatened – and very little more than a threat was ever necessary to bring James Boswell's black dog of melancholy howling to his side. He drank, he worked gradually – listlessly, by his own energetic standards – on his book, he contracted more venereal disease, he shopped out the black-haired gardener's daughter's illegitimate child with as much decency as he could muster, and he wondered where the exit lay.

It had been under his nose since childhood. Margaret Montgomerie was, in 1767, 29 years old to James's 27. She was directly related to him: they shared the same grandfather. She was, in fact, his first cousin. When they renewed their acquaintance upon his return to Scotland, she knew him as 'Jamie', although not for long: he hated the diminutive.

She was not beautiful. Other than that, they had little superficially in common. Her family was relatively poor, not peat-bog poor or even tenantry poor, but poor by the standards of an heir to Auchinleck. She was calm and strong willed. She had hair of midnight-black, careful brown eyes, a long, straight nose and a determined mouth. In 1767 they were corresponding idly; by the end of that year they were meeting at society events, and James began to feel affection and attraction nuzzling him from unexpected quarters. He began – while still pondering Zelide, and the gardener's daughter, and a handful of others – to take an interest in Margaret Montgomerie. And then his book was published.

An Account of Corsica, The Journal of a Tour to that Island; and Memoirs of Pascal Paoli was printed in Glasgow for a London publisher, Edward and Charles Dilly, in February 1768. Appended to a ramshackle and often inaccurate (although, for its time, diligently enough researched) history of the island was the memorable meat of the book: James Boswell's own account of how he, James Boswell, had travelled the length of this wild and wonderful place and had seen many strange sights before he, James Boswell, finally foregathered with the man of the European hour, Pasquale Paoli (the Corsican would have preferred the native, as opposed to the French, spelling of his Christian name). Of how he, James Boswell, spent an indeterminate but sufficient period of time with the great Paoli before speeding back to pursue his cause in Britain . . . as an ambassador, almost. As a semi-official ambassador.

It was a deeply, brashly personal piece of writing, but it was not – bafflingly not – egotistical. The word implies, and implied then, offensive behaviour, and James's use of himself in his account was far too transparent to give offence. His narrative was revealing, human and amusing. The writer was no abstract informant, no distant Olympian educator of the reader, but the main character in an earthly drama, a man with fears and pretensions and weaknesses. He was drawn by his own hand too starkly for smugness. He did not demean himself. He also patently possessed the considerable courage to attempt such a journey – but the courage was not stated; the reader must work that out, between the cheerful lines of self-mockery and impudent observation. Two hundred years later hardly a travel book would be written which did not begin from such a position; in 1768 it was unknown. 'Your history,' said Samuel Johnson of the book, 'is like other histories, but your journal is in a very high degree curious and delightful . . . Your history was copied from books; your journal rose out of your own experience and observation. You express images which operated strongly upon yourself, and you have impressed them with great force upon your readers. I know not whether I could name any narrative by which curiosity is better excited or better gratified.'

Boswell's preface to the original 'Account' has hardly been used in subsequent editions. It was one of the most extraordinary of its kind. 'I should,' he wrote, 'be proud to be known as an author, and I have an ardent ambition for literary fame; for of all possessions I should imagine literary fame to be the most valuable . . . The author of an approved book may allow his natural disposition an easy play, and yet indulge the pride of superior genius when he considers that by those who know him only as an author he never ceases to be respected.'

This was the unstated ambition behind the pen of anybody who had ever aspired to see themselves in print. Samuel Johnson had known those needs. Horace Walpole was at heart that flawed. It was writing so open, innocent and naïve as to be almost sacrilegious. 'Such an author,' he continued, 'when in his hours of gloom and discontent, may have the consolation to think that his writings are at that very time giving pleasure to numbers, and such an author may cherish the hope of being remembered after death, which has been a great object to the noblest minds in all ages.'

There it was. Take him, bright eyed, plumply gauche and plucking urgently at your arm, or leave him. Most took him. The book quickly ran to three editions in England and was widely circulated, in translation, on the continent. It was widely praised, then by the likes of Garrick, David Hume and Johnson, and later by such as Napoleone Buonaparte.

One damning comment would follow the book, as so many derogations followed James Boswell, down through the decades. Immediately after publication, he sent a copy to Horace Walpole, with a note which read in part: 'I dare say you have forgotten what you said to me at Paris, when I had the honour of giving you a few anecdotes of what I had just come from seeing among the brave islanders. In short, Sir, your telling me that I ought to publish something in order to show the Corsicans in a proper light was my first incitement to undertake the work which has now made its appearance. If it gives any pleasure to Mr Horace Walpole I shall be particularly happy.'

The curmudgeonly Walpole promptly wrote to his friend, the poet Thomas Gray, advising: 'Pray read the new account of Corsica; what relates to Paoli will amuse you much. There is a deal about the island and its dimensions that one does not care a straw for. The author, Boswell, is a strange being, and . . . has a rage for knowing anybody that was ever talked of. He forced himself upon me in spite of my teeth and my doors, and I see has given a foolish account of all he could pick up from me about King Theodore . . .'

'The pamphlet proves,' replied Gray, 'what I have always maintained, that any fool may write a most valuable book by chance, if he will only tell us what he heard and said with veracity. Of Mr Boswell's truth I have not the least suspicion, because I am sure he could invent nothing of the kind. The title of this part of his work is a dialogue between a Green Goose and a Hero.'

Horace Walpole (who would be remembered within decades not at all for his painstaking literary efforts, but for his relatively artless and unsophisticated collected private letters) and Thomas Gray could, however, cheerfully be ignored in the frothing wake of publication. Boswell skipped down to London to enjoy the notoriety. 'James Boswell, Esq.,' announced the *London Chronicle* in March, 'is expected in town.' Over tables of cod with oyster and shrimp sauce and bottles of claret and Madeira he discussed efficacious ways of fending off venereal disease ('. . . [an acquaintance] assured me that oil was an infallible shield') and thought privately of marriage to the woman who had agreed to translate his 'Account' into Dutch: Zelide, Belle de Zuylen.

He dragged himself briefly from London to visit Samuel Johnson in Oxford. The great man had just been reading a history of the distant Hebridean island of St Kilda which had been published in 1764 by a Highland minister named Kenneth Macaulay – a study as stylistically opposed to Boswell's 'Account' as it was possible to imagine – and James reminded Johnson of their tacit agreement to visit the Western Isles.

Boswell was still in London on 15 May, when a treaty was signed in Versailles whereby Genoa relinquished the sovereignty of Corsica to France. He returned to Scotland in June and commenced a fund-raising effort which resulted in 30 cannon and 150 rounds of shot, to the value of £700, being shipped from the Carron Ironworks in Stirlingshire to General Pasquale Paoli.

Fighting on two fronts, he finally gave up on Zelide. She would not marry him. She would never, of course, have married him. She may have been as confused about her own feelings for James Boswell as it was possible to be, but marriage was never, in the bottom of her heart, part of her complex desires.

Eventually, she would not complete the translation of his book. After an uncertain exchange of letters, they broke for ever from each other; she to a strange and silent marriage to another man and a life of distinguished literary hermitage, and James to a civilised, formal arrangement with Margaret Montgomerie.

It would be a stuttering courtship. No sooner had he got his cousin to sign a mock-serious affidavit to the effect that James was so much in love with her that marriage was impossible; that the marriage, given his temperament, would be disastrous; and that if, therefore, it looked like taking place she would submit to permanent banishment from Great Britain – no sooner had Margaret laughingly put her name to this bit of lovers' nonsense, than Boswell was telling Temple about the astonishing 16-year-old charms of Mary Ann Boyd. 'Formed like a Grecian nymph with the sweetest countenance . . .' No sooner had she inclined towards him than he was preaching not of their relationship but of Corsica. The island cause was as serious a rival for her attentions as any teenaged Irish girl. Throughout the spring and summer Boswell busied himself editing a collection of *British Essays in Favour of the Brave Corsicans*. It was seen by some as little more than a simple sequel to a publishing success. It was seen by others as a dangerous obsession. 'I wish,' Samuel Johnson told him, 'you would empty your head of Corsica, which I think has filled it rather too long.' If Johnson felt that way, how irritated was Margaret Montgomerie? Unlike the philosopher, however, she kept her counsel and tried to share James's passion. Unlike Johnson, she intended to marry him.

'How,' was Boswell's plaintive response, 'can you bid me empty my head of Corsica? . . . Empty my head of Corsica! Empty it of honour, empty it of humanity, empty it of friendship, empty it of piety. No! While I live, Corsica and the cause of the brave islanders shall ever employ much of my attention, shall ever interest me in the sincerest manner.'

Corsica – not the law, not Auchinleck, not Samuel Johnson, not a host of women – had given James Boswell the semblance of an adult identity. He was already known, as he would be known for the rest of his life, as 'Corsican' Boswell. It had given him renown, if not fame, and he would honourably acknowledge that debt. When the third edition of the 'Account' was published in October 1768 (just eight months after the first) he sat down in Auchinleck and added a fresh preface. 'When I first ventured to send it into the world,' he said, 'I fairly owned an ardent desire for literary fame. I have obtained my desire; and whatever clouds may overcast my days, I can now walk here among the rocks and woods of my ancestors with an agreeable consciousness that I have done something worthy.'

'Empty it of piety . . .' Corsica had also, at last, given him a faith. The havering between religious codes which had distressed James Boswell since his childhood was finally reconciled, in the light of a single great undeniable truth. Corsica brooked no apostasy; the Corsican cause was both absolute and tangible. 'They owe them [the Genoese] nothing, and when reduced to an abject state of slavery by force, shall they not rise in the great cause of liberty, and break the galling yoke? And shall not every liberal soul be warm for them?' James Boswell clung to Corsica because it gave him easy notoriety and because he felt a genuine sympathy for the politics of Paoli; but mostly he clutched the Moor's-head flag to his bosom as a reliquary. Beneath that banner he had, while in a condition of chastity, known all the sweets of being. Belief; after unrequited years of Calvin, Rome, Wesley and transubstantiation, finally he knew belief.

In August 1768 the French landed a powerful force upon the northern coast of their new acquisition. It was their clearest declaration of intent since the Treaty of Versailles in May: the French monarchy intended to make of Corsica not merely an autonomous adjunct but a strategically critical part of their nation. Their object at Versailles had been, unsurprisingly, not simply to relieve an old trading partner, Genoa, of embarrassing obligations, but to complete the conquest of Corsica beneath the *fleur de lys*. Opinion in Britain was divided. Edmund Burke pronounced, 'Corsica naked, I do not dread; but Corsica a province of France, is terrible to me.' 'Foolish as we are,' responded the statesman Henry Fox, Lord Holland, 'we cannot be so foolish as to go to war because Mr Boswell has been in Corsica.'

Both statements paid homage to the young Scot's proselytising; but only one could hold sway. It would be, for the moment, the latter. Paoli took what heart he could from British verbal support and from Boswell's Scottish ordnance and rallied his loyalists. An impressive series of defeats was initially inflicted on the complacent French (whose commanders took mental note to enlist as many of those fierce islanders as possible once the dispute was done) throughout the winter of 1768 and 1769. 'We are face to face with our last enemy,' Paoli told his people, 'we are not accustomed to count the number of our foes.'

But the numbers, as Paoli must have known, would be everything. France, relatively unencumbered at the time on other military fronts, reinforced, bought with francs and favours and promises an increasing number of malcontents and traitors, and on 8 May 1769, at a bridge named Ponte Nuovo which spanned the River Golo at the north end of the island, Paoli's mountain irregulars and sharpshooters were first distracted into a needless advance, then chased back down to the water and sundered. They fought demoniacally with knife, stone and bare hands against bayonets to hold the riverbank until night fell, and then they limped off into the southern hills, leaving behind in the rocks and scrub of the *macchia* more dead than they had ever known, and taking with them the knowledge that their battle was, for the moment, lost. It was the cruel nature of such contests. A guerrilla force could score one minor victory after another and never win the war; whereas a disciplined and replenishable regular army required just one major victory on its own terms and the spoils belonged to France.

James Boswell was, on that day, in Ireland, visiting relatives in the cousinly company of Margaret Montgomerie. He had travelled tremorous with anticipation at the prospect of meeting Mary Ann Boyd on her native turf. By the time he made landfall, he was writing to William Temple, 'She [Margaret] perhaps may and perhaps ought to prevent my Hibernian nuptials . . . I found her by sea and land the best companion I ever saw. I am exceedingly in love with her. I highly value her. If ever a man had his full choice in a wife, I would have it in her . . . and what weighs much with me, Temple, is that amidst all this merriment and scheming, I really imagine that she truly loves me.'

She did. Margaret Montgomerie, with her two-year dis-advantage on Boswell, with her miserly thousand-pound dowry and her entirely untitled church-mouse family, did love him. Enough to discuss with him his unexceptional philandering, his glooms and his occasional drunkenness, his fear of an ordinary future, and to absolve him of them. Enough to guarantee to mother his children. Enough to make sure that Mary Ann Boyd's palpitating little bosom did not get a clear run home on moonlit nights in Donaghadee.

On 12 June 1769 Pasquale Paoli and 300 of his followers marched into the placid, shambling southern Corsican coastal township of Porto Vecchio, where he boarded a British ship of the line which had been put at his disposal by Admiral Smith of the Mediterranean fleet. James Boswell had just arrived back in Scotland, where he was met by Andrew Erskine, who asked him if he had taken Margaret to Ireland in order to compare her with Mary Ann Boyd. Eight days later, six days after Paoli and his people had been put ashore in Livorno, where Boswell had com-menced four years earlier his journey into the heart of their land, he received confirmation of the battle of Ponte Nuovo and its aftermath. 'Quite sunk,' he felt himself unable to work at law that day. 'How sorry I am,' wrote Margaret to him the instant that she received the same news, 'for the poor Corsicans. I'm afraid the accounts of their defeat is but too true. I doubt not but you will see the General, as it's said he is on his way to England.'

'You know my unhappy temper,' he wrote to Margaret on 20 July. 'You know all my faults. It is painful to repeat them. Will you, then, knowing me fully, accept of me for your husband?'

'I accept of your terms, and shall do everything in my power to make myself worthy of you,' she replied two days later.

When James Boswell had read her reply he folded it closed again and wrapped it carefully, and at some uncertain time then or in the years ahead he wrote upon the wrapper 'vraye foi', before storing it with his other papers.

Paoli was in Milan, where great crowds stood outside his

lodgings and cheered; and then in Mantua, where a theatre audience stood as one to applaud as he entered his box; and then in Vienna, where he was received at the Court of Joseph II; and then – still skirting the sullen borders of France – in Holland, where he was the guest of honour at a dinner of the federal states; and finally at Harwich, where he made landfall with his small, exotic retinue of Corsican noblemen and priests and retainers on 18 September, arriving in London to the riotous acclaim of the mob two days afterwards.

He was a fortnight too late for the Shakespeare Jubilee. This three-day festival had been organised in Stratford-upon-Avon by David Garrick. Its timing was typically strange. Shakespeare had been born in 1564. Garrick, who was enjoying an eccentric temporary retirement from performance at Drury Lane, insisted that such a celebration, held five years after the bicentenary of the playwright's birth, could properly be called a Jubilee.

And so it was. At five o'clock on the morning of Wednesday, 6 September 1769, a blast of cannonfire by the Avon alerted the citizens of Stratford to the fact that the Shakespeare Jubilee was underway. All of the previous day and throughout the night society visitors had been arriving by brougham and post-chaise and private trap, and as the sun broke over Warwickshire members of Garrick's company wandered through the Stratford streets singing:

> Let beauty with the sun arise,
> To Shakespeare tribute pay,
> With heavenly smiles and speaking eyes
> Give lustre to the day.

Children ran around handing out programmes, the band of the local militia struck up, and a gaggle of dignitaries sat down to breakfast, after which they retired to hear an oratorio in the parish church.

At this point James Boswell arrived from London at the tiresome end of a confused, broken and uncomfortable journey on the Oxford fly. He was carrying a travelling bag, a musket, and a tall vine-wood staff with a vestige of curling root forming a hook at its top. The tip of the root had been carved into a bird's head. 'That bird,' he said, 'is the bird of Avon.' He was wet and dirty, he was still wearing the mud-spattered duffel travelling cloak used by postilion passengers, and his hair hung bedraggled about his ears. People whispered and pointed at him. He finally spotted Garrick, and they edged uneasily towards each other. James silently thrust a piece of paper into the maestro's hand. On it was written words to the effect that Boswell wished to remain incognito. They must not know who he was until he appeared, uniquely clothed, at the Grand Masquerade on the following evening. Then all would become clear. Garrick nodded and left. Who was that? people asked him. 'A clergyman in disguise,' he said.

On the following morning it began to rain heavily. A street procession of Shakespeare's characters was cancelled, and so Garrick declaimed verse endlessly inside the covered rotunda. A firework display failed damply. The Avon began to overflow, the surrounding meadows turned into swamp, carriages bogged down, and duck-boards were laid before the entrances to the rotunda. Men began to drink heavily.

At eleven o'clock in the evening the Masquerade began. At midnight James Boswell entered the arena. He was wearing, reported the *London Magazine* (whose anonymous correspondent was James Boswell), 'one of the most remarkable masks upon this occasion . . . the dress of an armed Corsican chief'.

He was dressed in 'a short dark-coloured coat of coarse cloth, scarlet waistcoat and breeches, and black spatter-dashes; his cap or bonnet was of black cloth; on the front of it was embroidered in gold letters, "Viva La Liberta", and on one side of it was a handsome blue feather and cockade, so that it had an elegant as well as a war-like appearance. On the breast of his coat was sewed a Moor's head, the crest of Corsica, surrounded with branches of laurel. He had also a cartridge pouch, into which was stuck a stiletto, and on his left side a pistol was hung upon the belt of his cartridge pouch. He had a fusee [the musket] slung across his shoulder, wore no powder in his hair, but had it plaited at full length with a knot of blue ribbons at the end of it. He had, by way of staff, a very curious vine all of one piece, with a bird finely carved upon it . . .'

Where is your mask? asked the Harlequins and Dominos. A mask is not proper for a bold Corsican, he assured them. He took from his pocket a sheet of paper which contained, to the audience's dismay, 46 lines of verse. He began to recite:

> From the rude banks of Golo's rapid flood,
> Alas! too deeply ting'd with patriot blood,
> O'er which, dejected, injur'd freedom bends . . .

There are conflicting accounts of the next stage in the proceedings. According to the *London Magazine*, the verses were 'well-suited to the occasion', all the way down to the concluding, 23rd couplet:

> With generous ardour make us also free
> And give to Corsica a noble jubilee.

Other sources suggest that a boisterous gathering, suffused with Garrick's poetry readings after two consecutive days, shouted him down. Whatever his reception, James Boswell considered it a job well done. He danced until the dawn, and on 8 September, while the *beau monde* was watching horses struggle through 18 inches of mud for the Jubilee Cup, he visited Shakespeare's tomb. And then he borrowed five guineas from David Garrick and made his way back to London.

Pasquale Paoli had been given comfortable lodgings in Old Bond Street by sympathisers. Immediately after breakfast on the morning of 22 September, Boswell made his way there. A footman opened the door to say that the General was indisposed. 'Stay,' said James, 'get me a bit of paper and pen and ink.' A small, dark-complexioned valet then came down the stairs. Are you Corsican? asked James in Italian.

'Si, Signor.'

'Oh, then there is no occasion to write. My name is Boswell.'

The Corsican valet started, seized Boswell's hand, kissed it and slapped the guest heartily on the shoulder, and then ran upstairs calling out: 'Mr Boswell!'

James followed him through an opened door. Paoli was standing in a nightgown and nightcap. The General strode quickly across the room and took James Boswell in a warm embrace, and the two men stood silently in each other's arms.

For weeks afterwards the Corsican republican and his friend circulated London. They drove with the Abbé Guelfucci in a coach from the centre of town, where crowds of boys scampered by the wheels and the commoners of London followed behind to hail the General, and Paoli smiled back at them, and bowed and waved 'while they paid him what honours they could'. They drove out of London through sparse hedgerows and copses to the rural village of Putney, and they drove round and back again across Westminster Bridge to the cheerful second welcome of a citizenry which, believing itself to be the possessor of a liberty unique among ordinary people throughout the world, also took upon itself the right to anoint and acclaim its fellow lovers of freedom, regardless of their country, class or creed. The mob of Wilkes took Pasquale Paoli to its heart, and not only because he had been done down by the French. And in October James Boswell negotiated him into a meeting with Samuel Johnson. 'I compared myself,' he said of that occasion, 'to an isthmus which joins two great continents.'

Communication between the two continents was difficult. Paoli spoke in Italian and Johnson in English, with Boswell interpreting. But their courtesy overcame all. 'From what I have read of your works, Sir, and from what Mr Boswell has told me of you,' said Johnson as Paoli entered the room, 'I have long had you in great esteem and veneration.'

Paoli, perhaps by way of apology for his slight English, spoke of how languages typify different people by conveying their unique ideas and manners.

'Sir,' said Johnson, 'you talk of language as if you had never done anything else but study it, instead of governing a nation.'

Paoli listened to Boswell's translation and shook his head. 'This is too great a compliment.'

'I should have thought so, Sir,' said Johnson, 'if I had not heard you speak.'

James Boswell had a further request to make of his two friends. On 25 November 1769 he married Margaret Montgomerie at her family home in Lainshaw, Ayrshire. Both bride and groom were dressed in white. Previously, he had drawn up a marriage contract. Peggie and he, the contract insisted, 'solemnly engage to be faithful spouses, to bear with one another's faults, and to contribute as much as possible to each other's happiness in this world.' This second Inviolable Plan had been signed earlier in London by two witnesses: Pasquale di Paoli, 'General of the Corsicans', and Samuel Johnson, 'Doctor of Laws, and author of *The Rambler* and other works.'

The marriage was not marred, but saddened by two earlier events. At the end of October Alexander, Earl of Eglinton, the kindly, generous overlord of Boswell's youth, had surprised a suspected poacher on his Ardrossan estate. The man was armed with a rifle, and as Eglinton approached he backed away, tripped, discharged the weapon, and shot the earl through the body. Eglinton died that same night.

And six days before James's and Margaret's nuptials, Alexander Boswell, Lord Auchinleck, father and father-in-law, had himself remarried at the age of 62. Like James, he had chosen a cousin: the 40-year-old Betty Boswell of the Fifeshire Balmuto branch of the family.

It was not unexpected, of course: Auchinleck had signalled his intentions to an astounded James in the summer. But it was no more palatable for that. Aside from his father's immense old age, James protested, where was the respect for the memory of a wife just three years dead? What about the impossibility of two married couples living under the same mansion roof at Auchinleck? And what of his inheritance? Would a first-born boy of a second marriage, or a new wife . . . he trailed into impossible fears. They were both groundless and pointless. Auchinleck had no intention of disinheriting his son. He was merely lonely and wished for a companion, and unlike his son (or many of his colleagues) he would not have sought satisfaction outside marriage. And James, and James's brothers, John and David, who claimed a similar nervousness, had no more chance of shifting this pillar than they had of raising Auchinleck House on a finger.

There was ultimately no deep rift. As Alexander and Betty Boswell displayed with the passing years an obvious disinclination to reproduce, and as the Balmuto cousin proved herself to be no usurper of family claims, the tenor of Edinburgh and Auchinleck life resumed. They may not have attended each other's weddings, but they lived apart happily enough ever after. James Boswell was not left in need of a second, or a second and a third, father. His friendships with the two older men are travestied by such claims. Both Samuel Johnson and Pasquale Paoli would certainly, throughout the years, provide sympathy when Auchinleck was simply exasperated, be indulgent when he was strict, and be prepared to debate when Alexander Boswell was eager only to inform. But those are not by definition the differences between good and bad fathers. They are certainly the differences between friends and blood-relations. For the rest of Alexander Boswell's life, James had a strong, severe, critical and affectionate father. When he died, he was left only with friends.

In the meantime, James determined to set up house separately from his father. Edinburgh's New Town was already being built at the other side of the old North Loch, but he preferred the clamour of the old, the noise and life of his early years, and he took a property in the Canongate, and shortly afterwards a cheaper set of rooms in James's Court off the Lawnmarket. He was not earning much money from the law: sums of £80 for a winter session or even as little as £100 a year found their way into his ledgers during his first few years of practice. But he still had a £300 allowance from his father, and he applied himself with the passion of a newly-wed whose wife is already pregnant.

The child, James Boswell's first legitimate offspring, shared the fate of one-tenth of his contemporaries by dying within hours of his birth in August 1770. They pressed on, James to his offices and tavern meetings and trips to Auchinleck to discuss with his father affairs of estate and the pruning of trees, and Peggie to the preparation of an Edinburgh lawyer's household. He continued to write occasionally for the *London Chronicle*, but literary London was, within months of his embracing his new responsibilities, an estranged world.

It seemed at first that not even Pasquale Paoli's visit would draw him out again. The Corsican, rather than having sunk like a latter-day von Neuhof into miserable obscurity, carried on his capable shoulders an international reputation which dilated by the day. Large areas of restless Upper America were named after him: townships were rechristened Paoli in Pennsylvania, Colorado, Oklahoma and Indiana, and a district of Texas south of Dallas became known as Corsicana. He was in receipt of a pension from the British government of £1,200 a year (four times the amount allowed to – for example – Samuel Johnson, as much on account of Paoli's extensive exiled household as of the good light which reflected on his unstinting benefactors). In September 1771 he arrived in Edinburgh. Boswell took him to the Carron Ironworks to see the founds which had cast his gifts of artillery, and on to Auchinleck. Walter Scott, citing some of Edinburgh's rich store of Auchinleck apocrypha, would many decades later suggest that the proprietor of that seat was unimpressed by the General and afterwards dismissed him as 'the landlouping scoundrel of a Corsican'. The phrase rings true enough. So, too, does Boswell's: 'He was two nights at Auchinleck, and you may figure the joy of my worthy father and me at seeing the Corsican hero in our romantic groves.' There is no contradiction in the stories: old age sharpened Alexander Boswell's iconoclastic tongue, but it did not diminish his hospitality.

And then Paoli left again, to charm and captivate the willing south, and James returned to pleasing domesticity. It would be six more months before he visited London, after a self-imposed absence of two-and-a-half years, on legal business. He went first to Paoli and received the customary bravura greeting. He strolled along the Strand and gazed for the first time as a married man upon the women of the street, and he felt a deep unease and vowed never again to visit London without the company of

Peggie. After some days he called on Johnson. The conversation wound round to the subject of St Kilda, that most distant of the inhabited Hebrides, about which Johnson had read a book four years earlier.

I had thought of buying it, said Boswell.

'Pray do,' smiled Johnson. 'We shall go and pass a winter among the blasts there. We shall have fine fish, and we shall take some dried tongues with us, and some books.'

Oddly, Boswell had been half-serious. A solicitor friend was under instructions from the laird of St Kilda, MacLeod of MacLeod, to sell his interests in the island of Harris, which included St Kilda and several other small islands. St Kilda was, however, Boswell was duly informed, excepted from the sale. He would have to find another way of tempting Samuel Johnson north.

For a month James Boswell made his rounds of London society. He was creating a template for a married, successful writer's time down in town from the provinces: dinners with magazine and book publishers, dinners with the great and good, dinners with old friends. He bumped into John Wilkes, by then returned, free from prosecution and an alderman of the city. ('Don't sit by me,' growled Wilkes, 'or it will be in the *Public Advertiser* tomorrow.') He felt the onset of middle-age – 'time was when I have sitten up four nights in one week in London. But I found this night very hard on me' – he conducted his business, and he returned to Scotland. What a fine thing it would be, he mused, to visit London every spring.

So he did. In March 1773 Peggie delivered a baby daughter, 'a fine, healthy, lively child'. They christened the girl Veronica. It seemed like reward at last for commitment and comparative sobriety. James Boswell tripped south to London in an unprecedented condition of paternal content. Once more he went first to the embrace of General Paoli, and immediately afterwards to Johnson.

His joy would soon become complete. In 1764, during Boswell's Grand Tour, Samuel Johnson had with eight other accomplices established an exclusive club. So exclusive that at first it was known simply as The Club, its founder members included Joshua Reynolds, Edmund Burke and Oliver Goldsmith. It would carefully adopt, as the years passed, new boys such as Edward Gibbon, David Garrick (after whose death The Club redefined itself as The Literary Club), and an acute Irish lawyer and man of letters named Edmond Malone, with whom James Boswell would strike a vital accord.

But that was in the future. In 1773 Boswell was not a member of this tavern gathering, which met every one or two weeks to drink and gossip and discuss the world of publishing and compete in the stakes of malicious invention. Entry was not an easy passage: in common with many such institutions, a member proposed and his colleagues then voted in secret ballot by dropping white or black balls into a bag. White signified approval and black signified disapproval, and the presence of just one black ball when the bag was emptied meant that the application had failed.

At the end of April, Samuel Johnson told Boswell that he was putting him up for The Club. On the night of 30 April he dined with some members, and after dinner they upped and left for the Turk's Head in Soho. Boswell sat and waited for the word. In less than an hour it came: all of the balls had been white. He dashed to Soho and into the Turk's Head. There were Garrick and Goldsmith and Burke and Reynolds, and Johnson, who stood when Boswell entered the room and walked behind a chair. He leaned forward and rested his huge forearms on the chair's back, as if it was a pulpit, and waved a meaty forefinger at James Boswell, 'pointing out the duties incumbent upon me as a good member of the Club'.

You must have got me in, Boswell suggested to Johnson later that year.

'Sir,' his friend replied, 'they knew that if they refused you, they'd probably never have got in another. I'd have kept them all out.'

Other than the birth and survival of his legitimate child or the chance to show Johnson Scotland, nothing could have made James Boswell happier. It was as good as a title to him. 'Were my places,' he would reflect, 'to be ranged after my name, as "Member of the Club at the Turk's Head", etc., I should make as great a figure as most peers.'

Within weeks, Johnson had made up his mind to visit Scotland.

Chapter Eight

CLEAN GYTE

Several of us [the English] have been, by Invitation, to dine with an eminent Chief, not many Miles from hence, in the Highlands; but I do assure you it was his Importunity (the Effect of his Interest) and our own Curiosity, more than any particular Inclination, that induced us to a Compliance. We set out early in the Morning [from Inverness] without Guide or Interpreter . . . but we soon strayed out of our Way among the Hills, where there was nothing but Heath, Bogs, and Stones, and no visible Track to direct us . . .

CAPTAIN EDWARD BURT, 'LETTERS FROM A GENTLEMAN IN THE
NORTH OF SCOTLAND TO HIS FRIEND IN LONDON'

He levered his aging frame down from the chaise on to the Canongate in the evening of Saturday, 14 August 1773, and wrinkled his nose at the smell. He entered Boyd's inn and sent a note to James Boswell, and then he ordered lemonade. (The Doctor had, a few years earlier, been made unhappy by his own consumption of alcohol and was, by 1773, abstemious.) The drink arrived, but it was too sour. He asked for sugar, and the waiter picked up a lump without using tongs. Johnson noticed that the waiter's fingers were dirty and promptly threw the lemonade out of the open window.

James Boswell arrived and decided that it would be diplomatic to offer him a room in James's Court. They walked arm in arm through the warm and odorous Edinburgh evening up the great highway to the Boswells' lodgings, where, to the Doctor's delight, Margaret gave him tea, vacated her own room for his comfort, and waited upon him beautifully. Later she would suggest scornfully, echoing Lord Auchinleck's 'Ursa Major' impression of Samuel Johnson, that 'I have seen a bear led by a man, but I never before saw a man led by a bear', but for the time Peggie Boswell was courtesy itself to her husband's friend.

The 32-year-old Boswell and 63-year-old Johnson departed for the far north four days later, leaving behind a mildly disgruntled wife and a father shaking his head in amazement. 'There's nae hope for Jamie, man,' Alexander Boswell is reputed to have grumbled to a friend, 'Jamie's gane clean gyte. What do you think, man? Whase tail do ye think he has pinned himself to now, man? A dominie, man – an auld dominie, that keepit a schule and ca'd it an academy.'

They could be forgiven for it, but they were wrong. If his journey to Corsica was the formative experience of his life, Boswell's 83-day stravaig through the Highlands of Scotland with Samuel Johnson would result directly in his culminating achievements: his two great published works. He did not consciously undertake it with that in mind. Cause and effect never much troubled James Boswell. He approached the journey as the last great adventure which, after marriage and the law, he had half-assumed would be denied to him – in that analysis his father and his wife were correct: James was playing truant from the dull pressures of everyday life. They could not be expected fully to understand, although Margaret had an inkling of sympathy, that the truancy was not entirely frivolous. Their husband and son had an unusually ravenous appetite for intellectual stimulation. Had it not been satisfied at least in part, for at least a month or two every other year, then not only would he have failed to write anything of importance ever again, but most likely he would also have atrophied and suffered a mental and – in short order – a self-induced corporeal death. He was driven by motives deeper than the desire to see the Cuillin of Skye. They could not, as by then they knew, have kept him behind for a throne. They were mistaken in simply assuming that Jamie was going to the Highlands because Samuel Johnson wished to do so. In fact, the reverse was true.

They crossed the Firth of Forth with James's servant, the statuesque Bohemian Joseph Ritter, and in the company of William Nairne, an advocate friend who was travelling as far as St Andrews. Johnson had still been toying with his affected Scottophobia in Leith ('Water is the same everywhere . . . when a Scotchman sets out from this port for England, he forgets his native country.'). Nairne bit his tongue and restricted himself to suggesting that Johnson might, while north of Berwick, forget England. At Montrose another waiter used his fingers to transfer sugar from a bowl to Johnson's lemonade.

'Rascal!' called out Johnson.

The landlord here, observed Boswell smartly, is an Englishman.

As they meandered north along the clifftops of the German Sea, through Laurencekirk and Monboddo to Aberdeen – where, significantly, James steered their conversation around to his friend's younger life – Johnson's regard for his companion grew. His 'gaiety of conversation and civility of manners,' he noted, 'are sufficient to counteract the inconveniences of travel . . . [his] inquisitiveness is seconded by great activity.'

Boswell, sending notes ahead of them to confirm comfortable accommodation, was occasionally concerned that Johnson might not have the stamina for the long trek ahead. He resorted to turning the racial tables with casual mockery:

'You're a delicate Londoner – you're a macaroni! You can't ride!'

It worked. 'Sir, I shall ride better than you. I was only afraid I should not find a horse able to carry me.'

At Slains and Strichen they turned west to Inverness, through the stern granite north-eastern villages of Banff and Fochabers, Elgin and Forres, to Nairn, where, hearing Gaelic (or Erse, as the Scottish branch of the language was then popularly known in the south) spoken and smelling peat fires for the first time, Johnson correctly surmised that he was crossing the border of the Scottish

Gaidhealtachd. On reaching the evocative hamlet of Cawdor, they called, by way of homage, on the Reverend Kenneth Macaulay whose book on St Kilda had interested Johnson seven years earlier. And there commenced one of the two major sub-plots of their journey.

Samuel Johnson was convinced that Scottish people had a wonderful propensity to fraud. Twenty-three years earlier he had been persuaded into one of the most embarrassing episodes of his career by a peg-legged Edinburgh scoundrel named William Lauder who, having been rejected by the academia of his native city, fled to London in the 1740s and there produced a series of fascinating essays which asserted that Milton's *Paradise Lost* had been lifted wholesale by its author from the little-known work of seventeenth-century Latin poets.

Johnson was converted by Lauder; so converted that in 1750 he contributed a glowing preface to the Scotsman's 'Essay on Milton's Use and Imitation of the Moderns in his *Paradise Lost*'. It was proved within the year that Lauder had himself carried out an extraordinary subterfuge. To make his point, he had translated bits of *Paradise Lost* into Latin and interpolated these extracts into the works of two obscure seventeenth-century Latin poets for the purpose of then quoting them back against Milton. Johnson was mortified, and unforgiving, and thereafter deeply suspicious of Scottish literary adventurers.

Kenneth Macaulay was the first on this Highland tour to suffer beneath the sceptical eye. Within a short time, Johnson was convinced that the Reverend in Cawdor had not written the History of St Kilda which had appeared under his name. There were some slight scholarly grounds for doubting Macaulay. At the time of his alleged visit to St Kilda (June, 1758) he was minister to Harris, which island maintained regular sea communications with St Kilda and whose laird was also master of the distant island group. Macaulay was also attached to the Society for Propagating Christian Knowledge, which showed an early interest in evangelising a place where it was rumoured – accurately – that papist traditions were slow in dying out. So there was little doubt that he had visited the place – but had he, whom many claimed to be almost illiterate, or another person armed with his information, written the book? Did it matter?

Samuel Johnson thought that it mattered. One William Lauder on this earth had been quite enough. Perhaps the aging Macaulay was overly reticent, perhaps he was none too articulate in English, perhaps his table manners offended: whatever the reasons, within hours Johnson was convinced that he had another Scottish charlatan on his hands.

'Crassus homo est,' he muttered to Boswell over the unfortunate Macaulay's dinner table. He is a crass man. 'Macaulay,' he would rumble later, 'the most ignorant booby and the grossest bastard.' It was the beginning of another, vastly more important, venture into detection. If the feeble old Kenneth Macaulay could get away with such chicanery up here among the lonely hills and the lulling peat fires and the impenetrable Erse tongue, such a comfortable distance from the critical gaze of London, what momentous quackery was being practised by that agile young humbug, James 'Ossian' Macpherson? Samuel Johnson's nostrils flared hungrily.

Their chaise rolled past flat sands and below the unhewn stone walls of the abandoned castle into the Royal Borough of Inverness: an impecunious island of English-speaking traders, soldiers and administrators in a sea of Gaelic-speaking agriculturalists. The houses which lined its narrow streets of worn and slippery stone were low and harled with crumbled mud and rubble, and windows were shuttered rather than sashed against the northern wind. Small Highland ponies dragged carts the size of wheelbarrows up from the river; barefoot women and children chewing raw vegetables roamed the town; and long-haired men strode in, with bonnets and filibegs flapping at their calves, from the outlying straths which curled away through the neighbouring hills to unimaginable pasturelands. Imported casks of French wine and brandy lined the wattle walls of the shops – or 'warehouses' – of the town, but otherwise little was sold in Inverness: a place of barter and self-sufficiency where money was scarce and 'a peddling shopkeeper that sells a pennyworth of thread is a merchant'.

After the comparative familiarity of the north-eastern coast, Johnson and Boswell had entered the Highlands. From Inverness onwards their journey would be by horseback or by foot, and they would travel through lands that Johnson liked to picture as being as remote even from Lowland Scots as Borneo or Sumatra; lands where, in the words of an earlier English visitor, the simplest request of a stranger would meet only with the phrase: 'Haniel Sassun Uggit.' ('Chaneil Sassuin agam' – I speak no English.)

They travelled west with two young 'civil and ready-handed' Highlanders along the south side of Loch Ness, between the water and the birch-covered cliffside on a clear summer's day, on the military road which had been built by General George Wade after the shockwave of the failed rebellions which had been commanded six decades earlier by George Keith, the Earl Marischal. They rode up through a cleft in the rocks and past the tumbling Falls of Foyers, and they found themselves on a high and windswept plain which led down again to the south end of Loch Ness and the garrison town of Fort Augustus. There the governor fed and bedded the five men, and they set off at noon on the following day, westward into Glenmoriston, along 'eleven wild miles' until they came across an innkeeper who kept on his shelves copies of the *Spectator* and a tattered treatise against drunkenness. They gave a military work party several shillings, and the men tipped their bonnets and bought whisky and fought, and on the following morning they saw blood on the ground where the soldiers had slept. They wandered on and up into Glen Shiel and examined the site of the Earl Marischal's final battle, where cold, lost and frightened Spanish soldiers had fled from loyalist Highlanders and English redcoats into the terrible winter snow. They rode downhill and stopped upon a riverbank in a green valley close by a hamlet of thatched stone houses built into each other like a honeycomb, and Samuel Johnson leaned back in the sun and the silence and the solitude and decided that, when he returned to London, he would write *A Journey to the Western Islands of Scotland*. This publication would, he made it clear, preclude any possibility of James following his 'Account of Corsica' with an 'Account of the Highlands': the market would not carry two such books. The decision would have been a more serious blow to Boswell – who was taking all the notes and who had certainly intended to publish – had he not been hatching plans of his own.

They took a winding track up the precipitous side of a mountain named Mam Ratagan, and as they reached the top and began a perilous descent Johnson grew nervous, so one of the Highlanders took his horse's bridle and led him along while attempting to divert the old philosopher with the sights.

'See,' said John Hay, 'the pretty goats!' and whistled to make them jump, while Johnson started and trembled in the saddle and Boswell, in the highest of spirits, laughed hilariously at the scene. Along the flat lands at the foot of the mountain – where a broad and open plain ran down to the village of Glenelg and the sea-strait which lay between the mainland and the island of Skye, whose black mountains were silhouetted against the fading light – Boswell spurred on his horse with a whoop and a halloo and made to gallop out of sight towards the inn. Johnson's nerves snapped. He called Boswell back 'with a tremendous shout' and chastised him for his thoughtlessness. They passed the towering barracks outside Glenelg, where a sergeant and a few footsoldiers loitered in the dusk, and arrived at the inn 'weary and peevish'.

About my riding forward . . . offered Boswell. 'Had you gone on,' rejoined Johnson, 'I was thinking that I should have returned with you to Edinburgh and then parted, and never spoke to you more.' It was the first and the last moment of real dissent between the two men. On the next morning Johnson retracted his comments. If he had insisted on returning, he said, he would have been 'ten times worse' than Boswell. 'Let's think no more on it.'

A sailing boat took them from the Glenelg narrows down the Sound of Sleat to the harbour at Armadale in Skye, where Sir Alexander Macdonald – dressed, thanks to his Hanoverian sympathies, in the tartan which had been denied his tenants since the 1745 uprising – met them on the shore and proceeded to offer them the strangest and most inhospitable of weekends. There was an insufficiency of bedroom space. There were no carpets on the lord's floors. There was no claret and – with Johnson limiting himself to lemonade – no toasts other than those which James offered silently to himself with some highly unsuitable port. When two gentlemen visitors entered the room Sir Alexander left them to lean against the wall while he threw himself fork-first into a liver pudding, and Boswell finally took it upon himself to make room for them at the table.

They spent an unsettled weekend. Both men grew increasingly annoyed with Sir Alexander Macdonald and with his refusal to entertain the notion that life in this place could be better for everybody, tenant and earl alike. James attempted to relieve the boredom by relating in the drawing-room his memories of the scion of the family, the Marcellus of the North, Sir James Macdonald, whom he had known in London in 1763 and who had died a romantic young man's death of fever in Italy four years later, but that only made the ladies weep. They strolled on Sunday up to the parish church at Kilmore and examined the monumental memorial inscription to Sir James inside that simple, one-roomed building, littered about with the crooked gravestones and slabs of broadsword-bearing Macdonalds long gone from the earthly kingdom which once they had ruled from Lewis to Tiree. Then they returned once more to the dull and mean-spirited house of their ignoble descendant, where James drank punch to be social and then port to get drunk, and after four days they left for more genial company.

The road north took them beside a well-populated coastal strip studded with houses of stone and turf, over rough moorland and down into Broadford, where at the foot of a conical mountain named Beinn na Cailleach they entered the home of Lachlan Mackinnon of Coirechatachan. 'Old Coirechatachan,' reflected Boswell happily, 'had hospitality in his whole behaviour.' Beef collops followed, and fricassee of fowl, fried chicken, ham, haddocks, herrings, bread pudding with raisins and lemon peel, port-wine syllabubs and a large bowl of punch.

En route between Coirechatachan and the smaller island of Raasay, they were joined by a Skye minister named Donald Macqueen, and Samuel Johnson permitted himself an early sortie against the perfidy of James Macpherson. The case of the Badenoch man was becoming urgent. He had followed the success of the Ossian legends with a *History of Great Britain and Ireland* which purported to trace all of the nation's civilised assets back to the ancient Celts, and earlier that year he had taken what many – Samuel Johnson included – considered to be an impertinent step too far by publishing a new translation of Homer's *Iliad* in the Ossianic style. The cornerstone of Macpherson's reputation was the authenticity of 'Ossian'. If that could be dislodged, down he would fall. Samuel Johnson, to Boswell's initial discomfiture, was determined to dislodge it.

Reverend Donald Macqueen having established himself as an educated man and one well versed in such Highland phenomena as second sight, Johnson asked him about Fingal. Macqueen insisted that he knew some passages in the original Gaelic, but he did not believe that Ossian had composed the verses as published by Macpherson. Johnson, who was firmly of the prejudice that Scottish Gaelic was an unliterary tongue which had never aspired to print, nodded knowingly, and James Boswell, compromised by patriotism and by a lingering affection for his old acquaintance, as well as by a nagging doubt that the answer to the controversy might not so easily be found, looked quietly on.

They crossed to Raasay on a boat rowed by men whose ancient shanties held, if Johnson could only have known it, the clue to the Ossian mystery; men who sang the songs of their forefathers, songs from land and sea which James Macpherson had cobbled together and bastardised in florid, loose translation – the divers fruits of a rich and venerable culture which he had blasphemously offered to the world as if they were the single work of one man's imagination. In that respect the Badenoch schoolteacher was a fraud, and worse than a fraud: he betrayed his heritage for gain. Samuel Johnson was not altogether wrong about James Macpherson but, as Boswell knew full well, he would never be entirely right about the literary claims of the Gaelic language. James Boswell, who possessed an open mind, a barrister's training and a genuine, enlightened intellectual curiosity, would come closer than the lexicographer and philosopher to an understanding of the Ossianic enigma.

Raasay was a merry place. They were well catered for by the laird in his palatial mansion-house which stood among trees and looked over greensward towards the white-tipped sea. They climbed the central volcanic peak, on top of which Donald Macqueen and Malcolm MacLeod of Raasay, a sprightly 62-year-old who had assisted Charles Edward Stuart 27 years before, sang a Gaelic song, and Samuel Johnson and James Boswell skipped and hopped and attempted a reel. James left Johnson behind and strode off to the medieval fortress at the north-east of the island, where he was pleased and proud to observe a small room in a vestigial tower, 'a little confined triangular place' with a round hole in one of its flags which opened directly on to the tidal rocks below. 'I did not imagine,' he mused, 'that the invention had been introduced into Scotland till in very modern days, from our connexion with England.' Upon his return to Raasay House, he told Johnson of this discovery. 'You take very good care of one end of a man, but not of the other,' laughed his companion, who had actually eaten extremely well since their departure from Armadale.

Life in Borneo or Sumatra, he could have reflected, would hardly have been so amenable. They progressed through Portree on Skye to Kingsburgh, a rambling country-house at the north-west of the island, whose proprietor, Allan Macdonald, a hugely impressive figure dressed in tartan vest and filibeg and hose adorned with gold buttons, with his jet-black hair tied behind and falling in ringlets about his temples from beneath a large blue bonnet, welcomed them in. He took them to his parlour and handed them drams of Holland gin before a blazing fire, and at suppertime his wife entered the room.

'She was a little woman, of a mild and genteel appearance, mighty soft and well-bred,' according to Boswell. 'She is a woman of middle stature, soft features, gentle manners and elegant presence,' according to Johnson. Despite her married status, she was introduced as Miss Flora Macdonald. Over roast turkey, porter, claret and punch, the starstruck travellers urged the heroine into tales of the escape of Charles Edward Stuart, before retiring to an upstairs chamber where, they were informed, Samuel Johnson would be sleeping in the bed once occupied by the fleeing prince.

James watched his bulky friend at rest on this pallet, looked at the wall and was startled to see a Hogarth print of John Wilkes grinning back at him, and found it difficult to put his thoughts into words. He informed Johnson of his confusion.

'I have had no ambitious thoughts on it,' smiled Samuel.

Later the next morning, shortly before they left, James came upon a slip of paper on the table in their bedroom. It contained four words pencilled in Johnson's handwriting: 'Quantum cedat virtutibus aurum.'

With virtue weighed, what worthless trash is gold. Johnson, the Hanoverian by necessity and Jacobite by sentiment, the pragmatic Tory who hated what Charles had done to his cause as much as he grieved over what history had done to Charles, found in the accomplished, unpretentious character of Flora Macdonald the stuff of true legend, and with the willing assistance of James Boswell he proceeded to broadcast that legend until it achieved global proportions and the name of the mild little woman from South Uist became a byword – 'a name that will be mentioned in history,' he guaranteed, 'and if courage and fidelity be virtues, mentioned with honour.' Before 1773 Flora Macdonald had been little known beyond the Highlands and Islands of Scotland and the handful of London salons which had entertained her in house-arrest following Charles's successful escape. Following 1773 she was – unwillingly – all but canonised.

Samuel Johnson passed his 64th birthday in the gaunt, grey rock of Dunvegan Castle, and as September drew onwards and the weather worsened they moved southwards down the western coast of Skye, still accompanied by the good Reverend Macqueen, to the farm at Ullinish; and Johnson tried once more to goad from the minister the truth about Ossian.

Macqueen had come round to admitting that Macpherson's work 'fell far short of what he knew in Erse'. 'I hope they do,' pounced Johnson. 'I am not disputing that you may have poetry of great merit, but that Macpherson's is not a translation from ancient poetry.' And then, with the interested Boswell standing by, bright-eyed and making mental note, he struck. 'You do not believe it,' he told Macqueen. 'I say before you, you do not believe it, though you are very willing that the world should believe it.' Macqueen sat silently. 'I look upon Macpherson's "Fingal",' Johnson pressed on, 'to be as gross an imposition as ever the world was troubled with. Had it been really an ancient work, a true specimen of how men thought at that time, it would have been a curiosity of the first rate. As a modern production, it is nothing.'

Ossian's verse has some beauty in it, Macqueen put in lamely –

'Ay, radaratoo, radaratee,' sang Johnson.

'Macpherson's translations are far inferior to Ossian's originals,' the minister later suggested to Boswell.

By then, James understood. 'Yes,' he gently replied, 'because they are not the same. They are inferior as a shilling is to a guinea, because they are not the same.'

Donald Macqueen shuffled unhappily away.

In Johnson's absence on the following morning, Boswell broke the puzzle. In the company of another Gaelic speaker, he persuaded Macqueen to read out some indigenous Gaelic verse on the subject of Cuchullain and asked the independent witness to compare it with Macpherson's English renderings on a similar subject. Macpherson's English was, said the witness, nothing like it.

But it had been similar. James told Johnson of the experiment, and reminded his friend that he himself had asked only that Macpherson's 'Ossian' should be as faithful to an original as was Pope's footloose translation of Homer.

Johnson's hunch had, in fact, been vindicated. 'He has found names and stories,' said Samuel, 'and phrases – nay passages in old songs – and with them has compounded his own compositions, and so made what he gives to the world as the translation of an ancient poem.' That was correct.

'It was wrong of him,' added Boswell, 'to pretend that there was a poem in six books.'

'Yes, Sir. At a time, too, when the Highlanders knew nothing of books and nothing of six – or perhaps were got the length of counting six . . .'

That was incorrect. Johnson, the controversialist, had once more taken his conclusion too far. Boswell's more temperate explanation, born of his training and of a naturally fair and adept legal mind, was perfectly sufficient and perfectly accurate. With forensic care he had pursued Johnson's suspicions and had unravelled James Macpherson's epochal deceit. He took no satisfaction from the deduction, and while in the years to come Johnson proceeded to chase Macpherson with remorselessly overstated accusations (and, at times, with a large stick), Boswell – whose word as a Scottish contemporary would have helped to sink Macpherson's obstinate reputation in his own land – kept an uneasy silence. There were, after all, uncomfortable similarities between himself and the Badenoch bard, similarities which had little to do with their nationality. They had both once been young and optimistic and in search of celebrity in a difficult world.

They met with Donald Maclean, the young laird of the island of Coll, and together they journeyed futher south. They returned to the blessed household of Coirechatachan outside Broadford, where the Mackinnons insisted on Boswell and Maclean staying up until five o'clock in the morning drinking four bowls of punch.

James woke up at noon with a severe headache and cursed himself for being in that condition when his first duty should be to Samuel Johnson's comfort in Scotland. At one o'clock Johnson rolled jovially into his bedroom.

'What, drunk yet?'

'Sir, they kept me up.'

'No, you kept them up, you drunken dog,' laughed Johnson.

Lachlan Mackinnon, carrying a bottle and a glass, and Donald Maclean entered the room, assembled around the bed, and insisted that Boswell take a dram of brandy.

'Ay,' said Johnson, 'fill him drunk again. Do it in the morning, that we may laugh at him all day. It is a poor thing for a fellow to get drunk at night, and skulk to bed, and let his friends have no sport.'

Boswell took the dram of brandy, discovered that it cured his headache, got out of bed and pursued a normal day's activity. He was not, in other words, at that time an alcoholic. Having dressed, he wandered through to Johnson's room and picked up a prayer book. It fell open to reveal the lines: 'And be not drunk with wine, wherein there is excess.'

'Some would have taken this,' he noted, 'as a divine interposition.'

A few days later, across the low and barren hills from Coirechatachan and back in the green meadows of the Sleat peninsula, Samuel Johnson mentioned an epigram which had been recorded in Job Orton's *Memoirs* of the nonconformist divine Philip Doddridge. It was new to James and he noted it. That was no small thing: he did so with a wistful fascination. The lines might have served him as a catechism:

> Live, while you live, the epicure would say,
> And seize the pleasures of the present day.
> Live, while you live, the sacred preacher cries,
> And give to God each moment as it flies.
> Lord, in my views let both united be;
> I live in pleasure, when I live to thee.

For the most part, James Boswell enjoyed the freedom from guilt over indulgence which was usual in his time and his class; but his Presbyterian upbringing caused sporadic crises of lacerating penitence, and his native intelligence always posted signs of warning in his mind. Alcoholism and venereal disease were epidemic killers in the eighteenth century. But heavy drinking and sexual adventure were both normal and expected in most sections of society. Men and women of education were mostly left to discover their own balance between enjoyment and risk, as Johnson had himself determined to reduce his drinking when he found it to be damaging his powers of reason.

By the time they reached Armadale again, James had taken a morning dram each day for a week. It was a custom well catered for in the Highlands of Scotland and one which could comfortably be pursued without social disgrace anywhere else in Great Britain. In lines which he never published, he warned himself with perfect clarity of the dangers of such a routine. 'It really pleased me to take it,' he told his journal of the morning 'skalk'. 'They are a sober people, the Highlanders, though they have this practice. I always loved strong liquors. I was glad to be in a country where fashion justified tasting them. But I resolved to guard against continuing it after leaving the isles. It [the skalk] would become an article of happiness to me. I thought with satisfaction when I got up that it waited me, as one thinks of his breakfast; so much is a man formed by habit.' He was drinking too much, and he knew it; he enjoyed too much being drunk, and he knew that also. The knowledge would preserve him.

Pausing only to note Samuel Johnson's comment on Sir Alexander Macdonald leaving for the mainland 'with the blessing of his people' – 'You'll observe this was when he left [Skye]. It is only the back of him that they bless.' – and the existence of a dance called 'America', an intoxicating reel which began with just one couple and ended with the entire floor wheeling and spinning together, and which served as a physical metaphor for the contagious emigration fever, they took a boat in a difficult wind for Coll. Johnson retired philosophically below while Boswell sat above the waves with the seamen and ate bread and cheese and mutton and salt herring, and drank whisky, rum, brandy, beer and punch. At first he was exhilarated to discover that he had conquered sea-sickness, before becoming extremely ill. It was nothing if not an empirical life.

They made landfall in Coll after a terrifying storm, and while resting there they were told of the festive recreations of the islanders, in particular of a game which was played over ten days at Christmas time when all of the men on the island were divided into two groups, each headed by a local dignitary, and 'there is a ball thrown down in the middle of a space above the house, or on a strand near it; and each party strives to beat it first to one end of the ground with crooked sticks. The club is called the shinny. It is used in the low-country of Scotland. The name is from the danger that the shins run. We corrupt it to shinty.' No visiting traveller before him had noted, and very few after him would pay attention to, this unique commonplace of life in the Scottish Gaidhealtachd. Drunk or sober, melancholy or alert, little evaded James Boswell.

After two weeks of the morning skalk, one morning in Coll Johnson cast his eye upon the glass at Boswell's side and said, 'For shame!' It is, he added, becoming serious. Boswell agreed, and the ritual ended.

From Coll they moved to Tobermory in Mull, and there James Boswell, after weeks of thought, finally took the decision to write the book which would keep both his and Samuel Johnson's name alive for centuries to come. As in Aberdeen, he took advantage of a time alone to press Johnson on details of his early life. While the willing Johnson spoke, Boswell took diligent notes beneath his nose. 'I have them,' he told his journal, 'on separate leaves of paper. I shall lay up authentic materials for THE LIFE OF SAMUEL JOHNSON LL.D. and, if I survive him, I shall be one who shall most faithfully do honour to his memory. I have now a vast treasure of his conversation at different times since the year 1762 [it had in fact been 1763] when I first obtained his acquaintance; and by assiduous inquiry I can make up for not knowing him sooner.' From that autumnal hour in the Inner Hebrides, for the remainder of James Boswell's life he was able even in the blackest and the dullest times to elevate his eyes beyond hangovers and the tormented aftermaths of venery, beyond dreary advocacy, beyond Edinburgh and Auchinleck, and beyond mourning. By the standards of a later age, he died in middle-age; without that decision in October 1773 he might have died a younger man, and history would have known him, in its smallest footnotes, simply as Corsican Boswell: a will-o'-the-wisp which promised much, but dimmed and failed in the northern night.

The decision taken, they migrated south through the wind and rain to the rose-pink rocks of Iona and on to Lochbuie in Mull where Johnson, with the abstainer's irritation at a carousing friend, told James not to get drunk on 'poonch'. James duly did so and vomited violently (which he supposed had the same result as not having drunk the stuff in the first place), and on the following day Johnson solemnly assured him that none of the Club got drunk.

None of them?

Well . . . the assertion was unsustainable, Johnson admitted. Burke gets drunk, and is ashamed of it. Goldsmith gets drunk, and he boasts about it, particularly if whores are involved . . .

It came as some relief.

By 29 October, James's 33rd birthday, they had arrived in Glasgow by way of Loch Lomondside, and four days later they celebrated their return to civilisation by exchanging their pack-horses for a post-chaise and driving over the Cunninghame hills and down into Auchinleck.

Less than two years separated the birthdays of Alexander Boswell and Samuel Johnson. Both enjoyed and were accustomed to domination and control of their company. Each prided himself on a pointed turn of phrase. One was a Presbyterian and a Whig; the other was High Church of England and Tory. Auchinleck had never bothered to read a word of Johnson's work; and if it had not been for his son, Johnson might never even have heard of the Scottish law lord.

James was aware of the potential for riot. He asked Johnson to avoid the subjects of politics and religion, and Johnson agreed. But he may as well have asked his visitor not to draw breath. Johnson's very life revolved around the unregulated discussion of politics and religion, and so James was obliged to spend six uneasy days trying to keep friend and father apart. When the weather cleared, this could be accomplished by walking Johnson around the grounds and pointing out ancient trees and interesting cattle; when, as was more often the case, the westerlies trapped them within the tall walls of Auchinleck House, the tension mounted. Temporary relief was gained when John Dun, James's former tutor and the minister to Auchinleck, invited the two of them to dinner. It was only temporary. Before long, Dun was maundering about the 'fat bishops and drowsy deans' who populated the Church of England, and Johnson was snapping, 'Sir, you know no more of our church than a Hottentot.'

After four days the keg blew. Oliver Cromwell's head jumped

forth from Lord Auchinleck's collection of coins, and 'they became exceedingly warm and violent'. Politics having appeared, religion quickly followed. Show me, asked Johnson, any theological work of merit written by Scottish Presbyterian ministers. Auchinleck's legal training came to his aid. Alexander Boswell was quite unfamiliar with contemporary literature, even with contemporary religious literature. But he did recall having seen in a recent bookseller's catalogue a title called 'Durham on the Galatians'. It was worth a try . . .

'Pray, sir,' he hazarded, 'have you read Mr Durham's excellent commentary on the Galatians?'

'No,' admitted a baffled Johnson.

Lord Auchinleck nodded serenely, his point made.

Two days afterwards Auchinleck escorted Johnson and James to their Edinburgh-bound chaise. Both gladiators were restrained, civil and courteous. All three men were relieved. And on 22 November Samuel Johnson returned to his London writing-desk. He left behind him a middle-aged young man with much on his mind.

Chapter Nine

BIRTH, ALCOHOL AND DEATH

Any portion of Time appears shorter to us the longer we live. We all recollect how in childhood a period of one or two years seemed of large extent, whereas when we have attained to middle-age it bears no bulk in the imagination. The reason is, as I once heard observed by a man of strong sagacity, that the older we are, we have the longer measure to apply to any period of time. We measure it with our own life, and the more that is lengthened the shorter does the period which is measured appear.

JAMES BOSWELL, 'ON TIME'

His life was, by the measure of the eighteenth century, sliding towards its close. Harsh reminders of that fact would soon occur by the year, as friends and family were borne into the grave. The two men whom he did and did not wish to die, the two men closest to him and the two whose death would liberate him – his father through inheritance, and Samuel Johnson, whose last breath would open the door both to the publication of his Hebridean journal and to the preparation of a biography – clung obstinately to great old age. They might, he knew, outlive him. He was bored with the law and too often bored with everything

193

else. He drank fretfully and seriously and – for the first time – to forget discontent rather than to heighten life, and he put the patient Peggie into an annual pregnancy.

The children arrived like clockwork weathermen. After Veronica, Euphemia was born in May 1774 and Alexander in October 1775. David was born in November 1776 and died of a teething fever in March 1777. James was born in September 1778 and Elizabeth in June 1780.

He fathered children and at first did enough of his duty by the law to keep ends together, managing to earn as much – £300 – through advocacy as his father allowed him in a year, and he drank. And after drinking, he shamefacedly rediscovered prostitutes, and as 1774 drew to a close his ambitions seemed to be fogged and dim, and London a long way away, and the grand schemes of his hectic youth which had come close to fruition in the wind and sleet of the Western Isles were slipping from him like a lifebelt from a drowning man. And, of course, the black dog returned, howling through the long, winter midnight hours, and he dreamed, half-awake, half-willing the melancholy on himself, that he was confined from October to April in an old house in the far north of Scotland where tedium weighed him down and nervousness gnawed at his soul, and from where there was no escape until the warmer sun of springtime shone through the dreary sky.

He shook himself free of the waking nightmare and sought the easy company of John Johnston of Grange. He dined out with the Edinburgh quality and took whisky in to imprisoned clients who stood accused of sheep-stealing – he was always a defence lawyer, whose brief was too often to save moneyless men from those nightmarish gallows which had kept him awake for half a week as a young man in London – and his life was dissolving into a strained and shapeless folly when, in January 1775, it received a short respite. There arrived in the post a copy of the manuscript of Samuel Johnson's *A Journey to the Western Isles of Scotland*.

James knew of the book: he had been asked for and had given help to Johnson, who had taken few notes and who depended more on philosophical reflection and generalised comment than on observation. He finished it in one sitting, reading Johnson's words fondly before his flickering drawing-room fire: 'I had desired to visit the Hebrides, or Western Isles of Scotland, so long, that I scarcely remember how the wish was originally excited; and was in the autumn of the year 1773 induced to undertake the journey, by finding in Mr Boswell a companion, whose acuteness would help my inquiry . . .'

When he put the book down at three o'clock on that January morning, he felt tired and confused, but too warmly inclined for resentment. He told himself that 'Mr Johnson had spoken so handsomely of me, and that the public would soon read what he had said.' He wrote immediately to Johnson: '. . . you kept me up the greater part of the last night; for I did not stop till I had read every word of your book. I looked back to our first talking of a visit to the Hebrides, which was many years ago, when sitting by ourselves in the Mitre tavern in London . . .' He then offered a couple of basic corrections. Nostalgia and reflected glory were no substitute for true celebrity, but they were all that was available.

A Journey to the Western Isles was not well received by the critics, particularly in the north of Britain, but in March 1775 James decided to return to London for the first time in two years, half-hoping to discover an ounce of second-hand fame. He went first of all, on this occasion, to Samuel Johnson, where he quickly realised that if any middle-aged Scot was the talk of London following Johnson's book, it was not James Boswell.

Johnson had used the *Journey* – and Boswell's inquiries, duly credited – to press home a ferocious assault on James Macpherson. 'I believe they [the poems of Ossian] never existed,' he had written. '. . . The editor, or author, never could shew the original; nor could it be shewn by any other; to revenge reasonable incredulity, by refusing evidence, is a degree of insolence, with which the world is not yet acquainted . . .'

Macpherson had been shown a copy of the manuscript of the *Journey* before publication and had promptly attempted to get this sentence and others deleted. The issue was nicely complicated by the fact that the two men shared the same publisher, the expatriate Scot William Strahan, of whom Macpherson requested that 'you will use your endeavours with that impertinent fellow to induce him to soften the expressions concerning me, though it should occasion the loss of a few days in the publication'.

Johnson would do no such thing, and Macpherson next attempted to have an erratum slip inserted in the book, advising readers that no offence was intended by Johnson and 'should this work come to a second impression, he will take great care to expunge such words as seem, though undesignedly, to convey an affront'. Macpherson was bouncing pebbles off a battlement. Johnson wrote gleefully to Boswell that 'Macpherson is very furious; can you give me any more intelligence about him, or his "Fingal"?'

Macpherson, his reputation teetering on the brink of destruction, was furious indeed. He wrote to Johnson that 'his age and infirmities alone protected him from the treatment due to an infamous liar and traducer'. Copies of the Ossianic originals had, he said, lain for weeks with his former publisher, Becket and De Hondt of the Strand, 13 years earlier. Thomas Becket agreed in writing that he had been in possession of some 'originals of "Fingal" ', but had since returned them to Macpherson. They were no longer, it seemed, at large. How Becket, illiterate in Scottish Gaelic, knew the difference between originals of 'Fingal' and any other written samples of the language, he did not explain.

Samuel Johnson's response was to buy a wooden cudgel six feet in length, topped by a knob three inches in diameter, and carry it ostentatiously about London. He then wrote to Macpherson: 'Whatever insult is offered me, I will do my best to repel, and what I cannot do for myself, the law will do for me. I will not desist from detecting what I think a cheat, from any fear of the menaces of a Ruffian. What would you have me retract? I thought your book an imposture; I think it an imposture still.'

James Boswell was not impressed by Johnson's tactics. He knew better than his friend what James Macpherson had done, which had been to take loose fragments of Gaelic song and poetry, render them even more loosely into English, invent and add large linking sections of flowery blank verse, and offer them as a whole under the name of some mythical ancient scribe. That much was indeed an imposture. But it did not proscribe the possibility that James Macpherson had in his possession some sheets of written Gaelic verse. And, what was more, he was sure that Johnson was wrong in some crucial elements of his argument. 'I believe there cannot be recovered, in the whole Earse language,' Johnson had written, 'five hundred lines of which there is any evidence to prove them a hundred years old . . . It is the rude speech of a barbarous people, who had few thoughts to express.'

Boswell had been brought up within earshot of Gaelic. It was the first tongue of the inhabitants of the island which rose from the sea to the west of Auchinleck; it was in his time still much spoken in Ayrshire; and whole Edinburgh masonries – the town guard, the sedan-carriers, and much of the ministry – were dominated by Highland men. He even knew the words of one or two Gaelic songs. He knew and respected the 'Earse' mocked by Johnson as a venerable tongue of which much was still to be learned by the sophisticates of the south. These convictions did not spring from spurious patriotism, but from a cool and logical mind – and a capacity for dispassionate observation. Where had the Doctor been while Boswell was in the Highlands and Islands of Scotland hearing men and women of every class and occupation talking in Gaelic, singing in Gaelic, conducting all of their affairs in Gaelic, using Gaelic as a Frenchman used French, or a Netherlander Dutch – or an Englishman English? Johnson was playing fast and loose with too much of the evidence. Far from leaping blindly into action on Johnson's behalf, as the philosopher expected him to do, James wrote to rebuke his friend: 'It is confidently told here [in Edinburgh] that before your book came out he sent to you, to let you know that he understood you meant to deny the authenticity of Ossian's poems; that the originals were in his possession; that you might have inspection of them, and might take the evidence of people skilled in the Erse language; and that he hoped, after this fair offer, you would not be so uncandid as to assert that he had refused reasonable proof. That you paid no regard to his message, but published your strong attack upon him.'

What was confidently told in Edinburgh was not the truth. 'I am surprised that,' replied an exasperated Johnson, 'knowing as you do the disposition of your countrymen to tell lies in favour of each other, you can be at all affected by any reports that circulate among them. Macpherson never in his life offered me the sight of any original or of any evidence of any kind . . . Where are the manuscripts?'

This was the chatter which greeted James Boswell when he arrived in London in March 1775. He was able to tell Johnson that at least one distinguished Scot, David Hume, had finally come out against 'Ossian', declaring that he would not believe its authenticity 'though fifty bare-arsed Highlanders should swear to it'.

'No,' said Johnson, 'nor though fifty Lowlanders should; for you know that all Scotsmen to a man –' here he paused, and excepted present company '– nay, not all, but droves of 'em – would come and attest anything which they think for the honour of Scotland.'

This, thought James Boswell, was nothing less than outrageous.

He dined with Paoli and breakfasted with Garrick; he attended his first meeting of The Club since his adoption; he told tales whenever possible of Johnson in the Hebrides; and he noted at length the philosopher's pithiest comments. He read to the painter Sir Joshua Reynolds extracts from his own journal in the Hebrides, and the kindly artist commented that they were more entertaining than Johnson's book, which can have helped his mood only briefly. He got roaring drunk and lurched late at night into another meeting of The Club, where he found himself sitting next to the politician Charles Fox and so insulted the parliamentarian (you will be prime minister, he slurred, and get applauded, but that will not be so good as being heard and applauded here, because . . . because, there they may just be applauding the prime minister, but here . . . here, they will be applauding Fox . . . d'ye see?) that Fox got up and walked to another seat and Bennet Langton deliberately passed the bottle around the drunken member.

It was the beginning of the period of James Boswell's life which would haunt his reputation through posterity. Those who knew him liked him still and were patient with his unhappiness, even when it achieved outrageous proportions, even when it offended ladies at the table. They also saw the sober days. Your drunkenness, said Pasquale Paoli, discovering James nursing a hangover one London morning, is a vice which hurts the character and gives envious people an advantage over a man of parts. But Paoli had a Corsican's sense of honour and bounden duty in friendship, a loyalty which might have been sealed in blood. He would never relinquish Boswell and never fail to offer him accommodation, food and comfort. His reprovals were gently offered. The General prevailed upon his ally to go for a month drinking only water, after which time James began to weaken and the pragmatic Paoli allowed him three glasses of wine at a sitting. He met with William Temple, who was working as a West Country vicar, in Devonshire, and his oldest friend was so alarmed that he pledged James to sobriety, by which term they both apparently meant no more than six glasses of wine at a sitting. But even Samuel Johnson wearied at times, writing once to Margaret Boswell that her husband would soon be home and the better for it. Sensible, respectable acquaintances such as Johnson's friend Fanny Burney began to see him, and portray him in their diaries, as the caricature of an acolyte, as a drunken, fawning, played-out fool whose only purpose left in a sad life was to punctuate whoring and drinking with prowling after Samuel Johnson, pen and tablet clutched in shaking hand. Burney would have, and would take, the opportunity to put her record straight; many others failed to do so.

Even in the worst of times, it was quite unfair. The present is never happy, said Johnson to him one spring day, 'every part of life is at some time future'.

'Is a man never happy for the present?' asked Boswell.

'Never but when he's drunk.'

The truth was that London, James Boswell's Eternal City, was leaving him very quickly behind. The metropolis waited for no one: it absorbed fresh talent and rejected the old with alarming speed. It was no more to be blamed for its ghoulish appetite than was James Boswell for being chewed up and spewed away – London must feed itself, and in its hunger there was no room for sentiment. Boswell had been for a while a successful minor implant in a towering organism; by the 1770s his usefulness was apparently over. He was patently unproductive, and what once had been rash but corrigible talent now seemed no better than an idle boast. It hurt, and there was no apparent solution. New firmaments crept over the horizon: Edward Gibbon and Adam Smith (who had just published volume one of *The Decline and Fall of the Roman Empire* and *The Wealth of Nations* respectively) were elected to The Club, and James Boswell complained petulantly that they lowered its tone. It hurt, and so while he was in London he abused his old relationship with the city. London, which once had been the gay receptacle of hope and opportunity, became a sinister outlet for his worst behaviour. He half-consciously avenged himself upon its cool façades with daily conduct which he would have contemplated only on the darkest Edinburgh night, and not just because he was 400 miles from Margaret's bed. In short: he whored without passion in London; he drank without restraint in London; and he pissed and vomited on its genteel avenues.

But he never quite gave up on the place – how could he, who was in love with London? – and it in turn, for auld lang syne, kept always a small part of its heart open to him. It seemed, in those dreary 1770s, that he might never again be at the centre of the city's affections, but he might still be fun for a night. It led him on like a flirt, and he followed like a dotard. He sobered himself sufficiently upon each visit to dress cleanly and smartly and to go out wooing the town. He did just enough to ensure that when next he arrived, freshly in Fleet Street and eager to please, doors would still be opened to him; and then he returned to Scotland bleary eyed, melancholic and diseased.

Peggie patiently bore him children and cared for his household, and he felt himself rebuked by her dutiful goodness and found himself reminded of his love for her. He settled to a score of resolutions. He would drink moderately or not at all for weeks on end, and then enjoy a raging night chasing prostitutes up and down the Royal Mile, and then it was an idiot's wager whether he would restrain himself in time or give in to penetrative sex, with its necessary, inevitable consequence of an immediate full confession to Margaret so that she would understand why he stayed clear of her bed until the incubation period was done. Such frankness was commonplace: wives preferred painful honesty to gonorrhoea. He took to gambling and losing a week's earnings in a sitting. Margaret grew so anxious that she could not sleep until he returned home, and he upbraided himself again. 'Reason tells me that I cannot expect to be better restrained now than by former vows,' he agonised, 'and yet, like a man who has had several blanks in the lottery and fancies that another ticket will certainly be a prize, I flatter myself . . .'

He was still concerned about his inheritance of Auchinleck. His father's moods grew stranger. He would carp at James's expensive jaunts to London and still mutter asides about his journey through the Highlands with 'that brute'. At times her stepfather was even rude to Peggie; although his feelings softened when her first son – 'a big-boned fellow' – arrived in 1775 and was christened Alexander. Finally, Lord Auchinleck settled the estate upon his eldest son, and upon all future eldest sons who carried the name of Boswell, and both James and Peggie could breathe sighs of relief.

But between a written settlement and inheritance, what was there? And after inheritance, what milestones lay between him and his own grave? The numbing answer seemed to be: nothing but births, and countless bottles of Malaga, and visits to London, and deaths. David Hume had died in August 1776, just hours before an unsuspecting, sociable Boswell rasped the craw to his door. David Boswell died at the age of five months in March 1777, and James – who had grown used, like most parents, to expecting death rather than life from their newborn, so that their hardened hearts could not be pierced – laid out his tiny frame under a cloth on the drawing-room table and wondered at his perfect waxwork features. David Garrick died in January 1779, a few weeks short of his 52nd birthday. 'That stroke of death,' eulogised

Samuel Johnson, 'which has eclipsed the gaiety of nations and impoverished the public stock of harmless pleasure.'

And a fortnight after the actor's demise, James Boswell walked into the High Court of Edinburgh to be greeted by a group of surprised and concerned faces. A colleague approached him, and Boswell asked what this meant.

'I am told your father's dead.'

James was stunned. He 'knew not what to think or do'. Another man came forward and explained that he had been in a tavern on the previous night, when a card was brought in which bore the words: 'Lord Auchinleck died this evening at eight o'clock.'

Half of James knew then that a cruel hoax had been played: it simply was not possible for his father to die one evening in Edinburgh and for him not to be told until a chance meeting on the following morning. But the other half was giddy with anxiety. He sent word to his father's house, was assured that Lord Auchinleck would be at work by eleven o'clock, waited for him to arrive and clutched the old man's hand 'with great affection'.

In October 1777 James had begun to contribute a regular monthly essay to the *London Magazine*, using the *nom de plume* of The Hypochondriak. Between 1777 and 1783 he would contribute 70 papers, and three of them were on the subject of death. One of those essays, as chance would have it, appeared in the month of Garrick's expiration and a few weeks before his father's falsely rumoured end.

'It has indeed frequently struck me with a mixture of wonder and dejection,' he wrote with sorry foreboding, 'to think how very few men have even their worldly affairs so set in order, that their death would not occasion many perplexities and unhappy wants, which care might easily have been taken to prevent and supply . . . Death has put it out of the power of a man to do what it would have vexed him exceedingly to be told should be undone . . .

'The death of kind relations, or friends, is, in my apprehension, the severest affliction which can befall us in respect to this world, for it both impresses us with a lively sense of our own frailty, and deprives us of the best comforts to which we have been habituated; yet, with respect to the other world, and the dreary passage to it, we are really benefited by such affliction, if we make a right use of it, so as that it shall loosen our attachment to earth, and allure us to die with placid hope.'

He had too wishful a frame of mind to make a good columnist. James Boswell's 'dreary passage' to the other world was unalleviated by 'placid hope'. All of his hopes were excitable, restive and impetuous, and more likely to be agitated than calmed by the proximity of death. The affairs which he desired to set in order before the reaper came for James Boswell extended beyond provision for his family. He had to achieve; he was driven to become, in his own words, 'a celebrated man'; and he was ultimately capable of doing so because alcohol never held full dominion over James Boswell. He was too aware of the danger to allow it total conquest.

'I do fairly acknowledge,' he told the readers of the *London Magazine* in March 1780, in the first of four essays On Drinking (drinking and hypochondria received four articles each, against death's three and two apiece on religion and fatherhood), 'that I love Drinking; that I have a constitutional inclination to indulge in fermented liquors, and that if it were not for the restraints of reason and religion I am afraid I should be as constant a votary of Bacchus as any man. To be sensible of this is a continual cause of fear, the uneasiness of which greatly counterbalances both the pleasure of occasional gratification and the pride of frequent successful resistance, and therefore it is certainly a misfortune to have such a constitution.'

This was not the dissembling of a confirmed drunkard. Intelligent people of his time had necessarily to sue for terms with alcoholic addiction. Some would fail to connect even the symptoms of a hangover with the excesses of a night before ('awoke inexplicably at three of the morning again, feeling restless and obliged to drink several bottles of water'). It was a struggle, in the hard-drinking city of Edinburgh – whose traditions he frequently used to excuse his own collapses into oblivion – to stay sober for long; when a hearty breakfast was often cold corned beef, a couple of eggs, small beer and porter; and where the tavern was the office and the meeting-place. James found himself too often twitching by the fire at home after one evening glass of wine, longing to finish the bottle and call out for more, but frightened of the hang-over, and the morning porter, and the meridian drams, and the afternoon session, and the dinner-table claret, and the gin punch, and the curing skalk at dawn.

Often enough he won, and often enough he lost. He was not alone. Visiting Johnson in London in 1781, he noted that his old friend was back on the bottle. 'I observed he poured a quantity of [wine] into a large glass, and swallowed it greedily. Everything about his character and manners was forcible and violent; there never was any moderation; many a day did he fast, many a year did he refrain from wine; but when he did eat, it was voraciously; when he did drink wine, it was copiously. He could practise abstinence, but not temperance.'

It was not entirely drink which sent his Edinburgh legal career into a spiralling free-fall. Alcohol helped, but boredom did the trick; boredom was the root. By the early 1780s James could hardly pay his way in Edinburgh. He was afraid to approach his father for an increased allowance of £400 a year: the old man was growing stranger yet in age, and it was a matter of great surprise and joy when he so much as expressed a grudging interest in seeing his grandchildren at Auchinleck. He was eccentrically refusing even to lend books to his son. James had taken it to be a sign of irrevocable decline when Lord Auchinleck failed to raise a murmur against his son's spring jaunt to London in 1779 ('had he been quite himself he would have been violent against it'), and he was right. Boswell made it south that year, but shortage of ready funds kept him in Scotland throughout 1780. In 1781 he enjoyed two expensive months in the metropolis and returned reluctantly home to collect the bills.

How could he live in Edinburgh? Edmund Burke had asked him one evening at The Club. 'Like a cat in an air-pump,' Boswell had replied. 'In so narrow a sphere, and amongst people to whom I am so unlike, my life is dragged on in languor and discontent.'

'I know not if you will be at rest in London,' another friend had observed. 'But you will never be at rest out of it.' But as 1782 drew on, the awful possibility re-emerged that he might be forced by circumstance to spend a year away from the Eternal City. He was almost £400 in debt and short of prospects other than those promised by his father's lingering decline. He wrote to tell Johnson of his plight, adding the unsubtle hint that once he was in the capital he might find work to pay his way, and received no sympathy.

'To come hither,' lectured the Doctor from London, 'with such expectations at the expense of borrowed money, which I find you know not where to borrow, can hardly be considered prudent. I am sorry to find, what your solicitations seem to imply, that you have already gone the length of your credit. This is to set the quiet of your whole life at hazard. If you anticipate your inheritance, you can at last inherit nothing; all that you receive must pay for the past. You must get a place, or pine in penury, with the empty name of a great estate. Poverty, my dear friend, is so great an evil, and pregnant with so much temptation, and so much misery, that I cannot but earnestly enjoin you to avoid it. Live on what you have; live if you can on less; do not borrow either for vanity or pleasure; the vanity will end in shame, and the pleasure in regret; stay therefore at home till you have saved the money for your journey hither.' It was sound advice, and it was heeded for a summer. Then providence made it superfluous.

On the morning of 29 August 1782 James was riding from Valleyfield in the direction of Dunfermline along the north bank of the Firth of Forth, when a messenger arrived on horseback, hailed him down and handed him an express letter. He knew at once that it was his father and that this was no hoax. He felt calm at first and then, in the chaise to Edinburgh, nervous. He wished that it was all over, all done.

He arrived at Parliament Close and was told not to go hurriedly into his father's room as it was not an agreeable sight, and anyway Lord Auchinleck recognised nobody. James entered the chamber. His father lay unseeing as he passed the bed. Elizabeth Boswell sat by the curtains. He marvelled at her composure. They shook hands, and James said that he wished to go to his father's side. 'It will confuse his mind,' said Betty. 'Don't torture him in his last moments.' James stood back, frozen to the spot and unable to speak, and began to weep.

He went to his home and returned to Parliament Close on the following morning. 'Still alive, still here!' he said to himself. 'Cannot he be stopped?' And then he shook his head at the strangeness of the thought.

In the small hours of 31 August, Alexander Boswell was stopped. His breathing grew quick and loud, and then as sharply died, and the doctor closed the eyes on his lifeless face. James looked for and observed no appearance of transition, no sign of Alexander Boswell's soul lighting out for a better place. He made his way back to James's Court, and wrote throughout the early light to friends, and cried and sobbed into a book which once had been Lord Auchinleck's and now, like so much else, was his.

Alexander's body was carried to Auchinleck and interred there in the family vault. James organised the funeral in a cloud of mild derangement. He carried his father's coffin through the subdued crowds of tenantry to the church as if, he imagined, he himself was floating away, lifted elsewhere by unseen hands. Was this how those who walked to execution felt? He saw his mother's coffin for the first time as his father's mortal remains were levered out of sight, and he returned to Auchinleck House and fled from the serious faces of the schoolmaster and the minister, the relatives and neighbours, up into the loft of the mansion that his father had built to bring the Boswell family peace; and there, alone with his vanished boyhood in the dull glimmer from the attic windows, the tears once more coursed down his desolated face.

Within a week he had received a letter from Samuel Johnson. 'I have struggled through this year,' it read, 'with so much infirmity of body and such strong impressions of the fragility of life that death, wherever it appears, fills me with melancholy, and I cannot hear without emotion of the removal of anyone whom I have known into another state.

'Your father's death had every circumstance that could enable you to bear it; it was at a mature age, and it was expected;

and as his general life had been pious, his thoughts had doubt-less for many years past been turned upon eternity. That you did not find him sensible must doubtless grieve you; his dis-position towards you was undoubtedly that of a kind, though not of a fond father. Kindness, at least actual, is in our power, but fondness is not; and if by negligence or impudence you had extinguished his fondness, he could not at will rekindle it. Nothing then remained between you but mutual forgiveness of each other's faults, and mutual desire of each other's happiness.'

James finished the letter and felt a passionate urge to be with Johnson. He calculated the times of post-chaises between Ayrshire and the north of England, and from there to London. But Margaret, who had been chronically unwell since their marriage, had been coughing up blood all through the wet summer of 1782, and in the balance – a crucial assessment – he realised at this fraught time that he loved Peggie and his children better than he loved Samuel Johnson, and better than he loved the city of London, and he must stay with them. So for the present he con-tented himself with responding through the post. 'I came to this place with my wife and children,' Boswell replied, 'on Wednesday the 18 September and took possession of the seat of my ancestors on Dr Johnson's birthday.'

He inherited an income from the estate of roughly £1,600 a year. It was enough to repay the interest on his debts. On 29 October he became 42 years old. 'A man cannot be happy in the country whose mind is not tolerably sedate,' he had written in the *London Magazine*, 'either naturally, or from having seen and enjoyed a great deal, and exhausted his curiosity and eager desires.'

So it would ever be with the new laird of Auchinleck. His curiosity and eager desires were never exhausted, and they must be slaked elsewhere but Ulubrae. In the short term, even Edinburgh would do. After a weekend in Ayrshire, James's Court seemed like Temple Bar. But after a winter in James's Court, Fleet Street drew him like a siren to her song.

Boswell was startled by Johnson's appearance in March 1783.

He was pale and he breathed with difficulty. He was asthmatic; he was suffering from dropsy and from severe rheumatoid arthritis; he was taking opium against the pain; and he had taken to paring at his fingernails and joints with a penknife in maddened efforts to excise the agony. Suddenly reminded of his own literary intentions, James determined to note as much as possible of the 73-year-old's conversation. There was not much of it left. He lodged, as had become his habit, with the generous Paoli and visited Johnson in the day.

James was now possessed of a strangely new-found sense of his own worth. As the Laird of Auchinleck, rather than the Young Laird of Auchinleck, he felt himself to be a man of substance. He was revisiting London in a new persona. It was almost like starting all over again: if the city had begun to reject the sometime writer and young man of affairs, it could surely not ignore a Scottish baron. He stayed comparatively sober, and he cultivated the likes of Joshua Reynolds and Edmund Burke, and he walked the streets with an affected dignity.

And he began to ponder on the political career which he had promised himself in that distant early manhood. In the course of a noisy London soirée, James had found himself roaring into debate with a couple of peers of the realm, and Mountstuart, his old acquaintance from Italy, slyly mentioned that some people thought James Boswell to be rather like his fellow member of The Club, the new Whig secretary of state, Charles Fox.

'Why, you're so much uglier,' offered a nearby army officer.

'Does your wife think so, Colonel James?' asked Boswell.

It was worth more than a jest and a passing fancy. Landowners, after all, were expected to go into government. The burdens of state were a part of their inherited responsibilities. And Members of Parliament were obliged to spend at least some of their time in London.

He mentioned it to Johnson. 'Unless you come like your countrymen,' said the Doctor, 'resolved to support any administration, you'd be the worse for being in Parliament, because you'd be obliged to live more expensively.'

James was hurt by the suggestion that unaligned Scottish

members were open to offers. 'Sir, I should never sell my vote. And it would vex me if things went wrong.'

'That's cant, Sir. It would not vex you more in the House than in the gallery. Public affairs vex no man.'

Johnson was right: public affairs did not particularly vex James Boswell. But personal prestige vexed him enormously. Back in Auchinleck and Edinburgh, he worked throughout the last week of 1783 on a 'Letter to the People of Scotland on the State of the Nation' which supported the property rights which were supposedly under threat from Charles Fox's Whig administration, mailed it out, and sat back in the confident expectation that he had done himself some good with the Tory caucus.

By the early spring of 1784 a general election was in the offing, and on 17 March he made a doomed bid for the Ayrshire seat. His election address announced that his political principles were 'those of a steady Royalist, who reveres monarchy, but is at the same time animated with genuine feelings of liberty . . . as I am now the representative of a family which has held an estate in the county, and maintained a respectable character for almost three centuries, I flatter myself that I shall not be reckoned too presumptuous when I aspire to the high distinction of being your representative in Parliament, and that you will not disapprove of my indulging an ambition that this family shall advance rather than fall off in my time.'

'One thing I must enjoin you,' wrote Samuel Johnson to the aspiring politician, 'which is seldom observed in the conduct of elections – I must entreat you to be scrupulous in the use of strong liquors. One night's drunkenness might defeat the labour of forty days well employed.'

Drunk or sober – and he was chiefly sober – James Boswell stood no chance of adoption for the seat of Ayrshire. The pocket burgh was buttoned up by the vested interests of the Scottish establishment long before he, a novice in this new game, made his move. He got no more than a glance at power, was rejected by the great titled patrons, and he retired, cheerful in defeat, from British politics and wandered back down to London as no more than the Laird of Auchinleck.

Johnson was in decline, but bearing up well. Early in June they took a trip to Oxford together, and after their return Boswell consulted with Pasquale Paoli and others about the best means 'of preserving so valuable a life'. Paoli suggested a winter in Italy. Boswell then consulted Sir Joshua Reynolds, who agreed.

But Johnson – who had, in fact, been heard to express some such desire – had not the funds for an extended continental holiday. Wasting no time, James wrote to the Lord Chancellor, Edward Thurlow, requesting on behalf of all of Johnson's friends that the old man's pension of £300 a year be increased 'as would be sufficient to put him in a situation to defray the expense in a manner becoming the first literary character of a great nation and, independent of all his other merits, the author of the Dictionary of the English Language.'

A week later James received Thurlow's reply. 'I am much obliged to you for the suggestion,' wrote the Lord Chancellor, 'and I will adopt and press it as far as I can. The best argument, I am sure, and I hope it is not likely to fail, is Dr Johnson's merit . . . It would be a reflection on us all, if such a man should perish for want of the means to take care of his health.'

Exhilarated, Boswell rushed to see Reynolds, who suggested that the three of them – Johnson, Boswell and he – should dine together to break their plan gently to the Doctor. There was no need for that. Boswell went straight to Temple Bar and broached the subject:

'I am really anxious about you, Sir,' he said, 'and particularly that you should go to Italy for the winter, which I believe is your own wish.'

'It is, Sir.'

'You have no objection but the money?'

'Why no, Sir.'

'Why then,' said James, 'suppose the king should give you the money? I have reason to think he will.'

'Why should you think so?'

'You are not to be angry with me.'

'No,' assented a perplexed Johnson.

'Why then, I will tell you fairly what I have done.'

And he did, while Johnson listened attentively, and when Boswell had finished he cried out warmly, 'This is taking prodigious pains about a man!'

'Oh, Sir,' said James passionately, 'your friends would do everything.'

Tears started into the old man's bulbous eyes, and he shook with emotion as he searched for an answer, without success. Finally, he exclaimed in a quavering voice, 'God bless you all . . . God bless you all, for Jesus Christ's sake.'

Deeply moved, and with damp eyes, James Boswell took his leave, for the last time, of Samuel Johnson's apartments. On the following evening, which was supposed to be James's final night in London, they dined together at the house of Joshua Reynolds, and Johnson waxed warmly on the delightful prospect of either a capital grant of £1,000 or an increased stipend of £600 a year and decided that he would rather have the latter. They talked of Italy, and Boswell and Reynolds told him how greatly he would enjoy it.

'Nay,' he said, 'I must not expect that. Were I going to Italy to see fine pictures, like Sir Joshua, or to run after women, like Boswell, I might be sure to have pleasure in Italy. But when a man goes to Italy merely to feel how he breathes the air, he can enjoy very little.'

They left together in Reynolds's coach, and at the entrance to Johnson's court he asked if Boswell would go in with him. James declined from selfishness – he was afraid that a maudlin night with his sick friend would be too depressing. So Johnson stepped down on to the pavement and called out, 'Fare you well!' Then he walked away without looking back, affecting a 'pathetic briskness' to his step, and James drove back to Pasquale Paoli's house full of foreboding.

The High Tory of romantic Jacobite inclinations was shamefully rejected by the Whig government of a Hanoverian king. Early in September a deeply embarrassed Edward Thurlow reported to Reynolds that Boswell's application on Johnson's behalf had been unsuccessful. Thurlow added that he wished Johnson to know that he could draw on him personally for five or six hundred pounds, and that 'he wished the business to be conducted in such a manner that Dr Johnson should appear to be under the least possible obligation'.

Samuel Johnson was above all that. 'I could not,' he wrote to the Lord Chancellor on 9 September 1784, 'escape from myself the charge of advancing a false claim. My journey to the continent, though I once thought it necessary, was never much encouraged by my physicians . . . if I grew much better, I should not be willing, if much worse, not able, to migrate.'

Three months later, at seven o'clock on the evening of Monday 13 December, he was dead. James received the news in Edinburgh on the Friday. This time there were no tears, just a dull stupefaction and a slow sense of immense loss. 'It gave me concern,' he wrote, 'that I was conscious of a deadness of spiritual feeling, and indeed a cold indifference as to the awful subject of religion.' He could never raise the courage to put it into words, but James Boswell was convinced in his fearful heart that what he saw and felt and heard and smelled and tasted, the world that he inhabited and its mortal population, were all that he would ever know. His duty was to them.

On Saturday 18 December he received a letter from Charles Dilly, the publisher of 'An Account of Corsica', asking if he could have a 400-page book on Johnson ready by February. James wrote back to say that he was indeed prepared to make a book from his personal collection of Johnsoniana, but he would do it in his own time; he would write it 'deliberately'. In the meantime, however, there was his journal of a tour to the Hebrides . . .

In the received wisdom of the publishing world, Samuel Johnson had been perfectly correct: the market could not bear another account of a visit to the Highlands and Islands of Scotland, let alone a second account of the same visit. The fact that by the time of his death most people had forgotten Johnson's *Journey to the Western Islands* was irrelevant; it alone should have muddied the waters for several decades, and the Highlands had not been left wanting other recorders – as well as Macaulay's recent work on St Kilda, Edward Burt had published his *Letters from a Gentleman in the North of Scotland* in 1754, and Thomas Pennant his *Tour in Scotland* as recently as 1771.

Boswell's *Journal of a Tour to the Hebrides* appeared on 1 October 1785, and it eclipsed them all. The first edition sold out of 1,500 copies within 16 days. He had intended to prepare it immediately after the unhappy Christmas of 1784, which he spent in a state of 'amazement' at Johnson's death, but concentration did not come easily. He travelled south from Auchinleck in March 1785 in search of he knew not what. At Carlisle he had a dream in which Johnson appeared to him in unexpected good health.

'You are very well, Sir,' Boswell called out to the wraith.

'Oh, no,' came a weak reply, followed by, 'I have written the letter to Paoli which you desired,' and then the apparition faded, protesting all the while that it, he, Johnson, would do anything and everything to show his love and regard for James Boswell.

That was the last that he saw of his friend and mentor of 20 years. It was a fitting resolution, more satisfactory by far than that strained and miserable night-time farewell in central London; which is, of course, why it occurred. To the very end, Samuel Johnson had protested that nobody could ever replace Boswell in his affections. 'They that have your kindness,' he had written to James in his final illness, 'may want your ardour.'

He went first to Lichfield, to receive the sacrament at the cathedral in Johnson's birthplace, and then to London, where he got drunk. In the middle of May he sobered himself sufficiently to be received at the Court of George III. Wearing what he was pleased to think of as a baronial scarlet suit, he swapped small-talk with the nobility until George himself, a monarch who was, in the words of J.H. Plumb, just two years away from getting out of his carriage in Windsor Great Park and addressing an oak tree as the King of Prussia, made his singular way to Boswell's side and bluffly mouthed the question framed by his advisers for the occasion: 'How do you go on with your account of your friend?'

'Sir,' replied Boswell, 'I am going first to give my log-book, my journal kept *de die in diem*, of the curious journey which Dr Johnson and I made through a remote part of your majesty's dominions – our Highlands and Islands. It will be more a journal of Dr Johnson than of what I saw. Whenever it is finished, I shall take the liberty to present it to your majesty.'

This flummoxed George, who had been given to expect a full biography from Boswell, not inconsequential vapouring about a traveller's journal dressed up as literature. The king, however, bluffed bravely on. 'But when are we to have your other work?'

'Your majesty,' preened Boswell smoothly, 'a little ago remarked that people were sometimes in too great a hurry before they had collected facts. I mean to avoid that fault, and shall take time, as I intend to give a very full account of Dr Johnson.'

'There will be many before you,' observed George.

'I wish first to see them all, Sir.'

'There will be many foolish lives first,' continued George, unwilling to let his insight go. 'Do you make the best?'

'I cannot presume to say that I shall do that, Sir. But I shall do as well as I can.'

James Boswell was concerned with two preoccupations throughout the summer of 1785. One was the preparation for print of his Highland journal, and the other was a vain desire to establish himself – who had failed at the Scottish Bar – as a lawyer in London. The latter was the failure which any of his friends might have warned against, although few enough did so; the former, with the help of Edmond Malone, managed to do what success in southern legal circles was intended to achieve – it established his name in London.

Edmond Malone was that quiet, assiduous Irish lawyer (and Shakespearean scholar) who Boswell had met at what had become, in the 1780s, The Literary Club. Malone worked self-lessly as Boswell's editor for the last ten years of James's life. He did so not for money or for prestige, but from friendship (the two men got on well together, as if the easy-going Malone was a John Johnston with literary expertise) and from an understanding that the raw material with which he was dealing held a promise which few others could grasp. Essentially, Malone, like any great editor, had an eye for unpolished genius.

Malone also understood that the essence of this first project lay not so much in its unrivalled qualities as a travel book, but in the dramatic tension created by two forceful characters voluntarily losing themselves in the wilderness. It was thanks to Malone that Boswell's catholic, all-seeing diary of events became as much a picture of Johnson and the author as of the condition of the Highlands in the years of turmoil which followed 1746. He deleted many of the 'small particulars', such as that unique account of the feudal form of the game of shinty on the island of Coll, and the loving descriptions of meals, and the – admittedly semi-libellous – asides at the expense of several hosts. Less necessarily, he tightened Boswell's prose. By the 1780s this was a perfectly tuned vehicle for its author's message. It would be almost impossible to number or to trace the hundreds of thousands of words which James Boswell had by then written, in the form of journals, memoranda, letters, essays, legal manuscripts and ephemera; and all were clear, stylish and appealing, and would remain so for centuries. As the 'Journal' would prove, he had become, in the 20 years between publication of his first two books, a great writer without anybody – James Boswell included – realising the fact. His syntax and narrative did not need to be polished by anybody. It is only fortunate that he found in Malone an editor who may not have entirely grasped his native brilliance, but who was sufficiently dazzled to leave an idiosyncratic masterpiece in a state approaching grace.

Throughout July, August and September they revised and rewrote, and corrected proofs together, and when the book appeared Boswell had dedicated it to Edmond Malone. Pointing out that the only previous recipient of such an honour from his pen had been General Pasquale Paoli, to whom 'An Account of Corsica' had been devoted, Boswell prefaced the 'Journal' with a short address to Malone. 'You,' he wrote, 'have obligingly taken the trouble to peruse the original manuscript of this Tour, and can vouch for the strict fidelity of the present publication . . . But I have a still more powerful inducement to prefix your name to this volume, as it gives me an opportunity of letting the world know that I enjoy the honour and happiness of your friendship.'

The reviewers chiefly sensed that they were in the presence of great originality, but consequently struggled to identify the work. They were not alone in their confusion. Boswell's old acquaintance Edward Thurlow, the Lord Chancellor, would tell James that he had 'read every word of it; and yet one cannot tell how. Why should one wish to go on and read how Dr Johnson went from one place to another? Can you give me a rule for writing in that manner?' Boswell could not, of course, rationalise the mystery of an original and irresistibly attractive style – he was hardly aware of it himself – and nor could the newspapers. While the *Journal of a Tour to the Hebrides* was selling in extraordinary numbers, the critical sheets sought largely in vain to locate its appeal. And when they tripped over that appeal and stopped to examine the item, they mostly mistook it for something entirely different and utterly irrelevant, and tossed it away again. 'Was it meritorious,' asked the *English Review*, 'was it right or justifiable in Mr Boswell to record and to publish [Johnson's] prejudices, his follies and whims, his weaknesses, his vices? . . . Mr Boswell provides fuel for that passion for minutiae, for trifling anecdotes, which takes place of all nobler views and pursuits.'

The *European Magazine and London Review* echoed Thomas Gray's idiotic opinion of an 'Account of Corsica', that 'any fool may write a most valuable book by chance', when it blithely suggested that 'The journal of a tour to the Hebrides with such a man as the late Dr Samuel Johnson cannot fail, if faithfully executed, to contain many particulars curious and interesting to philosophical minds.' And the satirist John Wolcot, writing as Peter Pindar, took the Boswell-as-grovelling-acolyte-before-Great-Men caricature to new levels:

> Nay, though thy Johnson ne'er had bless'd thine eyes,
> Paoli's deeds had rais'd thee to the skies,
> Yes! his broad wing had rais'd thee (no bad luck)
> A tomtit twittering on an eagle's back.

James Boswell was listening, of course; he always listened. But he was paying little heed. It was a malicious age, in which to court attention by getting work published was to invite bad caustic verse. It hurt for a day and was, if not forgotten, dismissed as one of celebrity's irksome side-effects. Boswell had other irons to heat. In the endpapers of the 'Journal' readers and critics alike would have found a confident advance notice. 'Preparing for the Press, in one Volume Quarto,' it announced, 'the Life of Samuel Johnson, LL.D., by James Boswell Esq. . . . Mr Boswell has been collecting materials for this work for more than twenty years, during which he was honoured with the intimate friendship of Dr Johnson; to whose memory he is ambitious to erect a literary monument.'

He was introduced to the English Bar in 1786 at the age of 45. His career there slid inexorably to a halt, as his 'Life of Johnson' took enormous shape. If one would not make him, the other must. 'I am sadly discouraged,' he would write to William Temple from London, 'by having no practise nor probable prospect of it; and to confess fairly to you, my friend, I am afraid that if I were to be tried, I should be found so deficient in the forms, the quirks, and the quiddities, which early habit acquires, that I should expose myself. Yet the delusion of Westminster Hall, of brilliant reputation and splendid fortune as a barrister, still weighs upon my imagination.'

Brilliant reputation and splendid fortune – the two might yet evade him. Two successful books published in three decades would guarantee no lasting fame. He was impelled to write another by three separate demons: the urge for notoriety (which he considered, rightly if immodestly, to be his due); a genuine wish to perpetuate the memory of that worthy man, his friend; and whatever genie it is which makes natural writers (and never was there a more natural writer) turn for comfort to the ink and vellum. Of the three the last was the most powerful. James Boswell could, with similar application, have made a great success of the law in Edinburgh or in London. He was articulate and charming and well trained, and his family background gave him every advantage. He did not do so because the law was, simply, not his vocation. Similarly, his last great book need not have been on the subject of Samuel Johnson. He had flirted with other topics, including the biographies of at least a dozen of his other acquaintances, a history of the Union, and an account of the 'civil war' (his term) which began when Charles Edward Stuart landed on the island of Eriskay in 1745. These were cast aside when Johnson died, through no lingering, misplaced sycophancy but because writing the life of Johnson most attracted him. It attracted him partly because he felt that talents such as Johnson's should not be forgotten, but mainly because the preparation of such a biography would most satisfy his own artistic impulses. Without that inspiration, a 'Life' of sorts might have been pre-pared, but it would not have set the standard against which all other biographies would be measured, and virtually all found wanting, for the next 200 years. Writers in James Boswell's time were not considered to be artists. Artists were not considered to be artists. Only poets and actors were, grudgingly, allowed a ha'penny-worth of temperament – and then only some poets and actors; most were happy to take their places in the masonry of craftsmen and skilled artisans. It was a sensible precaution, which prevented for a decade or two much indulgence and affectation, and which failed the eighteenth century only in refus-ing to the likes of Boswell a fair appreciation of the true and irrepressible source of their accomplishments.

He worked through hangover, disappointment and mourn-ing. He saw Hester Thrale Piozzi's *Anecdotes of the Late Samuel Johnson* published in the spring of 1786 and run to four editions within a year. He was dispirited to be hoaxed by his fellow English lawyers into acting upon an invented brief. He heard, in August 1786, of the demise of his old friend John Johnston of Grange – 'a loss that never can be made up to me'. Six months later Sir John Hawkins published his *Life of Samuel Johnson*. It was an injury compounded by insult. At the same time as he made a valiant attempt to shoot James Boswell's fox, Hawkins actually managed to mention his rival just once in a bulky text. Johnson had been accompanied to the Highlands, he said, by one 'Mr Boswell, a native of Scotland'. According to Hawkins's daughter, James called around to protest:

'Surely, Mr *James* Boswell?' he asked.

'I know what you mean,' replied Hawkins. 'You would have had me say that Johnson undertook this journey with *the* Boswell.'

Deterred only slightly, if at all, and sustained by Malone,

Paoli, Joshua Reynolds and other supportive members of The Club, James Boswell laboured on through the months and years, compiling, ordering, researching and sitting at his London desk with pen in hand and – for entire weeks on end – a glass of water by his side. 'Did some "Life" . . . Laboured at "Life" all day, yet did no more than seven pages . . . Some "Life". Only water.'

He considered returning to Scotland but was assured by Malone that if he did so he would hang himself within six months, and so he took a house in Cavendish Square, a house with Corinthian pilasters running down its elegant façade, where he was joined by three of his children and by Margaret. It would be another failed experiment. 'I am absolutely certain,' he wrote to Temple in a perfect summation of his engrossment, 'my mode of biography is the most perfect that can be conceived . . . My wife is, I thank God, much better; but is it not cruel to keep her in this pernicious air?' It was. Neither her Scottishness nor her health would survive the London smog. She returned, terminally consumptive, to the north.

And there, in Auchinleck, Peggie Boswell sickened and grew afraid for the future. The family's debts had been merely alleviated by inheritance of the Boswell country seat. She had a husband in whose talents she firmly believed, but who had worked for years, to the detraction of virtually everything else, on nothing more promising than a biography of an old friend. What 'Life' could repay the obsession of half a decade? She pleaded with him to retire to Scotland, but he would not go. London had him by the neck. It was Samuel Johnson's legacy to the Boswell family.

He visited Scotland whenever he could drag himself from the city which had wooed and finally won him, for he also loved the woman with whom he had ventured into a Georgian partnership, and by the spring of 1789 he knew that Margaret was dying. 'I found,' he wrote to William Temple from Auchinleck, 'my dear wife as ill, or rather worse than I apprehended. The consuming hectic fever had preyed upon her incessantly during the winter and spring, and she was miserably emaciated and weak. The physician and surgeon-apothecary, whom she allows occasionally, though rarely, to visit her, told me fairly, as a man able to support with firmness what they announced, that they had no hopes of her recovery, though she might linger they could not say how long.'

Boswell intended to stay with Margaret until the end. He rode about the Ayrshire countryside from house to house, from one drinking party to the next, unable to write or to concentrate on his affairs or to return to law, until one night he fell from his horse and damaged his shoulder. Margaret, strong and serene even in illness, told him bluntly to take himself back down to London. He did so, and had been there for a week when a letter arrived from his daughter Euphemia which said that her mother was sinking fast. He set off immediately by post-chaise, and sleeplessly covered the ground between Cavendish Square and Auchinleck in sixty-four-and-a-quarter hours. As his carriage rattled up through the trees and past the stable-block, to pull in before the great front door, Euphemia rushed tearfully down the steps to announce that Margaret had died four days earlier.

She lay peacefully, her countenance undisturbed. He could not believe that death had taken such a shape. He knelt beside her, talking to her, and when they came to take her away he protested that they must not do so: she was still real to him, and she was almost all that he had. There must have been some cruel deception; he had to stay and talk to dear, dear Peggie . . .

'What distress,' he wrote to Temple, 'what tender painful regrets, what unavailing earnest wishes to have but one week, one day, in which I might again hear her admirable conversation and assure her of my fervent attachment notwithstanding all my irregularities . . . I cried bitterly, and upbraided myself for leaving her, for she would not have left me. This reflection, my dear friend, will I fear pursue me to the grave.'

Chapter Ten

LIFE

I have often thought that there has rarely passed a life of which a judicious and faithful narrative would not be useful. For not only every man has, in the mighty mass of the world, great numbers in the same condition with himself, to whom his mistakes and miscarriages, escapes and expedients, would be of immediate and apparent use, but there is such uniformity in the state of man . . . that there is scarce any possibility of good or ill but is common to human kind . . . We are all prompted by the same motives, all deceived by the same fallacies, all animated by hope, obstructed by danger, entangled by desire, and seduced by pleasure.

SAMUEL JOHNSON, 'DIGNITY AND USES OF BIOGRAPHY'

One morning in October 1790 the celebrated novelist and, at that time, second keeper of the Queen's robes Fanny Burney was making her way to St George's chapel in Windsor when a friend approached her and said that an associate from happier days, James Boswell, was in the town. Would she, who had also known Samuel Johnson well, care to receive him?

Miss Burney thought not. She was in bad health, she wished to retire from the royal service but was being controversially prevented by her mistress's lackeys from doing so, and she was nervous of Boswell's reputation for recording anecdotes of all he came across. But yet . . . 'But yet I really wished to see him again, for old acquaintance' sake, and unavoidable amusement from his oddity and good humour.'

So she agreed to meet Boswell outside the chapel at the close of the service. She waited by the gate, and he approached, much plumper than of old, but: 'We saluted with mutual glee: his comic-serious face and manner have lost nothing of their wonted singularity; nor yet have his mind and language . . .'

'I am extremely glad to see you here,' cried James, 'but very sorry to see you here. My dear ma'am, why do you stay? – it won't do, ma'am, you must resign! – we can put up with it no longer.'

Fanny Burney laughed and looked long and hard at this vision from her past, and then she suddenly remembered where they were, that they were surrounded by a host of other people, and that James Boswell was uttering comments which, while being designed to greet and comfort an old acquaintance, might be construed as close to treason, and she hurried away.

James followed. 'If you do not quit, ma'am,' he urged at her shoulder, 'very soon, some violent measures, I assure you, will be taken.'

She stopped out of earshot of the chapel gate and asked after Sir Joshua Reynolds ('his spirits are very good'), and about Edmund Burke's *Reflections on the French Revolution*, which she understood to be on the verge of publication.

'Oh,' said James Boswell, 'it will come out next week: 'tis the first book in the world, except my own, and that's coming out very soon; only I want your help.'

'My help?'

'Yes, madam; you must give me some of your choice little notes of the Doctor's; we have seen him long enough on stilts; I want to show him in a new light. Grave Sam, and great Sam, and solemn Sam, and learned Sam – all these he has appeared over and over. Now I want to entwine a wreath of the graces across his brow; I want to show him as gay Sam, agreeable Sam, pleasant Sam; so you must help me with some of his beautiful billets to yourself.'

Fanny protested that she had none of Johnson's letters to hand. James 'proposed a thousand curious expedients to get at them', but she was adamant in refusal and hurried on.

James followed still and told her that his 'Life of Johnson' was almost printed, and as they reached the railings of the Queen's Lodge he took a printed proof-sheet from his pocket, and as people passed by staring at this strange couple, Fanny Burney apologised for not being able to ask him in. The Queen, she said, was waiting upon her. So James, standing at the gate of the Queen's Lodge in Windsor, offered to read extracts of his work out loud.

'There was no refusing this: and he began, with a letter of Dr Johnson's to himself. He read it in strong imitation of the Doctor's manner, very well, and not caricature. But Mrs Schwellenberg was at her window, a crowd was gathering to stand around the rails, and the King and Queen and Royal Family now approaching from the Terrace . . .' Fanny Burney apologised hastily and, 'with a step as quick as my now weakened limbs have left in my power', hurried dizzily into her apartment, leaving James Boswell proclaiming to passers-by at the gate.

'My "Life of Dr Johnson",' he had written to Edmond Malone five months earlier, '[is] the most important, perhaps now the only concern of any consequence that I ever shall have in this world.'

Chapter by printed chapter, he sent the book from a new house in Great Portland Street to Malone for editing and revision. Little else mattered. He kept up his legal presence in Westminster Hall as a desultory pretence, a kind of homage to the wishes of his dead father and wife, but 'the chambers cost me £20 yearly, and I may reckon furniture and a lad to wait there occasionally £20 more. I doubt whether I shall get fees equal to the expense.'

On the other hand, 'you cannot imagine,' Temple was told, 'what labour, what perplexity, what vexation I have endured in arranging a prodigious multiplicity of materials, in supplying omissions, in searching for papers buried in different masses, and all this besides the exertion of composing and polishing. Many a time have I thought of giving it up . . . Methinks, if I had this magnum opus launched, the public has no further claim upon me; for I have promised no more, and I may die in peace, or retire into dull obscurity.'

He was still enormously in debt. He had taken out a £1,500 mortgage against a tract of Ayrshire land to extend the Auchinleck estate, and sums of several hundred pounds were owing to friends and indulgent publishers across the country. His eldest son, Alexander, was at Eton College, James at Westminster School, and Elizabeth was boarded at a lyceum for young ladies in Chelsea. These all were fee-paying establishments. His two other daughters lived with him. The estate now cleared a profit, after taxes, administration costs and interest payments, of less than £900 a year. In January 1791, with all of the 'Life', excepting Johnson's death, written and with two-thirds of it proof-read, a man named Robinson offered him £1,000 for the copyright. 'I am really tempted,' he wrote, and was discouraged only because he considered the price to be marginally too low. Two thousand pounds would almost certainly have clinched the publishing bargain of the eighteenth century. Instead, he spent £16 8s on national lottery tickets, waited to collect the £5000.00 jackpot, and won nothing.

The Life of Samuel Johnson, LL.D., comprehending an Account of his Studies and numerous Works was published finally by Thomas Baldwin in London for Charles Dilly on 16 May 1791. Boswell dedicated the book to Sir Joshua Reynolds. In a devotional essay to the painter, he explained that the 'Life' might be found by many to be heavier going than the *Journal of a Tour to the Hebrides*, and for the reason for this the critics could look to themselves . . .

'It is related of the great Dr Clarke,' Boswell told Reynolds and the literate classes of Great Britain, 'that when, in one of his leisure hours, he was unbending himself with a few friends in the most playful and frolicsome manner, he observed Beau Nash approaching, upon which he suddenly stopped. "My boys (said he), let us be grave; here comes a fool." The world, my friend, I have found to be a great fool.'

The 'Life' had a steady childhood. Seventeen hundred copies had been sold by the end of 1791, earning Boswell almost £2,000.

The *Quarterly Review* instantly dubbed it 'the richest dictionary of wit and wisdom any language can boast'. The *Edinburgh Review* added that it was 'a great, a very great work, one of the best books in the world'. Edmund Burke told a friend that in his opinion Johnson appeared a more significant person in Boswell's writing than in his own. King George III was frankly baffled. Night after night throughout the summer of 1791, he would amble into his queen's dressing-room and quiz Fanny Burney on the subject matter – 'What? What? Eh? Who? Who?' Fanny Burney herself considered that James's 'loquacious communications of every weakness and infirmity of the first and greatest good man of these times' was reprehensible. But when, a year after publication, she found herself seated next to the biographer at a Chelsea breakfast, 'he soon insensibly conquered, though he did not soften me: there is so little of ill design or ill nature in him, he is so open and forgiving for all that is said in return, that he soon forced me to consider him in a less serious light, and change my resentment against his treachery into something like commiseration of his levity; and before we parted we became good friends. There is no resisting great good-humour, be what will in the opposite scale.'

Boswell entertained the other guests at that breakfast party with stories and hilarious impressions of Samuel Johnson. He was accurate and, as Miss Burney testified, irresistibly witty (Bennet Langton tried the same tricks and failed dismally). In such fading city footlights he span tales of his past, and people of the 1790s were startled to glimpse the Boswell who had entranced the good, the great, the bad and the ordinary 30 years before. In such dim, candlelit rooms he whiled away the closing of his century. Auchinleck was further than ever from being the Ulubrae of his father's dreams, the place wherein all Boswells unto the end of time would find a perfect peace; the big house was deserted and melancholy and haunted by too many spectres. He could not find the energy, in the shade of so many who had loved both him and this untouchably beautiful place, to commit himself to estate work there, and so he rode off to drink in the drawing-rooms of his landed friends and returned too drunk, too hungover to do much but drink again and stare depressively out of the broad western windows across the rolling plains to Arran and the other world, until his thoughts came round again to London, and the Carlisle post.

More friends died. Joshua Reynolds sank before his eyes, half-blind and in great pain, and passed away in 1792; in the same year as John Dun, James's favourite tutor and latterly the minister of Auchinleck who had buried his mother, his father, and his wife. 'I feel no pleasure in existence,' wrote James, 'except the mere gratification of the senses.'

And yet he did not collapse into the helpless alcoholism portrayed by the traducers who were not born when he was making London laugh, and learn, and come alive; or even into the more likely chronic, drifting, half-mad melancholy. He attended the breakfast parties and the meetings of his precious Club. The 'Life' went steadily into a second impression, and a third, and finally it dawned upon him that, after all of his travails, he had succeeded in conquering the Eternal City. London was his, and he revelled in the fact, and – as before – he used the author's introduction to his book to tell the world of the inner ambitions and ultimate satisfaction of this transparent writer.

'There are some men,' he wrote in an 'Advertisement' appended to the second edition of the 'Life', 'I believe, who have, or think they have, a very small share of vanity. Such may speak of their literary fame in a decorous style of diffidence; but I confess that I am so formed by nature and by habit that to restrain the expression of delight on having obtained such fame, to me would be truly painful. Why, then, should I suppress it? Why, out of the "abundance of the heart", should I not speak? Let me then mention, with a warm but no insolent exultation, that I have been regaled with spontaneous praise of my work by many and various persons eminent for their rank, learning, talents, and accomplishments . . .'

Why suppress it? Why not speak? He had been a brilliant travel writer and was now a great biographer. He knew at last what Edmund Burke had hinted at: that his work was the product of his own genius, not of Samuel Johnson's, and not a happy accident, not the result of Thomas Gray's gormless but assiduous taker of notes. Why not alternate the affectionate hours spent with his children with rollicking evenings over the punch bowl in the company of the London society which he had spent a lifetime cultivating, and which now, finally, opened wide its arms to an old man of sensational accomplishment rather than to a young one of indefinable and occasionally tiresome promise. In the 1790s, as in the raffish days and bonfire nights of the 1760s, few people claimed to find James Boswell tiresome.

He nurtured other plans: a life of Reynolds, and a visit to America, and one whose perfect symmetry called out to him but slid away in the political maze. Perfect symmetry, he knew well enough, evaded the lives of men. But it enticed him like a southern wind . . .

In 1789, following the French Revolution, the ban on exiles to Corsica was repealed. In the summer of 1790 Pasquale Paoli made his sad farewells to his friends in Great Britain and returned to his native island through a French republic which greeted him with rapture. He arrived in Bastia to the reception due a mythical hero from his people's past, and then the marriage with France, even with revolutionary, republican France, went wrong. Paoli was a Corsican nationalist. He was also, after 20 years, more a friend of London than of Paris. There could be no common ground between Pasquale Paoli and those who had once bartered for his country as if it was a slave at auction, even when they claimed a change of political philosophy.

By 1793 the Franco-Corsican alliance was in disarray and Britain was once more at war with France. Paoli seized the opportunity to exploit the years of petitioning achieved by himself and by James Boswell. The British Mediterranean fleet, local representatives of the greatest sea power afloat, had hovered off the coast of Corsica for months when in August and September the General wrote two letters, one to Admiral Samuel Hood and the other to the British foreign secretary, William Wyndham Grenville. Give me, the letters requested, 'English protection for Corsica's political existence'.

Hood wasted no time. On 13 September his ships invested

Calvi. The young captain of HMS *Agamemnon*, Horatio Nelson, commanded a landing party, and a burst of French shrapnel cost him the sight of his right eye. But Calvi fell, and so in short time did the rest of the island, and the Anglo-Corsican kingdom was proclaimed.

James Boswell would not live to see its unhappy end, but he revelled in its birth. At the beginning of 1794 the talk in London was of who should accompany Pasquale Paoli as a representative of the British crown in Bastia. James wrote to Henry Dundas, the Scotsman who had just become secretary of war, suggesting that both Paoli and the Corsicans would welcome him and that his qualifications for the post were such 'as almost to preclude competition'. Will you make me, he had asked Rousseau so many years before, your ambassador to Corsica . . ? Il ambasciadore Inglese, the men and women of Sollacaro had cried in unfeigned welcome . . . The English, they were once our friends, but now are so no more . . .

Dundas's reply cut through the reverie. There was still to be no place in the diplomatic for James Boswell. The job went instead to an amiable buffoon named Sir Gilbert Elliot, an earl of Scottish descent who, as viceroy, estranged Pasquale Paoli and most of Corsica within 12 months, and, in September 1796, fled this turbulent, unhappy place once and for all ahead of a detachment of the French Army of Italy commanded by a Corsican whom James Boswell had never met: Napoleone Buonaparte. Elliot would later be given the governorship of India, a more malleable colonial property. Such was the diplomatic. When he ran to easier tasks Pasquale Paoli's dream, and that of James Boswell, was dashed forever. But by that time James would never dream again.

'Do not suffer yourself to be melancholy,' his 16-year-old son James wrote to him shortly before his 54th birthday in 1794. 'Think not on your having missed preferment in London or any of these kind of things, the unreasonableness of which you yourself upon reflection must be sensible if you consider that your manner of living has never been that of a man of business and that, in short, you have been entirely different in every respect from those who have been (in that line) more successful – they who have obtained places and pensions, etc. have not the fame of having been the biographer of Johnson or the conscious exultation of a man of genius.

'They have not enjoyed your happy and convivial hours. They have not been known to Johnson, Voltaire, Rousseau, and Garrick, Goldsmith, etc., etc. They have not visited the patriots of Corsica. In short, would you rather than have enjoyed so many advantages have been a rich, though dull, plodding lawyer?'

'I must acknowledge,' a good father replied from Auchinleck to his good son, 'that "thou reasonest well" . . . London has for these thirty years and upward been the object of my wish . . .'

We suppose now that it was a tumour in his stomach or in his bladder, possibly accompanied by uraemia in the kidneys. He had been in London at a meeting of The Literary Club early in the spring of 1795 when he returned to Great Portland Street so 'weak and languid' that he shocked the son of William Temple, who was lodging with him.

He took to his bed, and early in May he began from there to write a letter to William Temple. 'My dear Temple,' he began. 'I would fain . . .' He dropped the pen. Young James Boswell picked it up. 'I would fain,' dictated Boswell, 'write to you with my own hand but really cannot.

'Alas! my friend, what a state is this. My son James is to write for me what remains of this letter . . . The pain, which continued for so many weeks, was very severe indeed, and when it went off, I thought myself quite well, but I soon felt a conviction that I was by no means as I should be . . . I feel myself a good deal stronger today notwithstanding the scrawl.'

He fought for life. For days he would insist upon being fed in order to build up a strength which would never return, only to vomit instantly. He asked to be lifted from his bed, but fainted when it was attempted. At two o'clock in the morning of 19 May 1795 James Boswell died, surrounded by his sons and his two eldest daughters and his younger brother, David. He had suffered much, David said of the last five weeks of confinement, but hardly at all at the end. He died in the arms of the city that he loved and which had, at the close, repaid his devotion; and he found his final peace in the vault at Auchinleck.

Alexander Boswell succeeded to the Auchinleck Estate, became a Conservative Member of Parliament for Ayrshire, and erected a public monument to the local poet Robert Burns – a contemporary but not an acquaintance of his father. He died from wounds sustained in a duel in 1822. James Boswell Junior was called to the English Bar and became the literary executor of Mr Edmond Malone, whose editions of William Shakespeare he saw through to the printing press. Veronica Boswell died of consumption at the age of 23, four months after her father's death. Euphemia became an eccentric composer of poetry and opera. Elizabeth married her second cousin, William Boswell, Sheriff of Berwickshire, and bore three sons and a daughter.

James Boswell's will, touchingly unrevised since 1785, left to William Temple, Edmond Malone and Sir William Forbes of Pitsligo, an Edinburgh banker and an acquaintance of his later years, 'all my manuscripts of my own composition, and all my letters from various persons to be published . . . as they shall decide, that is to say they are to have a discretionary power to publish more or less.'

Temple died in 1796 without having seen the papers. Forbes saw them, could make little of them, scribbled words like 'reprehensible passage' in the margins of some of the journals, and died in 1806, having effectively washed his hands of the responsibility. Malone took care of the manuscripts with the intention that young James should have a final say as to their destiny. But James Junior died in 1822, just ten years after Malone, and the papers were left in storage.

How the letters to Temple turned up in the 1840s at a shop in Boulogne where they were being used as wrapping-paper, nobody will probably ever discover. It seems likely that his private journals crossed the North Channel to Malahide Castle in Ireland when his great-granddaughter, Emily Boswell, married into the family of that house. For the full span of the Victorian era they were left as untouched as the bearer of a fatal malady. They surfaced there after the First World War; another batch appeared in the winter of 1930 in the Aberdeenshire dwelling of a direct descendant of William Forbes; and in 1949 Yale University bought the lot.

He died at the close of his time. James Boswell was survived for a few short years only by some of those who had known and loved him. James Macpherson died in 1796 in the large house which his Highland fantasias had bought for him in Badenoch, still encircled by unresolved controversy and still muttering darkly about the original manuscripts which he kept in a big trunk upstairs. John Wilkes died in 1797 as a city chamberlain, and former Lord Mayor, of London. Pasquale Paoli returned to England after falling out with Sir Gilbert Elliot at the end of 1795, just months before the final annexation of Corsica by the French republic. He died in London in February 1807 at the age of 82 years, was buried in the Catholic cemetery at St Pancras, and was honoured with a memorial bust and epitaph in Westminster Abbey. On 2 September 1889 his bones were disinterred from St Pancras, placed on a British frigate, and shipped to Corsica to be laid in a mausoleum in his birthplace, Morosiglia, amid chestnut woods and rushing streams and the daunting heights which James Boswell, alone among his race, had dared to climb.

Immediately after receiving the news of his author's death, Edmond Malone composed a short obituary for the *Gentleman's Magazine*. Aside from its subject's 'considerable intellectual powers', the article suggested that people should recall James Boswell as a person possessed of 'an inexhaustible fund of good humour and good nature . . . as ready to exert himself for his friends as any other man'.

He was an honest mortal who sought, in a vicious world, to give and to receive pleasure; and he made his honesty into a form of art. It remains the best way to explain him.

BIBLIOGRAPHY

Eighteenth-Century Scotland
Domestic Life in Scotland in the Eighteenth Century, Marjorie Plant
A History of the Scottish People, 1560–1830, T.C. Smout
The Social Life of Scotland in the Eighteenth Century, H. Grey Graham
The Making of Classical Edinburgh, A.J. Youngson
A Century of Scottish History, Sir Henry Craik
Webster's Analysis of Population – 1755
The History of Auchinleck Village and Parish, Dane Love
Mutiny, John Prebble

Eighteenth-Century England
Eighteenth-Century England, Dorothy Marshall
England in the Eighteenth Century, J.H. Plumb
The Age of Johnson, Thomas Seccombe
London Life in the Eighteenth Century, M. Dorothy George

Eighteenth-Century Corsica
Pasquale Paoli, Peter Adam Thrasher
Granite Island, Dorothy Carrington

Contemporaries
Life and Letters of James Macpherson, Bailey Saunders

233

Life of Flora Macdonald, Revd Alexander MacGregor
Fanny Burney's Diaries, Fanny Burney

Boswelliana
Portraits, Sir Joshua Reynolds
Johnson and Boswell, Hesketh Pearson
Boswelliana, Charles Rogers
James Boswell, D.B. Wyndham Lewis
New Light on Boswell, ed Greg Clingham
Who's Who in Boswell, J.L. Smith–Dampier
The General Correspondence of James Boswell, ed R.C. Cole
Boswell's Column, James Boswell

Also, as mentioned in the author's preface, the complete set of surviving journals and miscellaneous private writings collected and anthologised, chiefly by Professor Frederick A. Pottle, for Yale University, and now sadly almost all out of print in Great Britain.

INDEX OF SUPPORTING
CHARACTERS